Intrépide

Intrépide

Australian Women Artists
in Early Twentieth-Century France

Clem Gorman and Therese Gorman

Intrépide: Australian Women Artists in Early Twentieth-Century France
© Copyright 2020 Clem Gorman and Therese Gorman
All rights reserved. Apart from any uses permitted by Australia's Copyright Act 1968, no part of this book may be reproduced by any process without prior written permission from the copyright owners. Inquiries should be directed to the publisher.

Monash University Publishing
Matheson Library Annexe
40 Exhibition Walk
Monash University
Clayton, Victoria 3800, Australia
www.publishing.monash.edu

ISBN: 9781925523928 (paperback)
ISBN: 9781925523942 (pdf)
ISBN: 9781925523935 (epub)

www.publishing.monash.edu/books/i-9781925523928.html

Design: Les Thomas

Cover image: Gladys Reynell, *Pensiveness*, c.1913. Oil on canvas, 73.0 × 60.0 cm. 25th Anniversary Gift from the Friends of the Art Gallery of SA, 1994, Accession No. 944P9. © Ms Jessica Ivanovic.

A catalogue record for this book is available from the National Library of Australia.

CONTENTS

List of Plates vii

Foreword *by Wendy Sharpe* xi

Acknowledgments xv

Introduction: Intrepid Women – The Wild Geese of Australian Art xvii

Chapter 1   Iso Rae: At Home in Two Worlds 1

Chapter 2   Agnes Goodsir: A Witness to Paris 7

Chapter 3   Marie Tuck: A Very Determined Artist 16

Chapter 4   Bessie Gibson: A Safe Pair of Hands 22

Chapter 5   Dora Meeson: Progressive Feminist, Traditional Artist . . . 28

Chapter 6   Alice Muskett: Multi-talented and Generous 34

Chapter 7   Ethel Carrick: A Team Player 37

Chapter 8   Ada May Plante: An Undervalued Talent 47

Chapter 9   Margaret Preston: A Driven Woman 54

Chapter 10 Kathleen O'Connor: A Solo Act 62

Chapter 11 Anne Alison Greene: A Passion for Art and Teaching 70

Chapter 12 Bessie Davidson: *Une Australienne Française* 75

Chapter 13 Jessie Traill: A Comprehensive Vision 83

Chapter 14 Gladys Reynell: Freedom and Dedication 88

Chapter 15 Vida Lahey: A Pioneering Professional 94

Chapter 16 Mary Cockburn Mercer: *La Vie Bohème* 102

Chapter 17 Janet Cumbrae Stewart: Trailblazer 109

Chapter 18 Hilda Rix Nicholas: An Open-minded Traditionalist . . . 116

Chapter 19 Anne Dangar: Communard and Theorist 126

Chapter 20 Evelyn Chapman: A Pioneer War Artist 133

Chapter 21 Grace Crowley: A Major Australian Modernist 139

Chapter 22 Dorrit Black: An Influential Convert to Modernism 150

Chapter 23 Stella Bowen: The Symbiosis of Art and Life 158

Chapter 24 Madge Freeman: A Steady Achiever 165

Chapter 25 Constance Stokes: A Determined Career 171

Chapter 26 Moya Dyring: Artist, and Artist's Friend 181

Chapter 27 Betty Quelhurst: A Dedicated Artist and Teacher 191

Chapter 28 Margaret Olley: A Lover of Life and Art 196

Afterword 203

Appendix: Featured Australian Women Artists in Australian
  Art Schools, 1880s to 1940s 208

Notes 210

Bibliography 221

About the Authors 231

LIST OF PLATES

Plate 1　　Iso Rae, *Breton Girl with Goat*, c.1889. Pastel and black chalk on cardboard, 47.0 × 17.0 cm. Purchased with Funds donated from the Estate of Ouida Marston, 2011. NGV, Accession No. 2011.329.

Plate 2　　Agnes Goodsir, *Girl with Cigarette*, c.1925. Oil on canvas, 100.0 × 81.0 cm. Bequest of Mrs Amy E. Bayne, 1945. Bendigo Art Gallery, Accession No. 1945.2.

Plate 3　　Marie Tuck, *The Sewing Circle*, c.1910. Oil on board, 40 × 35 cm. Cruthers Collection of Women's Art, UWA, CCWA847.

Plate 4　　Bessie Gibson, *Portrait (Woman Knitting)*, (n.d.). Watercolour on wove paper, 20.2 × 14.4 cm. Bessie Gibson Estate, QAGOMA 1:0903C. Licensed by Viscopy 2020.

Plate 5　　Dora Meeson, *A Harvest Sunset*, 1888. Oil on canvas, 20.0 × 30.5 cm. Collection D.J. Angeloro. © Mr Simon Hearder.

Plate 6　　Alice Muskett, *A Lost Halo*, 1897. Pastel on paper, 56.4 × 40.2 cm. NGA Purchased 1992, Accession No. NGA 92.801.

Plate 7　　Ethel Carrick, *The Fruit and Vegetable Market, Nice*, 1933. Ink paper lithograph, hand coloured in watercolour. 32.4 × 45.9 cm. NGA purchased 1994, Accession No. NGA 94.1460.

Plate 8　　Ada May Plante, *Man with a Pipe*, c.1940. Oil on canvas on cardboard, 84.0 × 73.4 cm. Gift of Miss Mary Lindsay in memory of A.M. Plante, 1977. NGV, Accession No. A6-1977.

Plate 9　　Margaret Preston, *White Gum*, 1953. Colour stencil. 52.0 × 41.0 cm. Cruthers Collection of Women's Art, UWA, CCWA 647. Licensed by Viscopy 2020.

Plate 10　Kathleen O'Connor, *Self Portrait*, 1928. Oil on board, 64 × 49 cm. Cruthers Collection of Women's Art, UWA, CCWA 36.

Plate 11   Anne Alison Greene, *L'Église Saint-Étienne-du-Mont, Paris*, 1935. Oil on canvas, 73.0 × 60.0 cm. QAGOMA, Accession No. 1:1176.

Plate 12   Bessie Davidson, *Mother and Child*, 1914. Oil on canvas, 91.5 × 73.5 cm. Gift of Margaret (Mrs Klasen) and Sybil de Rose 1992. AGSA, Accession No. 923P6.

Plate 13   Jessie Traill, *The Roadside, Flanders*, 1907. Printed in brown ink with plate-tone, from one plate, 24.8 × 19.9 cm. Purchased 1977, NGA, Accession No. 77.220. © Jessie Traill / Copyright Agency.

Plate 14   Gladys Reynell, *Pensiveness*, c.1913. Oil on canvas, 73.0 × 60.0 cm. 25th Anniversary Gift from the Friends of the Art Gallery of SA, 1994, Accession No. 944P9. © Ms Jessica Ivanovic.

Plate 15   Vida Lahey, *Building the Bridge*, 1931. Watercolour and gouache over pencil on wove paper on cardboard, 24.5 × 28.5 cm. From the estate of Mrs Gladys Powell, 1941. QAGOMA 1.0299.

Plate 16   Mary Cockburn Mercer, *Ballet*, c.1939. Oil on canvas, 94.7 × 66.3 cm. Gift of Robin Sherwood in honour of Dame Elisabeth Murdoch's 100th Birthday through the Australian Government's Cultural Gifts Program, NGV, Accession No. 2009.146. © Mrs S. Hudson.

Plate 17   Janet Cumbrae Stewart, *Studio Fairy*, 1920s. Pastel, 64.8 × 50.2 cm. NGV, Felton Bequest, 1930, Accession No. 4387-3. © Scott Cumbrae-Stewart.

Plate 18   Hilda Rix Nicholas, *Les Fleurs Dédaignées*, 1925. Oil on canvas, 193.0 × 128.5 cm. NGA, Purchased 2008, Accession No. 2008.926. © Bronwyn Wright.

Plate 19   Anne Dangar, *Pochoir Composition*, 1936. Gouache on paper, drawing in brush and gouache, 33.0 × 27.0 cm. NGA, Purchased 2002, Accession No. 2002.52.

List of Plates

Plate 20 Evelyn Chapman, *Ruined Church, Villers-Bretonneux*, 1918–19. Tempera on grey paper, 30.2 × 38.8 cm. Gift of the artist's daughter, Pamela Thalben-Ball 1976. AGNSW 197.1976. © Estate of the artist.

Plate 21 Grace Crowley, *Woman (Annunciation)*, 1939. Oil on canvas on composition board, 73.6 × 53.0 cm. NGA, Purchased 1972, Accession No. 72.482. © Ms Gail Kimber.

Plate 22 Dorrit Black, *On the Rocks*, 1935. Colour linocut on white wove tissue, 19.8 × 31.4 cm. Gift of Ann Vanstone through the AGSA Foundation and Maurice A. Clarke Bequest Fund 2010, Accession No. 20109G14.

Plate 23 Stella Bowen, *Self Portrait*, c.1934. Oil on cardboard, 55.8 × 45.5 cm. NPG, Purchased 2003, Accession No. 2003.18. © Sharon Gallagher.

Plate 24 Madge Freeman, *Still Life*, 1926. Oil on board, 46.0 × 36.0 cm. Collection Bendigo Art Gallery, Accession No. 1936.2. © Bill Freeman.

Plate 25 Constance Stokes, *Reverie*, 1950. Oil on Masonite, 67.8 × 49.0 cm. A.R. Ragless Fund, 1950, Art Gallery of SA, Accession No. 0.1448. © Lucilla d'Abrera.

Plate 26 Moya Dyring, *Fishermen*, 1966. Oil on canvas, 38.1 × 60.9 cm. Heide Museum of Modern Art, Accession No. 1982.89. Bequest of John and Sunday Reed 1982. © Judith Innes Irons.

Plate 27 Betty Quelhurst, *Winter Sun – Surfers Paradise Beach*, 1961. Oil on board, 88.5 × 119.1 cm. Gift of the artist through Queensland Art Foundation, 1996. QAGOMA, Accession No. 1996.124. © Ian Quelhurst.

Plate 28 Margaret Olley, *Morning Interior*, 1973. Oil on composition board, 60.7 × 75.8 cm. Gift of Gretel Bootes in memory of Gordon Bootes, 2010. NGA, Accession No. 2010.569. © Estate of Margaret Olley.

FOREWORD

In the early 20th century, artists from all over the world flocked to Paris, even from places as far away as Australia. Some Australian artists actually were in the inner circle of the avant-garde: John Peter Russell was friends with Claude Monet, Vincent Van Gogh and Henri Matisse; and Charles Conder 'hung out' with Henri de Toulouse-Lautrec in the seedier parts of Montmartre.

But what about the women? It was more difficult for them at that time to meld into the Parisian art world. A woman's reputation was everything. They couldn't really join the club of rollicking, unruly young men. Even now a male artist with wild hair and dirty screwed-up clothes is a tortured genius, but a woman is just a mess. In Australia, women couldn't sit alone in bars, etc. Art was considered a desirable accomplishment for a young woman, along with piano, dancing, sewing, and a foreign language – but not as a profession.

The private painting tutor of the French Impressionist Berthe Morisot and her sister Edma wrote this anxious warning to their mother that they were getting too serious: 'Considering the characters of your daughters, my teaching will not endow them with minor drawing-room accomplishments; they will become painters. Do you realise what this means? In the upper-class milieu to which you belong, this will be revolutionary, I might say almost catastrophic.'

The women in this book went much further: they left everything, some never to return. As Clem Gorman has remarked, 'In those times, to leave her home and travel half round the world to live and study art was remarkable in itself'.

In the formal studio photos, many of these women look very prim, all white gloves and teacups, but I have no doubt that there was more to them than that. It is hard for us to imagine how very far away and alien Paris must have seemed. Now, after approximately 24 unpleasant hours on a plane, you are there. You can be constantly connected by the internet and technology. In the early 20th century, it took weeks to get there. You were only in contact by long-awaited letters. It was such an enormous, brave step.

Some were supported by their family, but many travelled alone. Some would have found it a relief to be away from the constraints of family. Paris had a reputation as somewhere you could go to be yourself. In Paris, it seemed no-one cared what you did, as long as it was reasonably discreet. For many, it was a precious time to work hard and to soak up as much as possible in the private art schools or in the Louvre before returning home, sometimes with new and 'rather shocking' ideas gained from seeing the work of artists such as Cézanne.

Women were excluded from free tuition at the École des Beaux-Arts until 1897. So they paid for classes in the studios of established artists or at private académies. It is important to remember that, even then, there was not *one* art world, but many. We tend to think of the early 20th-century breakthroughs of Picasso and Matisse but forget that this was at the same time as the ultra-conservative French academic style. Traditional life-drawing classes were an essential part of academic study: women were not always allowed, however, as it was considered inappropriate and even dangerous for 'the weaker sex'. Without access to nude models, female artists could not hope to produce paintings that could be considered serious and win major prizes, state commissions or scholarships. For a respectable middle-class woman in the early

20th century to support herself as many of these women did was a considerable achievement.

The Australian artist Moya Dyring said: '[Paris] is the only place for a painter to live, everything is so accessible, one can find so much beauty'. When today I am asked, 'Why Paris?', I always reply (feeling that it sounds a bit insipid) 'Because it is so beautiful!' It is also a place where art is considered important. I first went to Paris in my 20s. I had just won the Sulman Prize (judged by Albert Tucker) as well as the Marten Bequest, a travelling scholarship with a three-month studio residency at the Cité Internationale des Arts. I spent weeks in the museums seeing great art for the first time, exploring the stunningly beautiful streets and filling endless sketchbooks with ideas and impressions. Over the years, I returned frequently to Paris. In 2010, I bought an apartment in the non-touristy part of Montmartre with my partner, artist Bernard Ollis, and I now live and work there part of every year.

This fascinating book introduces us to many intriguing women; many who have been marginalised or forgotten. Reading this I kept wishing I could talk to them, wanting to know more about why they came to Paris, what their life was like, who their friends were, etc. This book gives a tantalising glimpse of them and is a great introduction to their work.

Wendy Sharpe

ACKNOWLEDGMENTS

We cannot thank all these people enough. The old cliché 'without them this book would not have been possible' has never been more true.

Special thanks:
John Cruthers, Cruthers Collection of Women's Art (CCWA)
Wendy Sharpe
Jane Watters, S.H. Ervin Gallery
Janet Parker, Freelance Editor

Lucilla Wyborn d'Abrera, David Angeloro, Christopher Antonious, Wendy Bacon, Greg Bain, Professor Clive Barstow, John Berghouse, Peta Jane Blessing, Melissa Boyde, Martin Browne, Joan Bruce, Emma Cain, Eileen Chanin, Creative Secretarial, Lyla Cross, Ann Curthoys, Tansy Curtin, Tracey Dall, Kate Daw, Bridget Donnellan, Georgina Downey, Richard Dulieu Salon d'Automne, Anne Dunn, Rebecca Edwards, Claire Eggleton, Helen Ennis, Peter Fay, Denise Ferrer, Jude Fowler-Smith, Juno Gemes, Kate Hargrave, Sam Hill-Smith, John Hoar, Vivian Huang, Susan Johnson, Joan Keating, Nicholas Keyser, Annette Larkin, Mark Ledbury, Mary Lijnzaad, Norbert Loeffler, Margaret Mayhew, John McDonald, Paul McGillick, Linda Michael, Patti Miller, Denise Mimmochi, Gillian Minervini, Catriona Moore, Camellia Morris, Joanne Mullins, Musée d'Orsay Archives, Christopher Newman, Nick Nicholson, Tim Olsen, Harriet O'Malley, Vanessa van Ooyen, Diane Ottley, Courtney Pedersen, Maryann Phillips, April Pressler, Queensland Art Gallery Archives, Noel Quelhurst, Karen Quinlan, Eric Riddler, Julia Rodwell,

Luke Sciberras, Carolyn Skinner, Catherine Speck, Ann Stephen, Jan Stephenson, Meg Stewart, Angela Sullivan, Anne Summers, Elena Taylor, Heather Todd, Bronwyn Watson, Jin Whittington, Bronwyn Wright, Lisa Zito

INTRODUCTION

Intrepid Women –
The Wild Geese of Australian Art

This book represents our journey to rediscover some of the Australian women artists who lived and worked in Paris in the early 20th century, and to give them and their work the honour and respect they deserve.

For many years we have travelled to Europe and always found, without question, that our favourite destination was Paris. We live there for long periods and drink in all that the city has to offer – its galleries, history, architecture, lifestyle and people. We have found that we undergo something of an osmosis, whereby we feel that we experience and absorb much of what Australia's visiting women artists also experienced, last century, with the added ingredient that they were working as professional artists, making their mark in the then world capital of art. We tread in their footsteps, and we feel that we almost know them, that they were the embodiment of what we mean by 'Paris'. This is the experience we would like to share with readers.

The movement of Australian women artists to Paris in the first half of last century was a pilgrimage, a lay pilgrimage, but a pilgrimage nonetheless. To them, as to us, it must have seemed that Paris exuded art, lived art, breathed art, and this heady elixir was what drew these pilgrims to the ateliers of Montmartre and, later, Montparnasse. In Paris today, even ordinary citizens are proud of their knowledge of the city's cultural riches. It has lost none of its excitement as a city of art.

A few years ago, our son won the first of two residencies at the Cité des Arts in the Marais district of Paris, in a magnificent spot overlooking the Seine. We became familiar with that area and found two Australian women artists had lived on Île Saint-Louis, where the Cité was subsequently established in the 1970s, and that an atelier in the Cité was later set up to honour one of them: Moya Dyring. In the early 1950s, Margaret Olley lived on the island and she and Dyring worked closely together. The Dyring atelier in the Cité is for artists from Australia to live and work and enrich their practice, just like the two women all those years ago. As we wandered the pavements there we felt their presence and we imagined too, the major figures, including Alice B. Toklas and Gertrude Stein, who visited Dyring's studio and walked those same pavements.

The reasons for Australian women artists going there varied, as did their beliefs, but all experienced a powerful urge to grow, and to challenge themselves. Art has always flourished on the back of such pilgrimages, as influence and skills spread from one arts community to another. There is simply no substitute, even with today's technology, for going to the place where 'it's all happening', experiencing it for oneself, living and working in that environment, and bringing it all back home.

They found themselves in a huge city populated mostly by people foreign to them and communicating, of course, in a language that they also found foreign. They may often have expected Paris to make them sophisticated but, knowing what they went for, they studied and viewed and chattered, and garnered from Paris all that they needed. Not so much sophistication, as creative maturity.

These artists contributed significantly to French art, some more than others. They were, in a sense, our Australian 'wild geese', who flew to a creative feeding ground where the notoriously nationalistic French took them seriously and were pleased with their contribution, as the evidence will show.

The Left Bank was, and is, a student area. Even in medieval times, most of the monasteries and teaching centres were located there, and, from the 17th century, this morphed into the great Sorbonne, which in time became part of the huge University of Paris that today sprawls all over the Left Bank, from Montparnasse to the Gare d'Austerlitz. Hence, a long tradition of art and learning is associated with the area that attracted Australia's women artists.

Those of the women, a majority, who exhibited in the Salons – annual open art competitions that were located mostly on the Right Bank – would have had to carry their artworks across town to those Salons. The Metro was in its infancy from 1900 to 1914, but a network of electric trams covered the entire city by the start of World War I. We can imagine them, in their long flowing dresses, carrying sometimes large artworks onto and off public transport, or perhaps on long tramps over the bridges of the Seine.

Lucilla Wyborn d'Abrera, who published a biography of her mother Constance Stokes, described the Latin Quarter in these terms:

> It was Montparnasse with its myriad eating places, cheap student apartments and often squalid artists' communes that became the magnet for aspiring and mostly impoverished artists, musicians and intellectuals from everywhere. Naturally it would become the hub of left-wing views and activities because of the general permissiveness of its excitable, transient inhabitants.[1]

We chose a number of women to write about who would serve as exemplars for the rest. This number boiled down, after much to-ing and fro-ing, to 28, who between them represent pretty much every pathway that these women took as they delved into the already heavily explored territory of world art in its capital city. We have chosen to focus on the first half of the 20th century for two reasons. One: this was the period when women travelled to Paris from all over the world, in substantial numbers but not yet in the stampede that followed World War II, and two: this was the seminal period when Modernism was thrusting itself forward as a challenger to the established art world. During the late 1950s, a huge flock of artists invaded Paris, which, while still artistically vibrant, was no longer art's world capital, which had moved to New York. In other words, the first half of the century was exciting, a time of significant change – and a supremely stimulating time to be there.

This has been an exciting and exacting project. While many fine monographs, articles and exhibition catalogue notes have been written about many of these women, there has not been an attempt to bring together for a wider readership a representative sample of the cohort of women artists who lived and worked in Paris and were excited and influenced by French art, and much of what has been written is directed at art professionals.

We have endeavoured to see the women as a cohort, while also acknowledging their individual differences. And we are bringing to the fore, as stated earlier, some artists who had slipped almost into oblivion. We hope this book adds one more vital step in the process of giving them the respect and admiration they have earned.

In approaching this project, we first asked ourselves why we should study, and value, these women. There are a number of reasons. One, in view of the difficulties encountered by such women wishing to travel, live and work alone, we believe they are to be acknowledged for their bravery. The journey on the high seas, particularly in the years before World War I, could be daunting – not only for the cost, but also for the dangers that still remained for ocean travel in that period. Although some travelled with a female companion, their family, or a husband, many travelled alone, which must surely have created some anxiety. Two, the quality of their work, as we will show, gives us reason to admire their skill and their hunger to learn and grow as artists. Three, as Australia was then largely dependent on importing its culture from the more highly developed, older parts of the European world, they were emissaries who imbibed the best of European art in France and were eager to share it with their fellow Australians. Most of these women either returned home and made their contribution as exhibiting artists or as teachers and mentors, or, like Anne Dangar, sent back regular information by mail, which helped Australian art to overcome its provincial outlook.

Australia has been quick to honour many other outstanding artists in a variety of fields. One might think of Sidney Nolan, Nellie Melba, or Robert Helpmann, all of whom received imperial honours from the Queen. Yet these Australian women artists of the period in question have, in our opinion, received insufficient or sometimes almost non-existent recognition for their considerable contributions to both French and Australian art, as we intend to show in the following pages.

Women, in the first half of the 20th century, often had to overcome the objections of family, and the case of Stella Bowen is a good example of this. These objections were often very strenuous, particularly when Paris was mentioned … Paris, the home of bohemia, where women went unchaperoned, had lovers, painted nudes, and smoked cigarettes in public. Many were lesbians, maybe as many as half – though 'lesbian' in those times might not always have had sexual implications. They went, we believe, to escape the patriarchy and to live lives in which they could make their own decisions, their own mistakes, and openly love women, though it is a contestable assertion and evidence for any 'escape' from the Australian patriarchy of those times is not easy to find, since women in those times were reluctant, we find, to openly discuss their sexual orientation, unlike today. But all of them loved art, and they headed for the city that shared that love.

The identity of these women reflected the Australia of their times. Not only were they predominantly Anglo–Celtic in ethnicity, they represented, by choosing art as a profession and not as a hobby, a fringe element of the white middle-classes that was less ready to conform to the rather strict bourgeois morality of these decades. In this respect, even before they left home, they were already a cohort, although in many cases not yet known to each other. They all, also, self-identified strongly as artists, although some did not wish to be labelled 'Australian'.

We emphasise that Paris was the world centre of art during this period. For that reason, this book focuses on Paris, almost to the exclusion of London. Artists, as Anne Gérard-Austin asserts, mostly preferred Paris, the heart of Modernism, which attracted a good proportion of the Australian women.[2]

London had some excellent teachers, some of them progressive, like Claude Flight, some with strengths in a particular technique, like Frank Brangwyn. But most of the deservedly famous art schools were in Paris. Again, most of the major painters of the era, those who had created new ways of thinking about art, like Matisse, Degas or Cézanne, were or had been Paris based. Bessie Davidson was influenced

Introduction

by van Gogh, Bonnard and Vuillard; Bessie Gibson by Whistler; Kathleen O'Connor by the Impressionists; and so it went on. All the great models and mentors were there, and their art could be seen – the paint barely dry – in the many marvellous public and private galleries. English art was already well known in Australia and was influential in such Australian art schools as the National Gallery Art School in Melbourne; French art, on the other hand, was less well known but, paradoxically, more famous – and often more iconoclastic. Paris was the mecca, and, to the women, an exotic one.

We regret that readers will not find in these pages some of the artists they may have expected. Grace Cossington Smith and Nora Heysen come to mind, among others. These artists, while among the greatest Australia has produced, did not study, exhibit, reside, or find their inspiration in Paris, which is the focus of this book. Much has been written about them and, after much thought, it has been decided to concentrate on those women who absorbed, and often brought home, the rich heritage of art that was Paris in the first half of the 20th century.

We sought to find common elements in the work of the artists that have been chosen for this book. The great chasm, we thought, was between the traditionalists and the Modernists, but even that chasm contained quite a few artists who had a foot on both sides; for example, Constance Stokes. Colour was one feature that was common to most of them, but this was the era when colour was springing to the fore, partly because of the invention of paint in tubes, and partly because of the example of the Fauves, who pioneered the use of strong and vivid colour in their work. Another common factor was an intense curiosity, and if there was a dominant element that can be seen in all their work it was, according to Butel, the element of design.³ All of the women, she asserts, consciously designed their work and incorporated design elements into it, especially the Cubists. Design, in this context, we take to mean that art works were planned in advance with such elements in mind as the leading of the eye across a painting; contrasts between areas of high and low palette; and the use, or not, of perspective.

Some did not wish to be known as 'Australian'. But they were, and they were often brash, forthright, confident and optimistic, unafraid to venture into new realms. They had not slipped across the Channel, or sauntered down from Germany – they had come all the way from a tiny British outpost at great cost, personal and financial, often missing their families and loved ones.

There is a clear and sharp distinction between the France of the period before World War I and the France of the period between the two world wars. In the first period, often called the 'Belle Époque', a strict morality limited the freedom and enterprise of women, even in France. The term Belle Époque was and is used to signify a brief period of peace, prosperity, and cultural excitement and excellence never before achieved in France. It ended abruptly with World War I. After the war, the 'Jazz Age' of the 1920s ushered in significant new freedoms and choices for women – although not so many as is sometimes asserted. Agnes Goodsir's painting *Girl with Cigarette* has been cited as an example of the 'new woman' of the 1920s.⁴ World War I not only divided the last shreds of the 19th century from the rapidly developing 20th, it also gave some Australian women artists the occasion to display their humanity, compassion, and devotion to the country that had taken them in and given them opportunities – Iso Rae, Bessie Davidson and others served with distinction and

Introduction

zeal during the war, either as unofficial war artists or in hospitals or recuperation centres helping wounded soldiers.

After the war, there was an opening up of society, a time of festivity and exuberance. Many African–American jazz musicians travelled to Paris during this decade to escape American racism, and jazz was very fashionable as dance music in bars. This period saw the full flowering of the freedoms that Paris had always promised. All of this pleasure ended ultimately in recklessness and the Crash of 1929, the Great Depression and the rise of totalitarianism in Europe.

New women arrived, some of the earlier cohort remained or returned, rents started to rise, Modernism became more ubiquitous, moral standards started to change, feminism came more strongly into focus – all adding up to a new kind of world. Paris was still the great centre of art, and Australian women continued to make their mark and their contribution and to enrich their art.

In seeking to make these artists better known and respected among the art-loving public, it has not been our primary intention to critically analyse their work or to pursue in depth the extent to which some of them may have had some stylistic influence upon French art. We hope to have provided some basis for such discussions.

We approached the S.H. Ervin Gallery in Sydney's Rocks district to mount an exhibition of these 28 women, to augment the work of this book in promoting these women. In January of 2018 this exhibition was staged, to considerable approval in the visual arts world. The work of gaining respect for these artists will continue.

All Australians can be proud of the 'Intrepid Women'. They did what they did with fortitude and determination, and, in doing so, fulfilled not only their own creative passions, but also added to their ability to enrich Australian art.

The Pilgrimage of the Intrepid Women

The Preparation

Where the artists came from, and how they prepared for their journeys, were questions we asked ourselves in researching their lives. As shown in each chapter, most grew up in well-educated families. Some of the women, such as Grace Crowley, came from small rural towns.

Raising the funds to travel so far, and to live and work in France, was easier for some than for others, depending upon the level of family support. While some obtained travelling grants, and others were given funding by their families, some had to earn and save for their travel money.

All of the women we have researched studied art professionally in Australia before heading for Europe. The National Gallery Art School in Melbourne, under Bernard Hall and Frederick McCubbin during most of the period in question, trained and encouraged by far the largest number of them – more than a third of the total represented in these pages. Julian Ashton in Sydney trained several, including Grace Crowley; and the Brisbane Central Technical College, under Godfrey Rivers, taught a number – Margaret Olley attended this school. In Adelaide, Gladys Reynell, Bessie Davidson and Margaret Preston considered themselves so well trained and were so confident that in the early 1900s they set up their own art school, one of their students being Stella Bowen. In addition, some of the women exhibited in Australia before leaving for Europe, especially those who were a little older prior to their leaving.

In general, it could be said that the training in these schools, at least prior to World War I, was basically traditional, illusionist, naturalistic painting, without the distortion that was later used in much Modern art. In visual art writing, the term 'illusionist' refers to the fact that the painting is purporting to depict a scene exactly as our eye would see it, yet the painting is not the scene – it is still an illusion of the scene, merely paint on a surface (it is a descriptive term, not a movement title.) Some of the teachers had been attracted to Impressionism, notably at the National Gallery Art School, but Modernism, especially in its more potent forms such as Cubism, was hardly taught and little was known about its techniques.

One artist who left Australian shores with inadequate training under her belt was Kathleen O'Connor, who acknowledged that she was under-trained when she arrived in Paris, although she had studied at Perth Technical College.[5]

The Appendix shows the schools in Australia at which our subjects studied before leaving. They had, indeed, quite a prelude to their artistic journey, this giving all of them a reasonably sound grounding before venturing into the international art scene. In our opinion, too, many of the women had learnt enough about the French art scene and the great European galleries to be anxious to get over there, to learn, and to look, firsthand. The reasons for each artist choosing to go will be established in each chapter, and the extent to which they equipped themselves before leaving.

At Home in France

What did the women find in Paris? What were the conditions under which they would be living? How could they know if they were going to be disappointed?

Their first task on arrival was to settle in to their new environment. As Grace Crowley describes, most pressing was the need to find somewhere to live and work.[6] Before World War I, Montparnasse was still only partly developed, with numerous open spaces and many slum buildings. Between 1853 and 1870, the Emperor Napoleon III commissioned Georges-Eugène Haussmann to rebuild large areas of Paris that were considered overcrowded and unhealthy. The Haussmann buildings that now epitomise the city are monumental, multi-storied, made of stone and brick, and characterised by balconies and cornices. They are part of a complete redesign of the city, which featured the creation of the boulevards. Even today, however, many of the residential buildings on the Left Bank are not Haussmann, but smaller two- or three-storey buildings. Some of the buildings back then were little better than farm sheds.

Expatriates from all countries crowded into this area, mostly because it was cheap, and close to shops and markets, and, of course, for socialising. The spaces into which many of the Australian women moved were, as mentioned, primitive, often with no running water or toilet facilities. Women who had been brought up in fine homes in Australia must often have been mortified to find themselves without basic amenities, but if so, they have left very little record of any dissatisfaction. Perhaps it was enough just to be in Paris.

If the expatriate community in Paris, of which these women were a part, was perhaps a little divorced from the daily cut and thrust of local life, they did not mind: it was the artistic Paris they were absorbing, intrigued by the street life more than by the politics or the condescension of the majority *bourgeois* population in the essentially conservative city – save for the Left Bank and Montmartre. This city rumbled and buzzed around them, but they were in a Paris that was timeless and above mere survival, a Paris of the mind, a Paris that survives and flourishes to this day. So, as we have said, they wanted the schools, the galleries, the living artists, the great artists of the past, the mystique, the freedom (sexual, political and artistic), the cheap ateliers, the art societies, the kudos for having been there, the chance to prove themselves in a tough, competitive milieu and, for some, the mythic lure of bohemia.

The cheap ateliers must have been a major reason for the migration of artists across the Seine to Montparnasse from Montmartre. Gérard-Austin quotes art historian John Milner stating that the rue Notre-Dame-des-Champs in the 6th arrondissement accommodated 'more studios than any other street in Paris'.[7] The lower rents, of course, drew students and artists, and it was not difficult to find some wholly unsuitable living quarters, freezing in winter and baking in summer, up flights of stairs that had to be tackled in long dresses and heavy underwear. We walked along many of the streets where they had lived, including the rue de l'Odéon, rue Campagne-Première, and the rue Léopold Robert, mostly within shouting distance of the Boulevard du Montparnasse and the Luxembourg Gardens, and not far from the Boulevard Raspail. We imagined the Australian women walking excitedly, perhaps at times in groups, along these streets to and from galleries. We felt we had gained a glimpse of what their days might have been like.

The Parisian art schools were cutting edge, some of the best in the world. Moreover, some of them, for example André Lhote's school, taught new fashions – in his case Cubism – which attracted those who were seeking to break new ground. The women studied mostly at private art schools and not at the state-funded schools, those having at the time only recently been opened to foreigners. The Académie Julian was conservative but highly regarded. The Académie Colarossi was as good, had art classes in which models posed nude so as to enable artists to learn to draw the human body, and could offer students the chance to paint with or without tuition – the latter being cheaper, of course. The Académie de la Grande Chaumière was also popular and well regarded. All of these were located on the Left Bank near the Boulevard du Montparnasse, where René-Xavier Prinet also established the first French school exclusively for women artists. There were also clubs, such as the Paris Club of International Women Artists, which formed in the late 19th century to provide support and encouragement for women artists. Also in this milieu were the Modernists, including Albert Gleizes, operating schools and influencing many artists from all over the world.

They also found numerous Salons with an annual exhibition advertised competitively and judged by a jury of eminent figures. These Salons gave many of the women an entrée into the Parisian art world, enabling them to compete on their merits in what was a very competitive industry. This competitiveness is why the women worked so hard. That the women competed among themselves is confirmed by Anne Dangar's letters in *Earth, Fire, Water, Air*, where Dangar mentions competitiveness between Grace Crowley, Dorrit Black and herself, and in which Dangar asserts that Black appropriated some of Crowley's and her techniques.[8] Competing also with the best of the world, they proved their worth by their success. Sebastian Smee, in his Pulitzer Prize-winning *The Art of Rivalry*, outlines competition between some of art's greats, including Matisse, Picasso, Manet and Degas, pointing out how important rivalry was between, for example, Picasso and Matisse.[9] In her review on Radio National's 'Books and Arts', Kathleen Calderwood quotes Smee: 'Their [Picasso and Matisse] rivalry extended throughout their lives, where one would ignore or engage with the other's work, even stealing ideas and motifs'. She then relates how Picasso stole the idea of painting African masks from some he saw at Gertrude Stein's house, which Matisse had bought from a curio shop.[10] Such rivalry is, of course, a natural and stimulating part of the creative process.

Also there were the many commercial art galleries, in some of which the Australian women exhibited. Many group exhibitions, a pathway toward recognition, were mounted by the artists' clubs and societies. The art dealers and gallery owners played an important role in bringing the work of little-known foreign artists to the attention of the French art-buying public.

Once settled in, they began to do what is today called 'networking'. Jane Jacobs, in her book *The Economy of Cities*, advances a theory she calls 'spillover', by which she means the cross-fertilisation of ideas that occurs in the dense environment of a large international city.[11] She makes clear she is referring to the intersection of Boulevard du Montparnasse and the Boulevard Raspail, which she considered the centre of the artistic world of Paris. There one can still, to this day, find the places that were most frequented by the expatriate artistic community – Le Dôme, most famous of all, and its nearby rivals Café de la Rotonde and La Coupole. There, the artists would rub shoulders with Picasso or Trotsky or a Russian émigré whose intentions might not be honourable. And, of course, make full use of the bathrooms.

These were, overwhelmingly, serious women who were determined to succeed as professional artists. They sometimes had to accept loneliness, which can be the downside of a solitary art such as painting, although some shared an atelier. They spoke passionately about their art, as did the French. In short, for them art and life were not separate categories. They went for themselves, as a coming of age, a transitional step toward maturity – even for those who were not so young.

As an example of the value of 'spillover', Jacobs cites Picasso, who took some of his innovative ideas from artists from non-visual fields, especially poets. By no means the most skilful artist of his generation, she states, he advanced his work by what today might be termed 'appropriation'. These ideas, she claims, originated in conversations particularly at Le Dôme, which today features many photographs of him on its walls.

We may imagine this phenomenon – creative gossip, one might almost call it, or shop-talk – taking place among the Australian women and people they met through mutual acquaintances at café tables – or indeed, like Kathleen O'Connor, simply absorbed from adjoining tables. It is indeed probable that it would have led to developments in the work of the Australian women artists, who might have been impatient to walk back to their ateliers to try to put into their artistic practice some of the ideas or methods they had just heard about or discussed.

James Panero expounds a theory of 'ideas in the air', in a crowded urban environment where artists congregate in public places – he includes the cafés and places where artists met.[12] During our own times in Paris we have experienced the stimulation of ideas all around us – in galleries, in the architecture, in the fashions – and Paris during the early 20th century was truly an incubator of intellectual ferment. This was the period of the Russian Revolution in 1917, and intellectual movements such as Marxism, Freudianism and Jungianism, Surrealism, Absurdism, Dadaism, Feminism, Anarchism, Anarcho-syndicalism, Existentialism a little later, and a general atmosphere of iconoclasm. Many of the progenitors of new ideas were exiled from, or fled, their home countries and found refuge in this city.

Lenin and Trotsky, then still on amicable terms, were frequent visitors at Le Dôme during the Belle Époque. Hemingway lived in Paris for much of the 1920s, as did F. Scott Fitzgerald and, a little later, Henry Miller and the Surrealist André Breton, along with the poet Rilke. Oscar Wilde lived in Paris for the last few years of his life around the turn of the century.

Can it be said that there is a 'female sensibility' reflected in the work of these women? Dora Meeson was self-consciously a feminist, and Margaret Preston was one of several of these women who was, we believe, acutely aware of a feminine heritage – in her art and interviews she chose to highlight her femininity in a politically conscious manner.[13] But most of the others appear to have devoted their energies predominantly to the pursuit of a non-gender-specific art. A couple of the women, including Hilda Rix Nicholas and Constance Stokes, rejected the term 'women artists'. They wanted to be treated merely as artists, and judged on their merits.

It can be argued that in this period more women painted interiors than landscapes, and that a lot of women painted portraits and still lifes, while many incorporated decorative elements into their work. This could be partly because until World War I women were often kept indoors performing household work and having little chance to see a stag at bay or a valley in the French Alps. Painting portraits was a way for many women to earn a living so that they could maintain their independence. And it should be remembered that artists like Rupert Bunny also used decorative motifs, and some of the women painted more 'robustly' than many of their male contemporaries.

Nonetheless it could fairly be said that whether women painted different subjects than men or not, these subjects would tend to be judged as 'inferior' simply because they were done by women. As women they were sometimes expected by critics to paint only in that decorative style, or only interiors, though many of them went into the Luxembourg Gardens and painted *plein air* (in the open air). As women they have often been undervalued, sometimes devalued, not the least in their home country. And women certainly paint women with a different eye to that of men – not merely as objects of desire to the male gaze, but as people of beauty. Janet Cumbrae Stewart's nudes would be perhaps the prime example of this.

Did the women join the art movements currently sweeping Paris, or did they remain aloof, using the intellectual context to broaden their minds but not to change their beliefs? The evidence will show that some of the women, a few of whom had been traditionalists back home, did change direction, enthusiastically adopting Modernism, while others either incorporated some Modernist techniques, such as flat structure on the canvas, bright colouration, or slightly non-naturalistic figures, while remaining fundamentally within the illusionist sphere.

We note that the women who sold their work easily – Chapman is a good example – were mostly those who did not adopt Modernism, except, perhaps, a touch of Impressionism. Selling paintings in a market as competitive as Paris was far from easy, and it was not easy either to obtain exhibitions. Even when work was exhibited, sales were difficult. Those of the Australian women who sold well must, therefore, have earned considerable respect among the art-buying public and among critics.

It is fair to ask whether the work of the women reflected their Parisian and French experience: did their work change as a result of their pilgrimage? Emphatically, we believe it did. The women painted Parisian scenes and they often adopted, in whole or in part, the current artistic fashions then sweeping French art, as stated above; several of them wrote diaries emphasising the influence Paris was having upon them and their art; some of them remained in France. Some of the influences of Paris – which were, after all, what they were seeking by going there – may have shown themselves subtly in their later work, and perhaps in their teaching methods and their conversation – but the evidence, in our view, shows clearly the influences of their French sojourns.

It would have been difficult, in such a dense milieu, for any artist to stand out, particularly if that artist was not a Modernist. Yet, to be hung in a salon, or to be given an exhibition or asked to join a society, one had to stand out from the crowd. It is our contention that each of the artists chosen for this book did stand out, not only for the quality of their work, but often for its uniqueness. Several of the artists spent time in North Africa, and the exoticism of that area where ancient, fabled cities had risen from the sand, and the picturesque villages of 15th-century architecture of Arabian provenance with the bright light and dry atmosphere – which more closely resembled conditions in Australia than those in northern France – inspired them. The colour and vibrancy of their work made an impression on the French. Indeed, the work of Ethel Carrick and Hilda Rix Nicholas today sells for very high prices – especially their North African work – another touchstone of quality.

We have asked ourselves: were the Australian women as 'good' as the men, whether it be their Australian male counterparts or the great European masters? It is certainly not fair to compare young people from a remote colony with European artists steeped in a long and rich tradition, and anyone can assert that this artist is 'better' than that one. Art appreciation is a subjective activity, but there appears to us to be no reason whatsoever to claim that the Australian women artists were inferior in the quality of their work than their male counterparts. The best argument in support of this is the work itself: what the eye sees, theory cannot displace, and in the end art is for the eye before it is for the brain. The colourful, striking, thoughtful, sensitive, sometimes decorative art of the Australian women stands comparison with any other artists of their time.

Uniqueness is also a quality subjectively gauged. It will be argued that each of the artists created work that was unique, even though, as newcomers, they were initially learning, and often imitating, work that had been done by the masters, and that each had also something of themselves to contribute, as we will seek to show. The French art establishment, and the French art-buying public, might be better judges of this in a competitive environment. Many of the women were accepted by the salons and art societies, whose judgment it would be difficult to question. Certainly we would argue that their experience was unique, as much as their art. Their experience as expatriates was different than that of German, English or American expatriates, as, coming from a distant and raw post-colonial society, Paris must have been awe-inspiring. To become embedded in a great city and an international art scene must have seemed the most unique experience of their lives, and some, like Kathleen O'Connor, described it later in those terms.[14] They were finding themselves as free, self-regulating individuals. It would be hard, in our opinion, to overemphasise the significance of this experience. This is not to say that they consciously subverted the moral order in which they had grown up, but simply that they were able, in France, to choose their own paths. A few of them, such as Anne Dangar and Bessie Davidson, 'became' French. Although they did return to Australia from time to time, France was now their home and they spoke fluent French, had French friends, and were respected and accepted by the French art world.

Did they find bohemia, that mythical country that always lies beyond the rainbow, and where people live exciting lives outside the norm? No, mostly, but yes, some of them, some of the time. Mary Cockburn

Introduction

Mercer mixed with famous artists, travelled around Europe to some glamorous spots, and had some personal experiences that would, at the time, have been considered decidedly outside the norm. Stella Bowen married a famous English novelist, enjoyed parties and dance clubs and was involved in a three-way relationship – to the detriment, it has been alleged, of her art. Most of the women, however, particularly before World War I, were there to work. Some, like Kathleen O'Connor, loved the slightly bohemian atmosphere of places like Le Dôme café, but even Le Dôme was a commercial business where people went to drink good coffee and talk about art, Life with a capital L, and politics. For most of the Australian women, however, devoted as they were to their art, and seeming to wish to avoid, perhaps, the seamier aspects of some parts of the Latin Quarter, a tea party in a studio was about as wild and wicked as it got: only a few of the women dived into the nightlife and the louche world of the Left Bank, in those days a very poor area unlike today. Today, what was thought of as 'bohemian' then would simply be called an 'inner city lifestyle', and, for most of the women, just being there in the Parisian art milieu would have been exciting enough.

The reason for our extended sojourn in Paris in 2015 was to research local records of the Australian women, but it is unfortunate, and it was immensely disappointing for us, that there is scant information held in Paris about these Australian women artists – not at the Australian Embassy, not at the Salon archives now largely held at the Musée d'Orsay, and certainly not at any private archives, such as the Bernheim-Jeune. And what little information existed was often incorrect. We should emphasise that at the Musée d'Orsay the staff in the archive were extremely helpful and courteous, making available everything that we sought. Across the French archives we found little.

We have requested the Cultural Attaché at the Embassy to lobby the archives to redress this.

For us, as researchers and writers exploring the world of these women, it has been a very exciting and significant experience. Walking past the home of Ethel Carrick, for instance, we were reminded that she and her husband set up screens in their tiny backyard so they could paint from a nude model in private. They had all walked these sidewalks; they had peered at the great art of the past in these same galleries. Even today, the Left Bank remains a centre of art. The art schools are still there, artists in paint-stained clothes still take coffee in the rue de Seine, galleries still mount exhibitions that amaze and engross us – and artists still paint, *plein air*, in the Luxembourg Gardens. Artists still walk the streets or ride the Metro carrying their paintings toward some gallery. When we are there, the first half of last century no longer seems like history.

The Homeward Flight

It is highly likely that the women came home with an aura of Europe about them. They would have been wearing at least some French clothes, in styles that would take years to hit Australia; they would have been full of their French and European experiences; their art would have blossomed and, in some cases, changed radically, as for example through the Cubists; and they would have had an air about them, perhaps of triumph but certainly of knowledge and authority, of having been, as it were, grounded in European art. This last may be one reason why a number of them went into teaching upon their return: Marie Tuck, for instance, in Adelaide, and Betty Quelhurst in Brisbane. Dorrit Black created a gallery. Gladys Reynell established a pottery. And most of the returning artists exhibited, thus displaying

Introduction

what they had learnt in Europe. Some of these women are now held in major Australian galleries, although very few are on display, which suggests that they are still not given the full recognition of their worth that we, and many others, feel would be appropriate.

We believe their lives changed considerably as a result of their voyage to Paris. The greatest change was that they became fully professional artists; their skills honed, their knowledge greatly deepened, their experience enriched, their confidence strengthened. They were across the latest world trends and on their return, or on visits home, they were able to teach many younger artists the latest techniques of Parisian art.

None of the Australian women created a new '-ism', but then neither did most male artists, or most Americans, or most English. Maybe they arrived too late to participate in the creation of new movements, some of which had been developing since the mid-19th century. They were there to catch up with a Europe that had leaped ahead, and for some of them it was only when they returned home that their French influences began to shine through, and they began to experiment. The more conservative artists brought home high levels of skill that they were able to impart to their fellow Australian artists either by teaching or by exhibiting. Those who mixed some degree of Modernist influences with a basically illusionist approach demonstrated that there was a middle path. It is the opinion of some academic authors that it was the women, overwhelmingly, who brought these influences home from Paris in general – Crowley, Dangar and Black certainly brought back home to Australia the theory and the techniques of Cubism.

An artistic pilgrimage on this scale is unlikely, we believe, ever to happen again. Today, huge flocks of tourists crisscross the globe, and many cities are significant centres of art in their own right. Today,

Mexico City has a vibrant and original art scene, as does, still, New York, not to mention Shanghai, Tokyo, Sydney and Los Angeles.

The achievement of this cohort of women was not only to change and grow themselves, both as artists and as people, and to assert that women could be as good artists as men, but also to impact upon French art, as we will show, and to quite radically influence Australian art upon their return. This is, overwhelmingly, the reason why we need to study this cohort, and this is why some of the best of them have been gathered together here as exemplars of these achievements.

Chapter 1

ISO RAE

At Home in Two Worlds

Isobel (Iso) Rae
1860–1940
In Paris 1887–1890; in Étaples 1890–1932

Iso Rae was a woman attached to her family, and her art exhibited compassion for human suffering. Her faces reveal the lives that their owners have lived. She was a person of deep feeling, whose art was a valuable aid to our understanding of life during World War I.

If she was timid and shy, as was said of her, her art was as bold as she, perhaps, was not, as well as warm and sensitive. Her works, influenced by the prevailing fashions of Impressionism and Post-Impressionism, were infused with her own character and strength and by no means derivative. They were revealing and clear, the character and individuality of her subjects shining out from the pictures. She felt free to explore the people of her adopted land, and she has left a legacy of insightful, yet quietly passionate work, illuminating the society in which she moved. Hers is a legacy worth preserving.

We had heard of Rae through her connection as friend to Rupert Bunny and Hilda Rix Nicholas, among others, but had not seen any examples of her work until we came across her works in a Deutscher and Hackett catalogue. These are outstanding works and it was hard work choosing which one to use in this book. Rae had fallen almost into oblivion.

There were signs in her early life that she would be an artist, though not necessarily that she would move to Europe – travel in her time was not as easy or common as it was in later years. She grew up, like so many of the women artists of her period, in an upper middle-class family. It was common for young women of this background to apply themselves to art (though professionalism was much rarer – it is the crossover from amateurism to professionalism that so often marks out the women in this collection as exceptional). Qualities such as shyness and sensitivity, one might think, would not seem out of place in an artist – though it is sometimes said of artists that their work is an escape from the harsh realities of everyday life.

She studied art at a high level in Melbourne, including at the National Gallery Art School, where naturalistic techniques were emphasised. She did well there and won a number of prizes in the student exhibition of 1883, where the jury made special mention of her work.[15] Her teacher, Oswald Rose Campbell, used anatomy as the basis for art, and she learned to paint the figure under George Folingsby of the painting school. Folingsby organised life drawing classes, and Iso and her sister Alison were founding members.

Not content to remain in Australia, Rae left with her family for Paris in 1887. The exact reasons are not known, but it might well have been the lure of Parisian art, which was the magnet for others of the Australian women, as revealed in our research. As many Australian women artists were travelling to Paris in this period, it might not be surprising that a budding artist would want to join them. In Paris, she mixed with mostly Australian expatriate artists and art students, and made the obligatory pilgrimage to the great art galleries where she saw the work of major European artists, including, of course, the Impressionists, an important influence on her work. That she moved to Paris with her mother and sister might indicate the closeness she felt for her family, and also perhaps her desire to expand her knowledge of art. In 1890, she and her mother and sister moved from Paris to Étaples in Picardy, where a colony of international artists had developed.

In Étaples, she continued to learn more from the many expatriate artists there. She lived there for more than 40 years. The colony was a ferment of ideas and exploration, and while there she maintained contact with Australia through an occasional painting being included in the regular exhibitions of the Victorian Artists' Society. An exhibition in 1908 at Mrs Theo Anderson's studio in Collins Street included Rae's painting of a peasant girl carrying home a bucket of water. Her work was seen also in the New Zealand and South Seas Exhibition at Dunedin in 1889–90. From Étaples she also exhibited regularly at the Old Salon in Paris, as well as in London.

The mist through which her Étaples figures can be seen annoyed some critics, who suggested that she had carried Impressionism 'too far', but she was, overall, widely respected in both French and Australian art circles. Betty Snowden, writing in *Wartime*, noted: 'During her three years in Paris, Rae was influenced by the French Post-Impressionist artists'.[16]

During World War I, she worked as a nurse at a British Army camp near Étaples, where in her little spare time she drew the men and the camp. Although eleven of these drawings are held at the Australian War

Memorial Gallery, she was not an official war artist and she could not find time to paint, but her drawings and pastels tell of the life and style of a military encampment: British troops lounging, German prisoners working. She shows everyday events behind the lines: men preparing for battle, caring for the wounded, keeping the prisoners occupied and entertaining the troops with soccer games, films and live theatre. The gouache highlights in the night scenes create a red glow, imparting an air of mystery. The night works are drawn on a dark grey textured paper, heightening a sense of anxious waiting and the unknown. Betty Snowden quoted Rae: 'I cannot write of all the things we have been through since the start of the War. We are, I believe, the only English in this town now ... many people went. But we do not want to break up our home unless absolutely obliged to do so'.

Given the grim reality of nursing work in wartime, perhaps capturing vignettes of camp life provided Rae with something of an escape. The subjects include portraits, figure studies and many drawings depicting the day-to-day activities of the camp. The close family Iso Rae had included her sister, Alison, who also worked in the camp at the hospital. Their mother died in 1916, but she and Alison remained in Étaples.

After the war, Rae moved to the small village of Trépied, near Étaples. There, she painted a number of works, including her well-known *Market Scene at Étaples*. In 1932, alarmed by the rise of Nazism, the sisters left Trépied and moved to England, where Iso Rae died in 1940.

As Grace Joel commented in a 1906 issue of *Art and Architecture Australia*, 'Iso Rae is another Australian artist who left these shores ... She is little known on this side, since she has been a resident of France for 20 years. One would almost say that she is French'.[17] Her work, of course, came heavily under French influence. One of her pastels on paper, *Cinema Queue* (1916), is especially impressive, both for its qualities and for the insight it provides about the nature of that war. 'Here Rae has created [a] dramatic elevated night scene, with her use of strong glowing light against the deep black of the night, and gouache over pastel used to highlight the glow of lights in the dark', wrote Snowden. In the foreground, a line of men waiting to enter the cinema building at the camp draws the viewer's eye along the line to the building and then expands our vision to include the entire camp: lines of tents in the background, precisely spaced in neat, crowded rows, scattered figures in the close foreground providing the only variation from regimented lines and shapes, sober and restrained colours with strong lines and filmy outlines in the Post-Impressionist style. There is uniformity, in keeping with the uniform nature of military life. With their peaked roofs, the buildings in the middle of the picture echo the shapes of the city of tents behind them, and the men in the queue are stripped of their individuality by their uniform clothing and the neat row of the line in which they stand. Rae was one of the few women of the time to record the minutiae of war.

The Wikipedia entry for Rae notes that few (of Rae's) works were acquired by public galleries, because they were considered – according to art historian Sasha Grishin – 'too intimate, too personal and too feminine to be included'.[18]

Her *Breton Girl with Goat* (see Plate 1), completed in 1889, is a gentle study of a young girl herding a goat. Done with coloured chalk, this displays Rae's desire to record the lives of ordinary French people, using simple materials and unpretentious locales – perhaps first recorded in pencil and later elaborated. The colours are muted, as is the sense of slow, rural movement. In 2002, Terry Ingram, in the *Age*, asked:

'Whatever happened to Isobel Rae?'[19] She was regarded, he said, as a fine artist of the calibre of McCubbin, yet she had been almost forgotten. The article goes on to tell of a painting sold in a Leonard Joel sale in Melbourne the previous week. The painting was *Breton Girl with Goat*, and was considered to be of a very high quality. Ingram noted, 'the atmospheric approach and rendering of the bush had the same characteristics of a McCubbin influenced by the pre-Impressionists'.

Yet, although she had moved to France, Iso Rae continued a strong relationship with Australia through correspondence. Thus she lived, in a sense, in two worlds – as an *étranger* in France, but without losing her sense of herself as an Australian. Taking the bold step of living abroad yet remaining within the safe folds of her family, Rae kept her ties with her home country and painted, or drew, some of the most beautiful and sensitive work of any of the women artists in this collection.

Chapter 2

AGNES GOODSIR

A Witness to Paris

Agnes Noyes Goodsir
1864–1939
In Paris 1899–1939

Agnes Goodsir, we believe, saw Paris and its ways and people more clearly than any other of the Australian artists who lived and worked there. She was the witness of the Left Bank, and her images, personal and intimate as they often are, help keep the image of that time and place alive today. From the time of her arrival in Paris in 1899, she lived there for most of her life, except for a brief visits home in 1905 and 1927, and brief periods in other European countries, dying in Paris in 1939.

In most ways, Goodsir conformed to the image of the typical Australian expatriate artist in Paris. Like many of them, she had funds at her disposal, she was dedicated to professionalism, she enjoyed the carefree aspects of Parisian life, and she achieved lofty goals. She remained, like Bessie Gibson and others, resolutely conservative in her art, apart perhaps from a little fling with 'La Japonaise', one of the then-prevailing trends that she followed, another being the general move away from *plein air* towards studio interiors. This relative conformity, however, does not obscure her keen eye as an observer of the world she chose as her own, the Left Bank and its 'types'. She trained on the Left Bank, settled there, kept rather to herself as far as other artists were concerned – although there is some uncertainty about this – and prospered there, leaving us some indelible images of her milieu.

Finding Agnes Goodsir was not a detective story, as was the case with some of the lesser-known artists in this collection. She was almost emblematic. Many of the books about Australian women artists in Europe, as listed in the bibliography, seemed to contain information about her, often with an accompanying image, such as *Girl with Cigarette*. Several of Goodsir's better known works are at the Bendigo Art Gallery.

She contributed both to French and Australian art, and must be regarded as a major Australian expatriate artist of her period. Like some of her Australian contemporaries, she was also something of a paradox in that she was progressive in some areas of her life and conservative in others. As a lesbian, it may well be that her sexual orientation could have been a major personal driver for her move to Paris, though her ambition in her work, and her desire to thoroughly school herself in all that the Parisian art schools and galleries had to offer, should be seen as the dominant motivation.

It is interesting to compare her financial resources with those of Australian women generally. Her father sent her an allowance of £100 a year. This did end in 1906 when her father died, but by then she was on her way, and did not mind having to fill in the odd financial gap with teaching. Then, in 1909, her stepmother also died, leaving her a legacy. The amount of her funds has not been finally settled, and she also obtained an income from her portraiture.

Renting lodgings in Paris in those times was considered more expensive for a woman than for a man, possibly because women had to make sure they were safe in their lodgings. According to the Boston Art Students' Association in 1887, '… in almost every case it costs a woman much more to live in Paris than a man'.[20] This is, in fact, why the Left Bank became the area of choice for artists around the turn of the century, as Montmartre, their previous home, became more expensive, being on a hill with magnificent views. Once settled, Goodsir concentrated single-mindedly on her goal of becoming a professional artist in the world's most competitive art marketplace. As she stated, 'It's such fun, if you want a café there, the Rotonde and Le Dôme where Trotsky and Lenin, Red to the last corpuscle met and planned the future of Russia, students of all sorts foregathered, all nationalities, Arabs, Czechs, Greeks, Romanians, Italians'.[21]

Agnes Goodsir did not love modern art. She did respect it, but that was as far as she went. She was determined to work only in a traditional mode. Indeed, to earn a living as an artist in Paris, then as now, it is necessary to conform to naturalistic styles, with perhaps a nod in the direction of a not-too-modern style, such as Impressionism. She did, as mentioned earlier, admire the Japanese influences then fashionable, especially the artist Tsuguharu Foujita. She seems not to have worked with any of her contemporary artists, preferring to learn from the French and follow her own star. Her apparent aloofness, however, does not imply that she lacked enthusiasm, and she wrote on this subject in an interview: 'you must forgive my enthusiasm: it [art and Paris] just means everything to me. Nothing else is of the smallest or faintest importance besides that'.[22]

The major source of her art education in Paris was the Académie Colarossi, which seems to have been overflowing with Australian women. While there she completed her first *Self Portrait* in 1900. She also studied at the Académie Julian for a time. She was clearly more interested in skilling herself than in taking on theory or iconoclasm. It should be noted, however, that like most of her fellow Australian artists in France, she was not without training when she arrived, having studied for two years in Bendigo at the Bendigo School of Mines (although it would be interesting to speculate what standard of art training a mining school might offer). By 1905, she admitted that her work was primarily figurative, as her distinctive painting style was beginning to emerge. In paintings such as *Girl on Couch* (originally titled *A Letter from the Front*) in 1915, she demonstrated her ability to render a moment of quiet solitude. But, by the 1920s, this form of subject matter was gradually replaced and we begin to see her more mature work, focusing on the types of the Latin Quarter, especially portraits of women.

Her palette is described as being darker than that of her Paris contemporary Rupert Bunny. She may have arrived in Paris already attuned to a more sombre view of the use of palette, preferring a lower, or darker palette. Landscape painting was, according to Karen Quinlan, a relatively new area for her, and her interest in it may have been due to her French tutors. Whistler, according to Quinlan, was also a considerable influence, particularly in regard to his ability to capture light.[23]

Her interiors are particularly striking, despite the everyday calm she was able to depict in her subject matter. The Nabis group of painters – broadly speaking a group of Post-Impressionist artists who painted representationally but with strong elements of design along the lines of Japanese prints – are said to have had an influence on her, reflected in her intimate, still interiors and eschewal of 'ugliness'. Her work depicted the mood and characters of the Left Bank, and one imagines her moving quietly about, watching and studying people, sketching, and later developing the sketches into paintings. Strength of composition and skilful drawing are features of her work, as well as decorative qualities. Her portraits are deep and dark, however, and 'decorative' may seem too inadequate a term to use for her powerful art.

By 1905 she had completed her studies and was working professionally, soliciting portraits and selling work. She would continue to learn, but never to change direction. The one exception to this was her experimentation, in 1921, with her watercolour painting, under the influence of the Nabis group, with some of whom she worked, thus breaking her other longstanding custom of working alone and under her own star.

Portraiture, however, remained highly important for her, and her success at the Old Salon in 1926 took her to the pinnacle of her career. Her friend and teacher A.T. Woodward, in a letter to the Bendigo Art Gallery, stated: 'She lived the Left Bank life to the full and enjoyed a complete life as a free and engaged artist'.[24]

As she was not poor she could afford to have visitors to her atelier and furnish her studio comfortably. Yet Quinlan finds that a 'preoccupation with her immediate surroundings and lack of evidence to support any contact with other expatriates suggests that Agnes Goodsir drew inspiration from within her studio, shared between the familiarity of objects and the enduring friendship of her close companions'. Gérard-Austin mentions that Agnes Goodsir and Rachel Dunn were aware of the Australian expatriates, but also of being 'intimately preoccupied with each other'.

There appears to be rather a distance between the artist and some of her sitters, which is mentioned by Gérard-Austin. Nonetheless, it is difficult on the available evidence to make definitive pronouncements about her social life. In a tolerant city like Paris, unconventional liaisons hardly raised a ripple among the art-loving section of the population living close to the Seine, and despite the differing opinions about her sociability, Agnes Goodsir seems to have fitted into that milieu seamlessly. She loved the Latin Quarter types and painted them more lovingly and respectfully, perhaps, than was the case with some of her other sitters.

Although Agnes Goodsir was, as Quinlan attests, ambitious, she was not a self-promoter in the style of Margaret Preston. She relied on her ability as a painter of portraits and interiors and was successful without self-advertisement. This may be one of the sources for her reputation as self-effacing and shy. Certainly, her record of exhibitions and awards speaks for itself. She was exhibited at the New Salon between 1902 and 1904; at the Salon des Indépendants in 1911; the Salon de la Société Nationale des Beaux-Arts in 1921 – which attracted favourable reviews – and also sporadically over the years, winning a silver medal in 1924 for *The Red Cloak*.[25] She also exhibited in the group exhibition '150 Years of Australian Art' at the National Art Gallery of New South Wales in 1938. Her drive to achieve respect as a professional must have been proudly rewarded by this recognition. Her successful exhibitions, together with references from satisfied customers, must have ensured a steady supply of sitters. Many celebrated residents of, or visitors to, Paris sat for her, including the actress Ellen Terry, the pianist Katharine Goodson, the philosopher Bertrand Russell, Leo Tolstoy and, possibly, according to Quinlan, Benito Mussolini.

Like the Nabis painters, Agnes Goodsir omitted the chaotic and unpleasant side of life from her work. She concentrated on rich patterning, draped curtains, fabrics, porcelain, prints, fans, furniture and screens. In *Girl with Cigarette* (c.1925) (see Plate 2), Goodsir, according to Quinlan:

> ... emphasises an eclectic mixture of costume and interior. The sitter wears a decorative shawl over a jersey pullover, accessorised by 1920s headdress, fan, with a cigarette in hand. In contrast to fashion illustrations, the contentment of the sitter is more important than the costume on display. The comfortable blending of old and new imagery reinforces the day to day existence of the earthy and free spirited woman of the 1920s.[26]

Joan Kerr shines further light on this work:

> This is certainly not a dramatic painting, yet one is drawn to the beautifully controlled subject. Perfectly at ease alone in a restaurant, neither demanding nor returning our gaze, this is the understated version of the archetypal Parisian woman, the cool, beautifully dressed sophisticate of the boulevards who is neither the exaggerated siren of the movies nor your average Aussie.[27]

Goodsir's *Woman Reading* 'shows the seated figure of a woman against a predominantly olive background', notes the report by Karen Quinlan, curator of the 1998 Bendigo Art Gallery exhibition of Agnes Goodsir's work. 'Her pinched cheeks, eyes lowered to a book (perhaps the Bible) – and presence of rosary beads hanging on the wall to the left of the composition suggest recent bereavement. Paint is variously applied and in the background the thin paint allows the weave of the canvas to further emphasise subtle textures.'[28] This is arguably the most sensitive and delicate of her better-known works. Light falls on the face, leading the eye immediately to her look of inner calm and composure, and absorption in what she is reading. Her dark clothing –

again, the strong contrast of light and dark that is often seen in Goodsir's work – allows the viewer's focus to rest entirely on the face and, more than that, what the woman is thinking and feeling as she reads – not an easy task for any painter. A line of attention between the book and the face creates the balance of the picture. A major work of art.

She did have a tendency sometimes to crowd her canvases with decorative imagery, but this can be balanced against the honesty and integrity of her portraiture. Quinlan writes: 'Early paintings reveal evidence of her training in Paris. She endorsed a romantic style, a cool realism and an innate symbolism unmatched by other artists. All of what is considered her better work consists of interiors, including of course the many portraits'. She loved interiors and the play of light within them, Quinlan noted. Working in oils, her paintings for the most part unaffected by the fashions that raged through the Paris art world, Agnes Goodsir stood largely alone, though able to enjoy the company of others when not at her easel. Her desire to conform may have had much to do with this need to be respected by her artistic peers.

Agnes Goodsir did not ever really go home in any permanent sense. She did return to Australia for six months, in 1905, and she returned again to exhibit work in 1927. There are few references to her returns. She did contribute to Australian art, but from a distance. In 1905, she demonstrated to family and friends what she had learned in Paris, and, in 1907, six of her paintings were included in the first Australian Exhibition of Women's Work in Melbourne. Also, in 1927, she returned to Australia for a solo exhibition at the Fine Art Gallery in Melbourne and Macquarie Galleries in Sydney. While home, she painted a portrait of Banjo Paterson. In 1938, four of her oils were exhibited in the sesquicentennial exhibition '150 Years of Australian Art' at the National Art Gallery of New South Wales.

Agnes Goodsir may have been self-effacing, she may have been humble, and certainly conformed to an artistic narrative that was middle-of-the-road. She was a precise observer, and was demonstrably ambitious according to Quinlan, proud of her growing recognition and assertive in creating opportunities to paint portraits. In the Melbourne *Herald* of 3 July 1930, Muriel Segal called her 'perhaps the best-known Australian artist in Paris'.[29]

Chapter 3

MARIE TUCK

A Very Determined Artist

Marie Anne Tuck
1866–1947
In Paris 1906–1914

Marie Tuck was diminutive – around five feet tall – but she made up for her small physical stature with a strength of character. As well as her artistic talent, she had a passion for music and owned a silver-stringed spinet – a small harpsichord with strings set obliquely to the keyboard – which she prized. When she was struggling to raise the money to get to Europe there was no thought of selling it. Eccentric, religious, and devoted to the welfare of others, she stands out as one of the most admirable and more individualistic of these artists. A woman who knew what she wanted, Tuck worked hard and long to save for her time in Paris. She never asked favours and always gave more than she took, whether working as an artist or in what may have been her more influential role, as a teacher of art.

Tuck came to our attention when we heard that she had worked for ten years in Perth to raise the funds to go to France. We thought that a woman this determined must have deep self-belief, and this could mean deep talent. When we looked at her work, this was confirmed, so she was added to our growing list as an artist little known outside of South Australia but deserving of wider recognition.

One of seven children from Mount Torrens in South Australia, Tuck worked from her early years at a plant nursery and was able to study art under James Ashton at his Norwood School of Art in Adelaide. Not having money from her family, as so many of these Australian women in Paris did, she saved her pennies from teaching art in Adelaide and then in Perth, far from her family and home town. The slow passage of her time in Western Australia may have made her fear being, or seeming, 'too old' by the time she made it to France. It must have taken considerable courage for a woman in those days, alone and without financial resources, to set such a difficult goal and to stick to it, not only because of the long years of saving but also because of the perception in Australia that the Parisian art scene was bohemian, even louche. And louche Marie Tuck was not.

She finally made it to Paris, arriving in 1906 and not leaving until 1914, renting a studio at 55 rue de Montparnasse. All of her years of hard work were about to pay off. She settled in very quickly on the Left Bank, where it was cheap and where there were schools, galleries and artists' studios in abundance. She cleaned the studio of Australian expatriate artist Rupert Bunny to pay for her tuition with him. According to her second cousin Ruth Tuck, she also studied at an art school. It is clear that she was influenced by Bunny, who in turn had been influenced by French art – though classical and traditional, not modern – and her paintings show the influence also of

Post-Impressionism. According to Ruth, Marie Tuck spent summers in Brittany and at Étaples, painting.[30] She became the first Australian woman to gain distinction in the world of French art.

In 1908, she sent home to Australia a huge painting, *The Fish Market*, for the 11th Federal Exhibition of the South Australian Society of Art, which was promptly purchased by the Art Gallery of South Australia for 100 guineas, a considerable sum in those days, and well worth the massive effort it must have been to pack and post. This work established her reputation in her home state.

In the same year, she exhibited at the Old Salon. Her work was hung for the next seven years in salon exhibitions and in 1911 she received an Honourable Mention for *Toilette de la Mariée*, perhaps her best-known work, later sold privately in Adelaide. Tuck excelled in painting regional scenes, such as the peasants of Brittany and Étaples. According to Shirley Wilson, she developed a strong tendency toward Post-Impressionism, despite studying with Bunny, whose style was classical and decorative.[31] She always denied that she was influenced by any movement, but her paintings tell their own story. On this subject, Elizabeth Young, the art critic for the *Advertiser* (Adelaide) in 1972, said, 'Her painting style ranges from a neo-classical allegorical style to high-keyed, later, impressionistic, blue shadowed landscapes'.[32] This would seem to confirm, as her work suggests, that she moved away from Bunny's early influence toward Impressionism, despite his hatred of it.

During World War I, Tuck was back in Adelaide, teaching life drawing and painting at the South Australian School of Arts and Crafts. She insisted on nude models, which may have raised a few eyebrows in that city during its ultra-conservative phase, but she got her way, which speaks for her determination – and the esteem in which she was held. She built herself a studio in Adelaide and contributed the skills and knowledge that she had acquired in France. Students gathered at her studio where she worked them hard; but on Saturdays they ate sandwiches, drank mulberry wine and talked about the artistic life of Paris.

She mounted her only one-woman show in 1924 at the South Australian Society of Arts, to a lukewarm reception. The reviews of her work were mixed.

Her students were devoted to her and she must be regarded, both for her painting and her teaching, as having made a considerable impression on the art world of Adelaide, slow to change as it was. One of her students, the artist John Dowie, said of her: 'she had the dancing, broken touch of a painter interested in light and atmosphere. Her palette was high-keyed and pure … she … taught us what an artist should be'. Interestingly, Jeffrey Smart studied under her, according to the Art Gallery of New South Wales webpage profile on Smart.

Marie Tuck continued to paint until 1939, including several panels commissioned by Rheims Cathedral to replace works destroyed during World War I. Most of her work during this later period consisted of portraits and *plein air*, impressionistic works.

Her second cousin Ruth had some insightful comments about Tuck. She wrote that she was sometimes embarrassed when Marie took her, as a teenager, to the theatre, choosing a costume from the studio's property box, 'managing to make her usually demure little self slightly bizarre'. She remembered that when she would take food to Marie, when her much-older relative was ill, as soon as Ruth had left, Marie would take the food to less well-off neighbours.

As always, the work must stand by, and for, itself. *The Sewing Circle* (c.1910) (see Plate 3) draws the viewer's eye to the centre of the circle, which is the focus of the attention of the three servant women busily working. The servants, whose occupation is suggested by the background stairs leading to upstairs accommodation, wear clothing in muted, simple colours, in contrast to some of the garments, roughly painted, on which they are working. The closed and intent circle draws the three women close to the viewer, distancing them from the receding stairs and the bare, drab walls of their workspace.

In *Sortie des Communicants* (1910), the flowing white veils of the girls lead the eye to one girl, centre, who is reading her vows, while behind, pompous individuals in black parade contrastingly. Despite the girls being seated, there is a sense of movement throughout the picture. For all the comments about Impressionism not providing a specific focus, in our opinion this, and several others of her work, do. Her group scenes, however, do use Impressionistic techniques through flowing scarves or veils, dresses, or large cloaks, although in some of her works these devices are employed to draw the eye to just one individual, an exemplar for the entire group – and Tuck did enjoy painting group scenes.

In *Toilette de la Mariée* (1911), a kneeling maid's eye and hands lead our eye to the face of the bride, reflected in the mirror. The use of the mirror heightens the emphasis on the woman's face, increasing the focus on her as the principal subject. The light in the curtains, and in the young woman's dress, face and hat are all white and bright, while behind and below is the darkness in which the maids work as the light streams in from a window straight onto the bride-to-be as she metaphorically faces the light. Tuck has blocked the figures, confident in her forms, using blacks and browns.

In 1996, the Kensington Gallery in Adelaide held a retrospective exhibition of Tuck's work.

Tuck's best work displays an innate sense of composition and tone. Her compositions were structured in advance, emphasising a sense of dynamism and kinesis in the group. She used thick, short brushstrokes and gave priority to the light – always, the light informs the picture. Marie Tuck was evidently a deeply religious person, to whom artistic style was less important than her sense of the subject, the light and the intrapersonal dynamism. She was a caring person who gave generously of her gifts and displayed a lifelong determination in whatever she did. In 1940, she suffered a stroke, from which she never completely recovered. Although remaining staunchly Anglican, she gave herself to the Catholic Little Sisters of the Poor, on the grounds that Catholics knew how to treat death with dignity.

Chapter 4

BESSIE GIBSON

A Safe Pair of Hands

Elizabeth (Bessie) Dickson Gibson
1868–1961
In Paris 1905–1947

Bessie Gibson was especially talented, in our view, in her watercolours and in her miniatures. Not only did she have a penchant for warm colours and a clear though difficult to quantify sense of positivity pervading much of her work, but her style, never iconoclastic, suggested to us an observant engagement with her subjects.

Gibson exhibited a keen eye for the solitary figure estranged in an urban environment, where only the figure suggested warmth. Not so much a contradiction, we believe, but what could be called a synthesis of oppositions. In the description of her life and work in the program for the 2012 retrospective of her work at the Tweed River Art Gallery, her watercolours are described as exemplifying her flair for colour and fluidity of line.[33]

She is a more complex artist, perhaps, than may at first appear, and something of a forgotten artist among Australian women expatriates in Paris, judging from the absence of references to her in much of the literature. Although she was respected there, we found little evidence of influence in her home country after her return. Nor did she have influence, it seems, upon young artists in Paris, as far as is known. Although she fitted well into the Parisian artistic milieu, she was only one of hundreds, maybe more, painting in a traditional style. Her work was initially dependent upon Whistler's, but over the years she developed her own vision and for the quality of her later work alone, she is an artist deserving of renewed recognition and respect.

She began her serious study of art at the Brisbane Technical College in 1889 and studied there until 1905 where, through her teacher Godfrey Rivers, she had access to English Modernism. She left Brisbane for Paris in September 1905, having achieved success as a painter of miniatures under Rivers.

Bessie Gibson lived and worked in Paris between 1905 and 1939, with some visits home. Few Australian women artists have succeeded in capturing the essential solitariness of a large city better than her. To do so, she used a Post-Impressionist style that rendered her subjects remote, individualised, and separate – from the artist, from the viewer and from his or her immediate surroundings. She was a master at leading the eye, even when the subject toward which she was leading it was indistinct. The success she had in her lifetime meant her work could not be ignored, and as soon as we had seen some of it we knew she deserved a place in this volume.

As with several other of the Australian women artists, there is little evidence as to why she felt impelled to travel halfway around the world to a huge and potentially intimidating metropolis; but it is not hard to guess, as Paris was the 'glittering prize' of her day. As was said more recently about New York – if you could make it there, you could make it anywhere. And Gibson definitely wanted to make it. A relative of hers, interviewed on the BBC, stated that Gibson painted potboilers, including many images of the Seine and its picturesque water craft, to maintain her income.[34] Fortunately, that is not all she painted.

She had already decided, it seems, that Modernism was not for her, and she already had acquired a degree of skill. Unlike Bessie Davidson, whom she knew in Paris, she did not incorporate any elements of Modernism into her work. She received money from her family until she got on her feet, so she was never as poor as many of the artists who lived within cooee of her studio in rue Campagne-Première on the Left Bank, running off Boulevard du Montparnasse. (This was a street we visited several times because of the number of these Australian women who lived there.) She shared a studio there, for a time, with Agnes Goodsir, and lived next to Ezra Pound. Within the general area lived Picasso, Braque, Matisse and Brancusi, among other avant-garde creatives in various artistic fields. The original intention of her family, it appears, was that she would spend three years in France, soaking up influences and studying, so that she would return to Australia a better painter. In the event, she remained in Paris from 1905 to the outbreak of World War II in 1939.

Soon after settling in, Bessie Gibson enrolled at the Académie Colarossi, and also at Castelucho's, though possibly not at the same time. Castelucho was a Spanish artist, very much in the Whistler mode. Later, she also studied the painting of miniatures, which she had already studied in Australia and in which she excelled. She also studied under an American artist named Edwin Scott, another Whistlerian.

From the start she remained within the conservative world of the salon exhibitions. Whistler remained the major influence upon her work. Although he was American, many in the Parisian art world regarded him as a French painter because his style was considered to be French in its influences.[35] Gibson often painted on wooden panels, sometimes leaving parts of the wood unpainted, as was the fashion – Whistler had done it and, like him, she also used warm local colour for highlights.

'The living conditions for Australians and other artists living in Paris,' relates Anne Gérard-Austin, 'were far below what they would have enjoyed back home. Despite the attractions of the neighbourhood and its busy streets, the comfort of these studios … was indeed poor, with running water, in particular, lacking. Often the studios were on the fifth floor or higher, with no elevator'.[36] It ought not to be assumed, though, that Bessie Gibson's life on the Left Bank was all work and no play. Centres like Le Dôme must have exerted an attraction, as they did for other Australians, including her good friends Bessie Davidson, Agnes Goodsir, Anne Alison Greene and Kathleen O'Connor, who were part of her little social circle living within a brush-throw of the Boulevard du Montparnasse.

As for the work itself – in *Portrait (Woman Knitting)* (n.d.) (see Plate 4), a young woman knits, dressed in simple clothing and seated against a background that echoes the sombre atmosphere of her constrained pose and distant gaze. Her eyes are focused outwardly as if she is thinking of anything but knitting, and her hands are working automatically. The background is like those of Whistler, and all the emphasis is upon the character of the subject.

In *Luxembourg Gardens* (1908), one's eye is drawn to several lonely figures, mostly separate, in a wide, landscape, formal picture frame. The eye takes in the solitary figures, then moves to the park's furnishings, stone railings and various statues, while the palace in the distance is the final subject to be observed. In contrast to many other landscapes of the Luxembourg Gardens, the mood is rather melancholy, with subdued colours and few high keys. The figures, although central to the composition, are indistinct and not detailed, so they remain distant to their location, to each other, and to the viewer. This work relies upon Whistler's technique of space against objects. The work is seen as a totality because of a common tonality and the recurring pattern of the brush strokes.

Gibson was little known in Australia until the 1970s, when the growing attention paid to women artists brought her work to light. Although some of her paintings are held in Australian galleries, she did not teach in Australia, so far as is known, nor did she gather acolytes. She did, however, exhibit in Sydney and Melbourne after her return home in 1947. There appears to be no extant evidence as to how much notice was taken of her work, or whether she influenced any younger Australian artists. Perhaps there was not enough of her work available for this to happen.

Nancy Underhill suggests that Gibson's reputation may have suffered somewhat because she was a Whistler acolyte (although she was also mentored in Paris by New Zealand artist Frances Hodgkins). However, she was not without honour in Paris, nor did the influence of Whistler, as mentioned above, always dominate her work. She exhibited regularly at the Old Salon until 1939 and received an honourable mention there in 1926.

Is her work rendered less impressive by her frequent reliance upon Whistlerian techniques? It may be argued that the work of any artist stands or falls not according to its originality but to its capacity to hold the attention and galvanise the viewer. It is the viewer alone, we believe, who can 'validate' a work of art. And on this basis, Gibson's work stands tall in its own right – influences acknowledged but not determinative.

Despite her lifelong traditional tendencies, Bessie Gibson grew and developed her skills as an artist throughout her life. In the final analysis, she was an artist who demonstrated that an acolyte who absorbs and skilfully reflects a mentor's influence may be as worthy of respect as that mentor.

Chapter 5

DORA MEESON

Progressive Feminist, Traditional Artist

*Dora Meeson Coates
1869–1955
In Paris 1898–1900*

Dora Meeson was something of a paradox – on the one hand she was a strong suffragette who designed banners for the women's movement and marched in rallies, and on the other an artist who never advanced beyond Impressionism and worked closely with, and for, her husband George Coates and his work, according to Meeson.[37] We found that a number of articles that mentioned Meeson were primarily about Coates. While, of course, money is far from being the only criterion of artistic worth, Meeson's work today sells for six figures, while Coates's paintings sell for a few thousand.

Dora Meeson was born in wealthy Hawthorn, Melbourne, the daughter of a schoolmaster, who later became a barrister. She studied at the National Gallery Art School in Melbourne, during which time she won, perhaps equal first with George Coates, the National Gallery

Travelling Scholarship, but according to unconfirmed reports, withdrew in favour of Coates.[38] After time in London at the Slade School of Fine Art, she was in Paris from 1898. She studied at the Académie Julian under both Jean-Paul Laurens and Benjamin Constant. It was in London in 1898 that she met up again with George Coates, her future husband. Meeson evidently felt at home in Paris, but unfortunately for her, Coates did not.

Had she remained in Paris, where she studied between the years 1898 and 1900, she may well have advanced and developed stylistically more than she did. She did differentiate herself from her husband's work, creating a different style for herself and painting some extremely admired works. But her work, though highly regarded, remained till the end as it had begun – with Impressionism – while the Parisian art world moved on, exploring, experimenting, challenging, sometimes failing, but never content to rest. She and Coates were, publicly, opposed to Modernism. Nevertheless, in our opinion, she was one of the finest artists among the women.

Coates had a scholarship to Europe on which they lived for several years, enough time for the couple to find their feet and their styles. Coates had come under the influence of, among others, Renoir, Degas and Monet, all of whom were still living. Meeson admired and was identifiably influenced by Fantin-Latour, Renoir, Guillamin and Rodin. She may have been influenced in her work also by Coates, and through him the artists that he loved. 'George and I both favoured the full brush, in preference to the English style, which used a thin, smooth, chalky texture'.[39] Living and working in France was an exciting time for both Meeson and Coates, so close to some of the great artists who were working there. They decided not to have children, presumably because art was their focus, along with, in Dora's case, women's rights.

Dora Meeson's support for the suffragette movement was as strong as her love of art. They also decided to provide financially for Coates's mother, and this decision may have helped sway Dora to paint more conservatively in order to sell more pictures. As we've noted previously in this book, portrait commissions were one obvious way to make money from art and Coates did specialise in this area.

Coates's health was never robust, and the couple moved south during the cruel Parisian winters, leaving behind their bohemian milieu on the Left Bank. His health deteriorated, she wrote in her biography of him, during their time in Paris. He had been finding it difficult to live on his scholarship, he had not been getting enough commissions for portraits, and his studio was cold and badly ventilated. His health may have been the reason their stay in Paris was not longer.

In 1898, the year in which she arrived in Paris, she won the Concourse de Torse d'Homme, a high award for live model drawing.[40] She came second in the Concourse de Torse de Femme in the same year. Such success for a foreign artist in Paris, in her first year of residency there, was rare and noteworthy. Typically, in her biography of her husband, she mentions a painting there by him, a portrait of a Mrs Harwood, the wife of one of their American friends, but not her own work. In 1911, she exhibited works – *Partie d'une Frise* and *Printemps* – at the Société des Artistes Français.

She and Coates studied Old Masters in the Louvre and compared notes about all that they saw. It is indeed a little difficult to study Meeson alone, because their lives were so intertwined, both artistically and personally. According to the art blogger Hels: 'Neither Meeson nor Coates responded to developments in art after Impressionism and their work remained entrenched within the limits of carefully crafted, realistic art. There does not seem to be any acknowledgement in their paintings of Fauvism, Cubism, or any of the other late-Edwardian or post-Edwardian art movements booming across Europe'.[41]

Her work was magnetic in the quality of its use of light and in the way it made the ordinary seem mysterious. Her ability to capture water is also particularly impressive. Christopher Allen writes, 'Meeson's work, indeed, seems drawn between two styles of Realism and Impressionism. It is realism which predominates in the dramatic paintings of London Bridge, seen from down low at the level of the river'.[42] Later he writes: 'In a few paintings, the tension between the two styles is not happily resolved, and realistic boats in the foreground seem inconsistent with the impressionistic river beyond'. He goes on to make an insightful observation: 'she is always responsive to the light on her subject and never seems to consider it merely picturesque'.

It is possible to argue, given her prioritising of Coates, that she was anxious not to power past him, and, since he was a conservative artist, so would she be: but this is merely conjecture. Be that as it may, perhaps it is a shame that she was not a little more adventurous, especially considering her interest in women's rights. However, she did make a considerable contribution to the art of France, and also to that of England. And she did, in the end, also power past Coates.

She also made a significant contribution to Australian art. Her successes in France were reported to a young country by the media. In 1913, she accompanied an exhibition of 19 works by her husband, and 12 of her own, to Melbourne, where they were shown at the Athenaeum Gallery and seen by an estimated 4,000 people. Meeson was very satisfied with the level of sales from this exhibition, which she ascribed to the fact that most of the paintings were landscapes, and not highly priced. In 1921, after 23 years abroad, the couple held a number of successful exhibitions in Australia, including one at the

Athenaeum Gallery on 8 May 1931, and one at Melbourne's Fine Art Society, in Exhibition Street, in 1934.

A Harvest Sunset (1888) (see Plate 5), an early work, is mistily indistinct, with a suggestion of dilapidation – the garden gate lies on the grass so that, presumably, the grazing horse in the middle distance could escape. The high grass, richly painted in complex detail, crowds the canvas, almost obscuring the farmhouses in the background. A figure, blending into the vegetation, stands by the gate gazing at the horse, as the viewer is also invited to do. Subtle, muted colours reward a viewer's study, and the overall impression is one of natural fecundity, in which the agricultural ambitions of humanity struggle to triumph, night fades the light, and nature commands the ground.

In November 2013, the Castlemaine Gallery held a retrospective exhibition of her work, including her paintings of the Thames. This exhibition began the resurrection of a largely forgotten artist. The degree of her influence upon other artists is not easy to gauge at this distance. However, her success as measured in both respect and sales makes it clear that she had an influence, and that she brought back home from Europe the results of her study, observation and hard work.

In his article in the *Weekend Australian* of 2–3 November 2013, Christopher Allen discusses two of her works, *Afternoon on Chelsea Reach* (1910) and *Chelsea Reach* (1913): '[Meeson] reconciles industrial subjects with an impressionistic vision, discovering the ambiguous sublimity that a colossal power plant can have when distanced and abstracted by a veil of mist. The result is a kind of lyrical wasteland … an unexpected vision of "stillness"'.

It is fascinating to speculate on what she might have achieved had she followed her own narrative and not subordinated herself to her husband to the extent that she did. She may be compared to Stella

Bowen, whose art also suffered because of her attachment to a man. It is never, of course, possible to know what actually goes on within any couple's relationship, so it is pointless to try to be definitive as to her motives, or the forces to which she was subjected. However, maybe it is possible to say that compared to some other Australian women artists, those who travelled alone or with female companionship, she does not seem to have stretched or challenged herself as much as might be expected of an artist whose talent may have been far greater had it been fully unleashed.

Chapter 6

ALICE MUSKETT

Multi-talented and Generous

*Alice Jane Muskett
1869–1936
In Paris mostly during 1895–1898, 1910–1912, 1920–1921*

Alice Muskett stands out, even among these women, for what we see as her generosity of spirit and for the passion reflected in her art. In choosing a path of independence, never ceasing to educate herself, and always self-reliant, she became a role model that younger women artists could emulate. A strong-minded woman, she was highly skilled and made a pathway for herself as a professional painter, earning some honours and exhibitions along the way. She was talented in other ways and was an arresting figure, displaying generosity to other artists on many occasions.

Alice Muskett was born in 1869 in Melbourne but moved to Sydney with her mother Phoebe in 1885. Her mother died the following year and Muskett became Julian Ashton's second pupil. Ashton instituted life classes for women, the first in Sydney to do so. He painted a picture of his life class in 1893, showing her, auburn haired, among the students. She was regarded as very beautiful, with a lively and entertaining nature. From 1890, she exhibited each year with the Art Society of New South Wales, of which she was a Council member in 1894, and with the newly formed Society of Artists, Sydney, from 1895.

On her first visit to Europe, she studied in Paris with the Académie Colarossi from 1895 to 1898, a long time at an art school in comparison to some other Australian women artists, and wrote home about her experiences there for the *Daily Telegraph*. She exhibited with Paris salons and her work was shown in the 1898 Exhibition of Australian Art in London. Her 1898 *Study of Roses* is with the Art Gallery of New South Wales. It was from viewing *Roses* that we determined to include her, delighted to have helped save a fine and sensitive artist from oblivion.

Her strong character displayed itself in some of her down-to-earth commentary on the state of the visual arts in Paris: 'There are far too many pictures painted, it seems to me ... it is a thousand pities this same energy and talent is not put into applied art of some kind ... there are 777 oil paintings in the Academy this year ... frankly bad as a whole'.[43] She was also unimpressed by many of the Australian exhibitors, including Thea Proctor, Tom Roberts and Arthur Streeton, according to Joan Kerr.[44]

Returning to Sydney, she served on the committee of the Society of Artists. At the 1909 Society of Artists exhibition, the *Lone Hand* magazine reported: 'Miss Muskett's triptych *Gold, Frankincense and Myrrh* is a harmonious decoration rich in colour: as for her roses, she has always painted flowers most sympathetically'.[45] In 1910, she was back in Paris. She returned again to Sydney in 1912, this time exhibiting with the Society of Women Painters. She went again to

Europe in 1920, returning once more in 1921. In 1928, she endowed an annual prize – the Philip Muskett Prize – at Ashton's, in honour of her brother, to encourage landscape painting. Kerr reports that Muskett continued to show regularly with the Society of Artists and contributed paintings to the first Australian Exhibition of Women's Work in Melbourne, including *The Shrine*.

Her pastel *A Lost Halo* (see Plate 6), created in 1897, shows a young woman, narrow eyed, head lifted to look out of the work, illuminated from her face down through her dress by a pale white light in an otherwise sombre picture, in which a dark cloak and background are only partly relieved by a faded gold crown or halo. The impression is of lost innocence, and of a darkness into which arrogance can lead. Much of her work, however, is more light-hearted and light-spirited.

Alice Muskett suffered financially from the Depression and was unable to travel. She suffered a cerebral haemorrhage in 1933, and died in 1936.

It is not only the big guns of women's art who need to be remembered and celebrated. Alice Muskett displayed a strong and lively talent, emphasising the decorative in an imaginative manner and prioritising design over subject matter. Her work was initially brought to our attention by freelance researcher David Angeloro, for which we are grateful. Her contribution matters; she deserves to be remembered: artists of her calibre should not solely be relegated to history's footnotes.

Chapter 7

ETHEL CARRICK

A Team Player

Ethel Carrick Fox
1872–1952
In Paris 1905–1913, 1916–1952

Born in England, Ethel Carrick moved to Australia at the end of World War I with her husband, Melbourne-born artist Emanuel Phillips Fox. Originally from London, where she studied at the Slade School of Fine Art, she married Fox in 1905 and they moved to Paris, where they lived and studied until 1913. Although they were only married for 10 years, they were a close team, however, Carrick's work diverged in style from his fairly early on, hers in the direction of Post-Impressionism, according to Susanna de Vries.[46] Fox encouraged his wife's work, and she made serious efforts on behalf of his work, even after his death.

Their early married life was set against the backdrop of the Belle Époque. She worked often by his side and frequently in *plein air*, usually painting crowds rather than individuals. He died in 1915, and she returned to Paris in 1916, and between 1920 and 1940 she travelled extensively, lobbying curators to buy and exhibit her husband's work. Researching her life and work, as with Meeson and Coates, we discovered his name and work appearing wherever hers did, making it sometimes difficult to separate them as artists, and, in some texts ostensibly about her, his name and work occupy much more space.

Apart from her own painting, the indefatigable Carrick became a member of a number of groups dedicated to the advancement of art, or of women's art, especially between 1906 and 1912. She was a member of the Union Internationale des Beaux-Arts et des Lettres. She became a Member of the Salon d'Automne in 1911.

She networked with women's groups and with individuals for the purpose of assisting those artists and others who fell on hard times. Like other artists, including Bessie Davidson and Dora Meeson, she devoted much of her abundant energies to helping others.

Their marriage was, to all appearances, as successful as their art, and they were evidently enmeshed in both spheres. Nor does her promotion of him appear to have dimmed her own success, since her work today sells for hundreds of thousands of dollars. In this she may be seen to have differed from her compatriots Stella Bowen and Dora Meeson. Carrick gained immediate success with her brightly coloured and sharply observed market and crowd scenes.

It would be interesting to have been able to view a life of Ethel Carrick in a parallel universe, one in which she was not married to Fox – would her work, we wondered, have been even more individual? Would she have been more adventurous? Later in her life, after his death, she did begin to cautiously experiment with some new techniques and styles. In *Painted Women*, Anne Gray states, 'paradoxically the lower expectations [of women artists in Paris] gave them more freedom to experiment'.[47]

Despite her devotion to her husband, her work, with its marvellous colour and vibrant warmth, brought her to our attention years ago. Her work stakes its own claim for her to be recognised and respected, and there was never any possibility that she would not be one of our 'Wild Geese'.

Their life in Paris was not as poverty-stricken as for some other Australian women artists. In 'The Greatest Voyage', Anne Gérard-Austin writes, 'The couple was determined to choose something better than the average Paris studio, and selected one of the purpose built studios, equipped with a cold water tap, bare boards and a potbellied stove, and above it a comfortable apartment with a fireplace, a modern kitchen, and piped hot water'.[48] Few Australian artists were so fortunate. The apartment and studio were in the Cité Fleurie at 64 Boulevard Arago on the Left Bank. They loved their studio, which we visited in the course of our research. Susanna de Vries writes: 'Carrick found their life in Paris a delight ... At long last she was free to live the way she pleased. She worked just as hard as her husband and allowed little time for cooking ... they ... ate out a great deal. Their life together was companionable, home loving, [and] middle class'.

According to Gérard-Austin, Ethel Carrick was both energetic and independent, determined to devote her life to art and engaging with Modernism.[49] However, her work shows that the further reaches of Modernism, such as Cubism, were a field too far for her. Her love of *plein air* took her to the parks and gardens for which Paris is famous, particularly the Luxembourg Gardens, where her evolving engagement with Post-Impressionism manifested in loose brushstrokes and strong colours, possibly influenced by the Fauves.

One of the Parisian influences that shows in her work was her ready acceptance of Orientalism, then fashionable in the city, especially in the form of Japanese prints and designs, although the term was also sometimes used to refer to North African art and the art of Asia Minor, the former achieving a strong decorative influence upon much of her work.

She showed works at the Salon de la Société Nationale des Beaux-Arts and the Salon d'Automne from 1908. She exhibited with other international women artists in group displays entitled 'Les Quelques' in 1910 and 1911. Thus her work achieved notice and respect from the start. She and Fox made Paris their principal home, where she studied for a time at the Académie Julian. Throughout her years in Paris, she also gave her time and energy to the promotion of the work of artists in France. When Fox died, Carrick, though grieving, moved on, and in 1916 she left the studio she had shared with him and moved into a building occupied entirely by artists' studios, most of the artists being foreigners. She continued with her travels outside of Paris, particularly to the south of the country to avoid the Paris winters.

Later in life, she initiated a scheme of purchasing works through the French Australian Association to aid Australian artists in Paris who, owing to World War II, had suffered financial privation. This was just one of the impressive ways in which she sought to assist her fellow artists.

Apart from her *plein air* work, she achieved attention for her portraiture. In *Painted Women*, Anne Gray suggests that her paintings of women attempted to reveal an inner strength of character in her subjects, rather than merely depicting their physical appearances. Women in her paintings do appear to be enjoying their freedoms, albeit mostly in the company of men, and her women appear always to be at their ease.

One problem that did affect her life was the covert hostility she experienced from some members of Fox's family, due to the fact that she did not have children, as de Vries makes clear. His family was extremely child-oriented, and it is reasonable to assume, as de Vries asserts, that his relatives' attitudes were forcibly expressed to him, and likely through him to her, which must have been discomforting. Fox painted a number of works of his pretty sister Irene, posing with her equally pretty dark-haired daughter Louise contentedly cradled in her arms. Irene had little respect for Carrick's work, insultingly referring to it as 'daubs'. Carrick's response was that she didn't consider it essential for women to produce offspring and that women, too, could have careers. She may have found it disturbing that Fox desired children just as her own career was getting somewhere. She knew from the experiences of her female fellow students that the pram in the hall was the enemy of promise. As Susanna de Vries comments in *Triumphs and Travels*: 'One wonders just how much Mannie stood up for his wife against the barrage of disapproval from the rest of his family'.

Carrick became increasingly respected, and emerged from the older Fox playing 'Pygmalion' to her. She, too, used light effects skilfully in many of her best works, emphasising the play of coloured light across surfaces. As with many other Impressionists, she brushed figures on quickly, suggesting rather than clearly outlining form. This had the effect of offering the viewer a generalised idea of a scene as distinct from a naturalistic representation of it. Again, in accordance with the evolving principles of the style, she emphasised brushstrokes and surfaces rather than illusions of depth. In this, she was engaging tangentially with the Modernist tendencies of her time. So, at that time, her work did contrast to some extent with that of her husband.

Over time, however, as she learnt more about French art she began slowly to move away from Post-Impressionism toward more modern styles, as foreshadowed in the work described above. Like some of her expatriate colleagues, she was open to change and to new ideas, provided they could be seen to follow as developments from what had gone before. In short, she never ceased to search for an art that for her would be truer and more challenging.

Outside of France, Carrick developed an interest in North Africa, which she visited a number of times during the early 1900s, exploring her version of Orientalism. She exhibited a typical example of her North African work, *The Mosque at Tangier* (1911), at the Société des Peintres Orientalistes Français in Paris in 1913. On her return from Tangier, Parisians received Carrick's work with great admiration and praise.

Carrick began exhibiting in Paris and elsewhere from around 1906, and her work found immediate acceptance. She never stopped learning, and she charted an artistic course of her own. The Salon d'Automne was her favourite outlet for her work, and she exhibited there fairly regularly until well into the 1920s. Her only solo exhibition in Paris was at the Galerie de la Palette Française on the Boulevard Haussmann, where she showed 22 works in 1928.

Some of her work, both during and after her strictly Post-Impressionist phase, demonstrates a technique known as 'broken colour', where thick paint is applied directly to the supports – wood or canvas usually – with the colour of the support incorporated into the painting itself. In all of her work she was able to take advantage of the fact that colours were now being offered for sale in tubes for convenience, which at the least made *plein air* work much easier.

Anne Gray, in *Painted Women*, argues that Carrick consciously avoided competition with Fox, largely by painting with different techniques and materials.

By the 1920s, she had developed that ability, previously remarked, to bring out the inner qualities of a sitter, which she achieved partly by creating low keys using a darker palette. Moreover she was able to portray not only strength of character but also intimacy between two or more sitters, thus elevating her portraits to a higher level than mere observation and demonstrating that the best art is not only about technique, but also about emotion and empathy – qualities for which technique is merely a tool for their realisation.

Her work found favour in official circles, too. In the late 1920s, the French government purchased two of her works, including *Le Marché aux Fleurs à Nice* (c.1928).

Ethel Carrick, then, grew and changed, and this may partly be attributed to her apparent awareness of changing trends in what is a trend-conscious art form. She loved the fashionable movements of her time, and often emphasised fashionable currents in her work, revealing the breadth of her curiosity, her willingness to employ decoration, and her responsiveness to the fast-changing world in which she lived.

Although she and her husband paid return visits to Australia in 1908 and 1913, it was not until 1952 that she returned permanently to her adopted homeland of Australia, dying in Melbourne soon afterwards. Despite her long periods spent in Europe she made a considerable contribution to Australian art. She forged strong links with the Australian art world and, according to Gérard-Austin, described herself as an Australian. She enjoyed friendships with a number of Australian women artists, including Ethel Spowers and Eveline Syme. She was always constantly pleading with Australian galleries to exhibit Fox's work, rather than her own. It is safe to say, though, that her contribution to Australian art has been well received and respected.

Many observers may feel that her lifetime effort to avoid being valued artistically as highly as her husband did not succeed.

Acknowledging the strong partnership with Fox, Angela Goddard curated an exhibition of Carrick's and Fox's work in Brisbane in 2011 titled *Art, Love and Life*.[50] She was determined to emphasise, or have the public see for themselves, Carrick's extraordinary talent, which she considered to have been overlooked. The exhibition was reviewed in the *Sydney Morning Herald* by Katherine Feeney and also by John McDonald, in which he quotes Goddard's exhibition notes: 'Goddard states in her exhibition notes that while Fox was adept in employing the techniques of light that were characteristic of the current Impressionist movement, Carrick possessed a talent that, while by no means radical, was considered strong enough to be exhibited alongside the father of abstraction, Wassily Kandinsky'.[51,52] He further quotes Goddard in the notes: 'It's kind of a sad story in a way because she debases her own work and career in the interests of promoting his'. He quotes Goddard quoting Carrick: 'I want to lay stress on his work, which is so much the greater – my work is nothing in comparison with his'. As stated above, it is possible to conclude that her talent was strong enough to survive being submerged beneath that of her husband, who was a decade older and once one of her teachers.

In 2019, art dealership 69 John Street in Leichhardt published a brief biography of Carrick in which it was stated that, responding to changes in art from around 1908, Carrick painted, instead of idyllic park scenes, bustling markets and beachside resorts, and that Carrick later began to outshine her husband E. Phillips Fox, not only finding critical acclaim, but markets that wanted her work.

In *Manly Beach – Summer is Here* (1913), the blue of the ocean is picked up by the blue bathing costumes of some of the bathers, scattered among the chaotic crowd covering the beach. There is a broad focus on the beach rather than on the ocean. The eye is led among the brightly coloured crowd from the foreground into the middle distance by the arrow shape of the crowd grouping. If there is a precise focus, it is a woman in a light blue dress, reclining in a beach chair and holding a parasol as she gazes in the direction of the artist. There is a sense of movement, as of joy, among the crowd, created partly by the colour and the use of high keys, and partly by the physical attitudes of some in the crowd, who look as if they are moving or are about to move: the whole scene is one of transience, movement, evanescence. Soon this crowd will be gone, Carrick seems to be saying, and their joy is only of the moment.

The Fruit and Vegetable Market, Nice (1933) (see Plate 7) displays the technique of broken colour. The painting reveals the thought that has gone into its structure. There are three levels, the top and bottom levels leading the eye to the central level, the actual market, a broad, longitudinal site of social activity. In the foreground, figures – presumably buyers – appraise the market as they approach it. In the background, partly encircling the commercial hub, a fine modern building, possibly a town hall or college, encloses the marketplace on three sides, its rectangularity imposing a sense of authority upon the seeming chaos of the buying and selling. The market itself has almost a monopoly of rich and vibrant colour, where seated and standing figures in bright clothing seethe and huddle as they barter under straggling palms and ordered umbrellas shading the sun, which donates its brightness to the whole scene. The overall effect is peaceful yet busy, a lively and very social scene, somehow encompassed within the surrounding arms of the colonial authority represented by the building.

As a painter, and as a woman determined to promote the work and the wellbeing of others, she was tireless and energetic, and may be said to thoroughly deserve the esteem in which she has been held. As a team player, not only for the team of herself and Fox, but also for the team of artists, and women artists in particular, she was as unselfish as she was talented.

Chapter 8

ADA MAY PLANTE

An Undervalued Talent

Ada May Plante
1875–1950
In Paris 1901–1904

Fame is fickle, and some of our artists have not had the recognition their work deserves. Ada May Plante was a sensitive, highly talented, dedicated artist whose art, we believe, enriches the canon. Her apparent unwillingness to self-promote may have led to her being less valued, publicly, than her work may be thought to deserve. For artists, the balance between self-promotion, creative sensitivity, and integrity is often a challenge to negotiate. It has been said that when an artist is creating, he or she must be sensitive, thoughtful and true to their Muse, allowing their creative instincts to flow freely. When the work is, done, however, and the artist is seeking a gallery in which to exhibit, they must become capitalists, relentlessly selling the product they have created, utterly confident in its value and keen to enlighten the world with its transformative insights. Few artists combine both these attributes and, sadly, some of those who possess only the former attributes may tend to fall by the wayside in the space of public recognition.

We stated in the Introduction that one of the reasons for undertaking this book was to assist the growing trend to recognise and revalue those Australian women artists who have been largely ignored or misremembered – and another gem presented herself with our discovery of Ada May Plante. The public hardly know her, as Juliet Peers points out in her brief 1990 biography of Plante, one of the artists represented in an exhibition by the Victorian Artists' Society.[53] Plante's painting was *Portrait of a Lady*. She may be regarded as an artist who not only lacked, but was perhaps happy to lack, the killer instinct of an egoist when offering her work. The best that such artists can hope for, often, is some dedicated followers, an 'in crowd' who are proud of their good judgment in loving this artist's work. Plante always had such a band, and we believe they were correct in their judgment of the quality of her work. Her work demands to be respected, as does her artistic journey toward Modernism, and she is slowly acquiring a larger band of dedicated followers. We hope her inclusion in our book will fast-forward that process.

Originally from New Zealand, she came with her family to Australia at 13, and lived in Melbourne, attending Presbyterian Ladies' College and studying at the National Gallery Art School under Bernard Hall and Frederick McCubbin, winning prizes during her time there. She was a contemporary of George Bell, an influential Melbourne artist and teacher. She exhibited with the Victorian Artists' Society but then made the pilgrimage to London and later Paris, living and working in the latter city from 1901 to 1904. She shared a studio with Christina Asquith Baker and studied at the Académie Julian.

Her reasons for going to Europe are not well documented but it can reasonably be assumed that she caught the same bug as so many other Australian artists, both male and female: to be part of the world centre of art and the exciting things that were happening there, news of which filtered slowly back to Australia.[54] Fortunately for her, her family had enough money, despite some business setbacks, to send her to Paris and to supply her with a modest income thereafter. Not for her the 'romantic' poverty of the artist in a garret.

Peers states that her 'identifiable French work gives no evidence of contact with Post-Impressionism at this date, being mostly dark and conventional including genre scenes such as that exhibited with the Victorian Artists' Society in 1906, after her return'. It could be added, however, that some of these works also displayed vibrant colours. Plante first painted in what the *Australian Dictionary of Biography* calls a 'Whistlerian style of Impressionism', and was certainly familiar with the approaches of Cézanne and van Gogh, and other France-based artists before leaving for Europe, but later changed her style.[55] It may have been around 1925, or as late as 1930, that she began to display Modernist leanings. Peers writes: 'Arnold Shore is the source for the oft-quoted date of c1925 for the emergence of her modernist style', although others suggest that she saw the work of Cézanne and other moderns firsthand in Paris. In 1950, Adrian Lawler suggested that 'twenty odd years ago' – i.e. around 1930 – she was inspired by 'the enthusiasm of some of her younger artist friends' for 'the post-Impressionist conception of painting as the organising of coloured shapes'. Ada's translation and subsequent circulation amongst her associates of a French text on Cézanne places her in an active role in the lively debates on art characteristic of her circle. By 1931, Ada is shocking Arthur Streeton with 'raw and green' impressions and a portrait of William Frater, evidence that she had been thoroughly converted to Modernism. Peers also writes: '[Her Cézanne translation] provides a link between the regionalist search for identity and the art of Cézanne which, together with the injunctions for the artist to avoid the fashionable and superficial and to cultivate a deep association with nature, makes an interesting parallel for the lifestyle chosen by Ada Plante', and 'Plante shares the assiduous dedication to, and intimate knowledge of, a particular place, admired by advocates of regionalism and post-Heidelberg landscape painting'. Elsewhere Peers states:

> Painting modernist pictures would at first appear to be an unlikely activity for Ada Plante, a reserved character ... there is no self-destructive tight rope walk on the knife edge of café society, no articulation of political and social change ... No artist of her generation, in the recollection of contemporaries, cared less about propaganda, self praise and advertisement.

Her contribution to Australian art was probably more substantial than might seem compatible with her modesty and lack of assertion. With a strong desire to paint locally and regionally, she painted studies of buildings and landscape around Darebin, outside Melbourne, where she lived for a time after her return to Australia, and in other areas associated with her life, including Eaglemont and Research. Among her portraits are paintings of her close friends and family. After World War I, creative life in Melbourne collapsed into a kind of torpor for a time, asserts Phipps. However, the 'Pink House' – a coach house near Darebin called the Darebin Bridge House that Lina Bryans had bought and renovated, and where Plante lived from 1934 with other artists – was a lively centre of debate and work from the 1930s. This house became an unlikely cosmopolitan milieu for Modernist artists and writers.

Ada May Plante also joined and contributed to artistic organisations after her return home. She and her friend Eveline Syme were prominent members of the Post-Impressionistic Melbourne Society of Women Painters and Sculptors. There she quickly gained recognition by supporting the Modernist faction, and rapidly was acknowledged in her own right, according to Peers. Her legacy in Melbourne includes her activity within the Contemporary Art Society, later in her life.

It was five years before her death, at 69 years of age, and frail, that she held her first solo exhibition in April 1945. George Bell described it as 'an exhibition of considered effort and great distinction' – though 'considered effort' is hardly a rave review. Her work, however, must speak for itself, and, contrary to our view, some reviews have been less than wholehearted in their evaluation of her work. Alan McCulloch, quoted by Peers, wrote in 1945: 'A strong bond of sympathy unites Miss Plante to her subject matter: landscape, still life or figure study, she invests them all with the quiet charm of her personality'. For Arnold Shore, however, her portraits were, as reported in the *ADB* in 1988, 'charged with a sensitive perception of character'.[56]

Her most effective works, asserts Peers, are those in which there was both time and picture space for her to build up a tight design. She exhibited in the inaugural exhibition of the Contemporary Art Society in Melbourne in 1932, along with Baker, Bell and others. A memorial exhibition of her work was held at the Stanley Coe Gallery in Melbourne in 1951. Yet, this artist has somehow remained almost invisible to the present day.

Shorty, painted in 1945, shows an older man with a wistful expression, as if thinking of something in his past, smoking a pipe at a small table in a plain bar, a half-finished beer before him. He reclines against the wall and his hand resting on his thigh does not look relaxed. Pale colours again, which are, interestingly for this modern artist, segmented as much by line as by colour, form the background of a working-class pub. The sitter is not so much posing, as caught when absent, as if by a candid camera.

Man with a Pipe (c.1940) (see Plate 8) is very much in the same style as *Shorty*. Plante liked to paint some of the regulars at her local hotel. This is a character study and all of the items shown – the books, his clothing, the drape, the pipe, his pose – suggest a man at ease with himself, wise and thoughtful. Delineating the boundaries of all areas makes for a clear and uncompromising picture, perhaps much like the subject himself. His face shows the wear and tear of a hard life, possibly as a manual worker, while the books and the cravat suggest a desire to rise above his past circumstances. The subject's gaze is out of the frame, perhaps into a past he cannot share.

It is the face that draws and holds our attention, displaying the talent Plante has for depicting character. Thin, intelligent, somewhat ascetic despite the smoking and the drinking, this man is perhaps a pub philosopher, a working-class bloke who aspires to the finer things in life, someone with whom we might imagine holding a thoughtful and engaging conversation. Perhaps he is weak, addicted to alcohol and tobacco, but there is a thoughtfulness in his expression and in his eyes, which, to our mind, echoes the thoughtfulness of the portraitist.

Plante is another artist whom David Angeloro, a freelance visual arts researcher and writer, suggested to us. Liking what we found in research, we were both thoroughly impressed by her work. David feels she was a talent worth recognising but who, perhaps through her retiring nature, had been largely overlooked. We are grateful to him for his assistance and hence she came to be part of our lives.

Strength does not necessarily manifest in assertiveness: there is quiet strength, and this Plante displayed in abundance. We would certainly argue once again that Ada May Plante deserves far greater recognition than she, along with so many others, received in her lifetime.

Chapter 9

MARGARET PRESTON

A Driven Woman

Margaret Rose Preston (nee Rose McPherson)
1875–1963
In Paris 1904–1907, 1913–14, 1918

In many of the books that teach professionalism to students in creative arts faculties, it is written that when an artist is marketing their work it requires a hard-nosed approach to network and self-promote. This certainly applies to Margaret Preston, born Rose McPherson, who changed her name when she married William George Preston after World War I. She was an artist of fine sensibility who was sincere in her love of art and had an artist's sensitivity, yet who promoted herself and her art relentlessly throughout her long career. A creative arts faculty today would have nothing to teach her in respect of professionalism. She was a model not only of determination, but of self-belief, and of a deep and restless curiosity that obliged her to continually explore new ideas, and to challenge herself. Fortunately for her reputation, later generations have largely accepted her own valuation of her work and worth.

Although she was reputed to disdain housework, she expressed a domestic sensibility when painting household objects of everyday use.[57] Was this opportunism, or an artist's privilege of choosing a subject on the basis of its innate visuality? Perhaps a little of both, but we would suggest that in the end it does not matter, because the quality of her work, and her contribution to the advancement of art, trump all else. And although she learnt a lot in her career, she did so not as an end in itself, but in order to find ways of realising the visions that were constantly growing in her head and would not let her rest. To this extent, she was a driven woman, and what she needed was a level of technique that would give form to her visions.

Not that she was lacking in technique before she crossed the ocean. She had spent years studying art at tertiary level in Adelaide and Melbourne. Perhaps she went overseas partly to put the finishing touches to her skill and gain the confidence that would enable her to be fully professional. Most of all, however, we believe she went because she had to, driven by an inner need to realise her own best potentialities.

In 'From Eggs to Electrolux' in *Art in Australia*, she wrote that she painted 'against all opposition of friends and relatives'.[58] This demonstrates the inner determination of this artist to go it alone, backing her own judgment, and accepting the consequences of her actions. She also stated that she found it so easy to paint everyday objects that she would be 'the best still life painter in the world'. This immodest assumption convinced her to storm the world, and to this end she started saving for her trip to Paris and London.

The death of her mother, orphaning her, saddened her deeply, but it released her from family duties, and she set out to follow her dream. While it seems true that she sometimes travelled or worked with people of substantial financial means, it was her determined spirit that really created the financial resources for her pilgrimage, as she sold paintings in Australia before her departure. She felt obliged to succeed for her mother because her mother had given her so much help (despite opposition from others) with her training and had pushed her to become a professional artist. She did also inherit from her mother, states Ian North, and this gave her the final lift to enable her to cross the water in 1904.[59] She remained in Paris until 1907, returned for the period 1913–14, and lived there again for a time in 1918.

Margaret Preston took time, as many other artists did, to come to terms with Paris, a city that was so much bigger and more complex than Adelaide. However, she settled in and began studying intensely, as well as travelling around Europe to acquaint herself with the best in world art. She searched diligently for the best teacher, explaining in 'From Eggs to Electrolux' that she was 'this little Australian who worried and wanted to learn'.

In her article in the *Home* magazine, 'Why I Became a Convert to Modern Art', she wrote: 'Tradition thinks for you, but Heavens how dull! To keep myself from pouring out the selfsame pictures every year I started to think about it'.[60] So, a thinking artist is a modern artist. Deborah Edwards writes, 'The ferment in Paris did not shift her from tonal realism. But she did learn the subjectivity of vision, one step away from the illusionist approach. Everyday objects can become aesthetic objects for painters'.[61] This was long before Andy Warhol.

From the Post-Impressionists, especially Manet and Whistler, she learnt the primacy of design and an emphasis upon the surface of the artwork. From the start it had decorative connotations and flattened the picture frame, as in Cubism. In *Modernism and Feminism*, Helen Topliss wrote that Preston preferred to paint still lifes because she could experiment with these concepts.[62] North writes that, when seeking a teacher, Preston looked for someone moderate.[63]

She experimented with colour, seeking an aesthetic, rather than a realist feeling in her work. She developed a colour scale and colour came to be increasingly dominant in her work. In this, Gauguin and the Fauves were influences. Her bold graphic arrangements were startlingly modern and she was a key influence in the redesign of post-war interior design in Australia, argues Edwards.

It was during the 1920s that she celebrated the development of labour-saving devices for the home, presumably on the basis that these would help set women free from household drudgery. She painted them using fashionable techniques such as the decorative Japonaise style. All the while she was coming increasingly to the belief that if you fill a canvas you need to decorate it as well as teach or astonish.

Through all her work she never ceased to experiment, to achieve an art that was more than realism, but without going all the way either with Cubism or abstraction. She challenged herself, as Elizabeth Butel points out, especially in the area of colour. Further, she developed dynamic line and symmetry, the latter an important element of the decorative.[64] A letter from Preston to Norman Carter is quoted by Edwards: 'Decorative work – this is the only thing worth aiming for in this century … I am trying all I can to reduce my still life to decoration and find it fearfully difficult'.[65] Henri Matisse was one of her inspirations, from whom she derived the principles of Fauve design: colour, flattening of space, and rhythm. She used colour combinations to produce emotional sensations.

All this she owed to her Paris years. While studying there she, like some others of the Australian women artists, knew what she wanted, and used her teachers, and her own struggles and experiments, to achieve her artistic goals. Making the unimportant and the everyday emotional was no easy task because the viewer tends to approach images of these things without emotion, seeing them only as utilitarian, and it is a considerable achievement of Margaret Preston that she succeeded in these aims. Without the experience of Paris, it is difficult to imagine that she could ever have attained the level of skill, or the knowledge, to gain the confidence necessary to make the contribution that she did to Australian art. In her bold use of colour alone, she was indebted to the French.

In continuing development of her work she 'remained centrally committed to a commonplace attachment to materiality', as she writes, and she 'moulded these forms to [her] aesthetic'. She attempted, according to Edwards, to achieve a non-rational rhythmic 'life energy' as a 'counter to … mechanistic views of reality'. She did this while, as Edwards puts it, 'remaining immune to the claims of Impressionism'. Preston underwent a subtle yet profound conversion in Paris, one of which she remained in control while allowing the influence of teachers and mentor artists to guide her.

Edwards writes that when Margaret Preston returned, the influence of Cézanne had increased considerably, bringing a closer understanding of pictorial structure, a symbiosis of the eye and the intellect. Later, she was also to say that from Picasso she became aware of a tripartite progression of forms: first, the pure original forms of nature, then the forms elaborated by geometry, and finally the forms made of art. Her artistic catharsis, then, was to apply intellectual order to the acute observation of natural form.

Of her social life only some is known, which is in keeping with the strict morality of the times – notwithstanding the supposedly libidinous Jazz Age of the 1920s. She was perhaps attracted to friends and partners who had complementary strengths upon which she could draw. In Paris she re-established contact with many old friends, including Bessie Davidson and Rupert Bunny, the latter having some influence upon her ideas. Her *Still Life* (1926) in the collection of Art Gallery of NSW, features warm reds, oranges and pinks, all of which were favoured by Bunny. She had a degree of recognition in Paris: a traditional oil was accepted by the Salon de la Société des Artistes Français.

When she returned to Australia in 1919, her work was favourably received from the start, beginning with *Summer*, according to unattributed notes held in the archives of the Musée d'Orsay: She quickly became a powerful advocate for modern art.[66] Her preference for still life was seen as appropriately feminine and uncontroversial, making her one of the first Australian women Modernists to be widely promoted. In Australia, she seized every opportunity to promote her aesthetic. Her zeal earned her the nickname 'Mad Maggie'. In fact, she is one of the few of the Australian women artists given due treatment in Parisian art archives.

Another way in which she influenced Australia was by introducing Aboriginal themes and techniques into some of her work, especially her landscapes. A third was by her wide use of printmaking, to which she gave an art rather than a craft stature, investing her woodcuts with, according to Janine Burke, 'stark, powerful imagery and simplified composition'.[67]

Her moves toward Modernism were, according to North, in line with trends in Sydney during her time back there, though it was gathering pace slowly. Her return, and the return of others like her, helped move it along considerably, and she developed a following among young artists wanting to embrace Modernism, though the art-loving public was slow to respond to it.

Margaret Preston was such a self-promoter that the question of how we first found out about her barely arises. We knew about her before undertaking this book, and we had seen examples of her work for years, in the New South Wales and South Australian state galleries. However, as we began to research her, the breadth of her creativity and the range of her interests impressed themselves greatly upon us, and we understood why she was impregnated in our subconscious as an artist and to see that her career, ultimately, in our view, was based upon the quality of her work.

Like so many influential artists, Margaret Preston continued to explore, grow, and develop, never allowing herself to fall into a rut of repetition. She 'attempted to make an authentic, national art that was derived from Aboriginal culture and Australian landscape'.[68]

White Gum (1953) (see Plate 9) is somewhat uncharacteristic of Preston's usual work. She manages somehow to suggest vigour, even in a dead stump. It has a certain elegance, despite the harshness and its grey, leafless and twisted shape, and there is beauty in its curving voluptuousness. It challenges a viewer to admire that which might easily be overlooked. The brown background may suggest a forest fire. There is little colour in this coloured stencil, and the work speaks of Margaret Preston's ability to find beauty and a sense of life in the most unlikely of subjects.

Margaret Preston's polemical writing on art also influenced the future of art in Australia, especially with regard to Modernism. In working as hard to put herself and her ideas forward as she did to create her art, she was ahead of her time. She never adopted a bohemian lifestyle, nor did she spend time cultivating favours for herself at Le Dôme among the artistic milieu, preferring instead to talk directly to art lovers, but she did a service to all artists by demonstrating that it is not enough to have talent alone. And she directed attention to areas that would be pounced on by later generations of artists and art lovers: Aboriginal art, printmaking, and the art of the everyday.

Chapter 10

KATHLEEN O'CONNOR

A Solo Act

Kathleen (Kate) Laetitia O'Connor
1876–1968
In Paris 1907–1909, 1911–1914, 1918–1926,
1927–1939, 1951–1955

How does one choose a favourite personality to write about when writing a book such as ours? In so many instances we've thought this one, or that one, was incredible. The truth is that each artist is unique, and we have had a difficult time narrowing it down to the ones we have chosen.

There are standouts, and Kathleen O'Connor is one of them. She was an intriguing woman, full of contradictions. She hoarded all correspondence and documents, even down to receipts for bread and prescriptions for glasses. She loved name-dropping, and there is some evidence to substantiate her claimed links to well-known artists. She meticulously hid details of her private life, was untruthful about her age, and was not known to have an affair with either sex. When asked about personal relationships she would answer, 'Wouldn't you like to know?' In *Chasing Shadows,* Janda Gooding writes that O'Connor was seduced by the excitement offered by the European art world and was determined to pursue her artistic interests.[69] Perhaps by this time she had already decided not to marry.

Gooding notes that her thoughts of travel may have been influenced by articles in arts magazines, in which the authors describe the practical costs of board and lodging, models, studios and fees at schools such as the Académie Julian and Académie Colarossi, as well as the bohemian and romantic lifestyle in which women and art students could participate. O'Connor, says Gooding, was also bitter about how the West Australian establishment had treated her father, C.Y. O'Connor, an engineer who built the water pipeline from Perth to Kalgoorlie. He was accused of fraud, and committed suicide, only to have his reputation revived when it was later discovered the accusations were false. This perhaps gave impetus to her desire to travel to France.

Kathleen O'Connor worked alone, as most artists do most of the time, and lived alone, except for a short period sharing an apartment in Paris on the Left Bank with artist and teacher Frances Hodgkins. She did have a small circle of friends, mostly other Australian women artists, but liked her own company – she seems not to have been part of any 'crowd' or gang – although she sought the company of many Impressionists including Bonnard and Vuillard.[70] Such apparent contradictions as this only serve to heighten the sense of mystery and secrecy surrounding this artist. There is plenty of mythology about the lonely outsider who creates works of genius: Kathleen O'Connor produced works of beauty, sometimes of power, and always, in our view, of originality.

Kathleen O'Connor was born in New Zealand but came to live in Perth with her family in 1891. She studied art at Perth Technical School from 1900, under James Linton, an English artist who had been trained at the Slade School of Fine Art in London. She exhibited regularly at the West Australian Society of Arts from 1902. Even in these early years she was always the witness in her art, the disinterested viewer looking in on the scenes of the world, from an alienated viewpoint, never engaging with her subjects – often, in fact, obscuring their faces so as not to reveal character – as in many of her Luxembourg Gardens paintings. She travelled to Paris in 1907, remaining there for most of the time, with occasional short visits home, except for the war years 1914–18, until her final return to Perth in 1955. In Paris she also studied at the Académie Vassilieff prior to 1914. We were pleased to see that Western Australia had produced at least one local artist who had made it to Paris and developed a strong and vibrant talent, despite the difficulties created by the isolation of the west – the tyranny of distance.

She settled herself in an atelier in the rue de la Grand Chaumière on the Left Bank, and positioned herself within the expatriate artist community. She had been encouraged, according to Anne Gray in *Painted Women*, to travel and experience Europe by the example of such women as Marie Tuck.[71] While in Paris, particularly in the early years, she depended to some extent upon the expatriate artist community for moral support and encouragement as she caught up with the technical standards needed. This community, suggests Gray, may have included Rupert Bunny, who was also her tutor; Marie Tuck; Bessie Gibson; and Ethel Carrick and her husband Emanuel Phillips Fox. She also taught herself French. Thus, she seems to have lived a busy life, involving others, and, as Gooding notes, not always living a life outside society. She continued to maintain a strong relationship with her family in Perth as a comfort to her in her new surroundings, and possibly because she engaged in a long struggle with them to secure a small stipend to allow her to survive in Paris.

In 'The Greatest Voyage', Anne Gérard-Austin states that O'Connor provides an example of a strong-minded, upper-middle-class Australian woman determined to overcome obstacles to make it as a professional artist.[72] To say that she learned from the French would be an understatement: she learned everything of artistic importance from the French and was the first to admit that she had landed in Paris with poor skills tempered by high ambition.

Technically deficient she may initially have been, but from the start she displayed an obvious gift, and enjoyed making designs for painted velvet and silks for dress materials; indeed, she returned to this work after her return to Australia. She remained practical, too, in Paris; for example, doing interior work for Parisian homes to earn money to supplement her small income from her family. And all the while she was in Paris she wrote home about her experiences there and the fashions of the day, fabrics and fashion being another of her keen artistic interests. These articles were published in the *West Australian* newspaper between 1910 and 1913.[73]

Though an outsider by nature, with her little group she would paint *plein air* in the Luxembourg Gardens from about 1908 to 1914 – when the war drove her out – using the people she saw there as a way of improving her skills, as many artists do, observing the people of Paris in a detached way. She painted quickly, rarely reworking a painting because the people she painted would never form a group in quite the same way again, even if they returned to the gardens. These remarks are truer of her later work than of her earlier Paris work when she was still finding her way technically. The earlier Luxembourg Gardens works are usually painted from the same level as the subjects, while the later ones were usually painted from above.

Her sound interview, in her dry, precise voice, with Hazel de Berg at the National Library, provides some insights:

> I always loved drawing and wanted to be an artist. I could not help learning; everyone I met taught me something. I got an impression of something, not a literal portrait, but form was always important to me. I soaked myself in art and artists, most conversation bored me. Once I got to Paris I never wanted to live anywhere else; once you live a long time overseas you're not fit to go home. I didn't copy the Impressionists, but they influenced me; the French are the greatest painters. I knew many leading artists, Modigliani, others, but the War [World War I] changed Paris; all the studios went. I frequented restaurants and cafés, mostly at night, I saw many famous people but I had no need to talk to them. Growing as an artist is the same as growing as a person.[74]

One can understand how, listening and watching at Le Dôme, soaking it all up, she might not feel the need to talk.

She was in love not only with art but with the life of the streets, parks and cafés. In an article in the *West Australian*, she wrote: 'the dream of Paris life, the restaurant life, the café life, which to me is almost the most fascinating of all there is to see. Restaurants, dancing with lights, glasses glittering with reflections, and with it all the music of many voices … in Paris one feels at least part of a great whole'.[75] In 1911, Kathleen O'Connor had two works, of the Luxembourg Gardens, accepted by the Salon d'Automne, the first of regular showings there. She never ceased to challenge herself – for instance, experimenting with the use of tempera during the 1920s. In 1920 and 1921, she exhibited at the Salon d'Automne, mostly still lifes in 1921, which Janda Gooding, in *Chasing Shadows*, thought signalled a need to earn more money from her art. In the 1930s, she worked as hard as in earlier times. She exhibited with the Salon d'Automne again in 1932. She became more interested in group exhibitions later in the 1930s. In 1934, she showed with the Société Internationale des Femmes Peintres et Sculpteurs, and in 1937 at Musée de Jeu de Paume and Galerie J. Allard.

Returning once more to Paris in 1951, she had a solo exhibition at the Galerie Marseille in June 1953, as she was anxious to develop a legacy in France. She received much media coverage, some of which remarked upon the influence of Vuillard, but she sold little, which was a cruel disappointment to her.

Kathleen O'Connor's return visits to Australia always disappointed her, too, and she kept returning to France, coming home only when her finances ran out. In 1940, she caught one of the last trains out of Paris before the Germans entered – the train was bombed but she survived. Her return to Perth in 1948 disappointed her yet again – according to the *Australian Dictionary of Biography* she stated that 'this is not a centre of art', and promptly left for Europe once more. Her final return to Perth was in 1955 – that was it, the end of her 'authentic' life, according to O'Connor in the de Berg interview. She was warmly welcomed, at first, by the art community there. In 1948, she was given a retrospective exhibition at the Art Gallery of Western Australia, which was a critical and commercial success, re-establishing her in her home town. She found support from some, but not from others – the Australian art scene was beginning to focus on abstraction and she was beginning to seem out of date. However, during her final years in Western Australia she won several prestigious prizes, and another retrospective was held of her work at the Art Gallery of Western Australia in 1967.

There was one less pleasant experience, however, on her 1948 homecoming. She brought with her many of her works, and was charged so much import duty for them by Customs that she was obliged to throw a hundred or more of them into the ocean at Fremantle – a shocking homecoming for such a fine artist.[76]

The work itself had undergone a dramatic shift during the 1930s. In her earlier work, especially those paintings made in the Luxembourg Gardens, there had been an unavoidable tendency of rapid brushstrokes and sketchy outlines. For instance, in *Two Figures, Luxembourg Gardens* (1910–14), the two female figures are sketched in roughly with blue/grey and white paint using several different brushes. Charcoal underdrawing shows through, as does the now honey-coloured card surface. Around the figures she dashes in a neutral background, eliminating all depth of field in her random marks. In the last stroke, wet paint is scraped away to register the form of the easel. At a later date, she added a glaze varnish that had charcoal or oil colour deliberately added to achieve a lower, almost soiled tonality, across the picture surface.

In the 1930s, however, though retaining a high key palette, she abandoned the precision of her earlier works. Robert Hughes described her painting *In My Studio, Paris* (c.1937):

> When you look at it you see the delectable froth of light breaking up the forms and leaving them still somewhat legible. You can, for instance, read the jug and forms of the oranges or apple on the plate and a vase and a glass resting on a saucer and a bunch of spring onions, but what really counts is the exuberant action of the line, weaving and flickering through paint strokes of very high key colour and then anchored by the fat, prosperous curve of the beautifully painted jug. She had a gift for organising images as surface, a fine, voyeur-like sort of knitting that few local painters of the time could even approach.[77]

Self Portrait (1928) (see Plate 10) is a self portrait that almost seeks to obscure the sitter. Kathleen O'Connor gazes out of a dark ground, wearing what is presumably an overcoat, and a hat pulled down over her hair, as if she wishes to be encased within herself. Shades of dark brown and dark red militate against any suggestion of lightness of being. Her lips are slightly parted as if whispering something we are not meant to hear, and her eyes, slightly clouded, gaze challengingly at the viewer. This is a powerful portrait of a very private person.

Art can be the most social of art forms – art clubs, gallery openings, studio dinner parties, artist co-ops, groups of artists living together, friendship networks – but it can also be the loneliest. O'Connor did seem to enjoy a social life, among carefully selected friends. But, basically, she trod her own path, like one who knows her strengths, her limitations, and her goals. She was not a joiner, nor did others follow her. Yet her art reflects her joy, not only at living and working in Paris, but also in the act of painting itself. Her work, we believe, is essentially lyrical, graceful and full of the love of life.

Loners can contribute to the whole while standing outside of it. The *Australian Dictionary of Biography* states: 'O'Connor was a woman of firm character and opinions ... While influenced by Impressionism and the *intimistes* ... she remained an individualist, with a strong sense of form ...'.[78]

Kathleen O'Connor made a considerable contribution both to French and to Australian art. She deserves to be remembered as one of our major artists, and her work should be esteemed accordingly. Julie Lewis begins her biography of Kathleen O'Connor with the statement: 'In many ways Kathleen O'Connor remains an enigma'.[79] The artist would have liked that – she enjoyed keeping people guessing.

Chapter 11

ANNE ALISON GREENE

A Passion for Art and Teaching

*Anne Alison Greene
1878–1954
In Paris 1912–1914, 1918–1939*

Born in Bridport, County Dorset, England, the fifth of 11 children, Anne Alison Greene immigrated with her family to Australia in 1892, first settling in Rockhampton. The family then settled in Wynnum in Brisbane, where she and her sister Alice later set up the Moreton Bay Girls' High School (now Moreton Bay College).[80] Anne was an outstanding example to many of the young women she taught. Art and culture, a passion for both sisters, and core subjects at the school, drove them both to exhibit and teach. Anne is especially interesting because her teaching extended beyond the visual arts into other artistic fields, notably music. She later stated: 'I feel with my sisters that the importance of cultural subjects in character formation cannot be over-emphasised'.[81]

In Brisbane, she studied art at the Brisbane Central Technical College with Godfrey Rivers. Her serious art training began when she moved to London in 1911 and studied first at the Battersea Training School and later at the South Kensington School of Art. She moved to Paris in 1912 and lived there until 1914. After a return visit to Brisbane between 1914 and 1918, she returned to Paris and lived there until 1939. In Paris, particularly, she pursued her great love of Impressionism, in which style she painted extensively.

In Paris, she came under the influence of Émile Jaques-Dalcroze, the founder of eurhythmics, a discipline that awakens, develops and refines musicality through movement, ear-training, and improvisation. Eurhythmics was then introduced at her schools. She studied with Edwin Scott at Castelucho's School of Art, and after a time was appointed manager of that studio, which seems to indicate that she was, like many of the Australian women in Paris, a highly organised person.[82] Later, she established a studio of her own, in the rue Campagne-Première, in which location she also established the Paris version of her school, and began exhibiting. We became aware of Greene through seeing her marvellous portrait of Moya Dyring, after which we began to seek information about her.

Anne Alison Greene returned to Australia during World War I, making her way back to Paris in 1918, and it was during this period after the war that she determined to make her mark in her mentor city. She exhibited with the Société Nationale des Beaux-Arts between 1920 and 1939, becoming an associate member, and in 1928 she became a full member, regularly exhibiting there until 1939. She established a studio again and began teaching. Bessie Gibson, her close friend, bought several of her paintings, mostly in the Impressionist style.

Greene made a significant contribution to Australian art, especially in Queensland, and she held an exhibition of her work at Finney's Art Gallery in Brisbane in 1950. The Queensland Art Gallery purchased three of her works from the exhibition.

From the example of two of her better-known Paris works, Anne Alison Green might be assumed to use a dark palette. *A Winter Day in Paris* (1934) shows the Arch itself looking almost inconsequential, in contrast to its real-life, imposing presence. There is only one high key: soft light falling on an apartment building in the background, echoed along the tops of other background buildings falling away to the left of the picture plane. In the foreground, dark figures move slowly about their business, looking neither to left nor right. A sombre, turbulent sky hovers low overhead, threatening disruption, while a sparse, winter tree stands stark and bare to the left as if competing with the nationalistic shrine. Nothing enlivens the picture. Is Greene suggesting that a national monument should be shunned or downgraded? Even the mottled ground seems inappropriate next to a national monument. For a woman who loved Paris, it may seem odd that this painting does not evoke the glories or beauty of the city. And it is only the Arch's central position in a dark cityscape that leads the eye to it, otherwise it might blend into the apartment buildings.

L'Église Saint-Germain-des-Pres (c.1935), on the other hand, while not glorifying the medieval church and its intense history, does present a more buoyant, optimistic view of the city. From a peaceful sky of floating clouds light pours onto a row of apartments behind the church, leading the eye before the viewer takes in the church, with its steeple reflecting the light pervading the scene. Figures in the foreground have tiny high keys and seem to move purposefully – they may be enjoying themselves. A spear of dark foliage and a small structure lead the eye gracefully to the bright buildings. The church spire touches the sky as if bringing its light down to earth – surely what churches are supposed to do. The viewer's eye, having taken in the principal points, may wander off down the street, wondering what interesting shops and people may lie in that direction. Altogether, a happier view of the City of Light.

Another study of a Parisian church, *L'Église Saint-Étienne-du-Mont, Paris* (1935) (see Plate 11), displays a clear and compelling structure. The triangular shape of the church, reaching into the sky, is imitated by a triangle in the centre foreground of two lines of converging figures, leading the eye to the edifice and seeming to invite the viewer to want to approach the church in the distance. A low key palette of greys and browns allows the viewer to study the complex lines of this unconventional church in the heart of the Left Bank, as Anne Alison Greene avoids the temptation to introduce colour to make her subject more superficially attractive.

We began our study of Greene when, late in our research, we asked a curator at the Queensland Art Gallery if she knew of any artists we should consider. When she sent us images by Greene and we discovered where her initial roots lay, we found it hard to believe that this artist had not achieved recognition already. We learned more about her educational activities, the teacher who instinctively knew how to stimulate the very young in finding their creative capabilities and making available the tools to help them, according to *Design & Art Australia Online*.

In *The Long Weekend*, Tansy Curtin states, 'Anne Alison Greene depicts herself putting on makeup at her dressing table, a gesture that in Manet's *Nana* was read as indicating prostitution. In portraying herself with a lipstick Greene proclaims her status as a modern woman in charge of her destiny'.[83]

So settled and accepted was she in her adopted town, had she not been forced by ill health to return to Australia not long after World War II, Anne Alison Greene might in all probability have lived the rest of her life in Paris, with perhaps an occasional visit home to see family and to exhibit. Until her death in 1954 she was better known in France than in Australia, a tribute to her skill and her work ethic, and her work always received appreciative attention in the Paris media. She was one of the women who enriched Australian art as she brought Paris back home with her, showing Australians all that she had learned in the world capital of art.

Chapter 12

BESSIE DAVIDSON

Une Australienne Française

Bessie Ellen Davidson
1879–1965
In Paris 1904–1907, 1910–1965

Of all the Australian women artists, Bessie Davidson, to our minds, was the one who was arguably most successful within the French art world, and who perhaps most identified herself with that country.

Our research found that Bessie Davidson, one of the most highly regarded and influential of the Australian women artists who lived and worked in France, did not form fixed and final ideas, as some of the other Australian women had done, before leaving her comfortable existence in Adelaide for Left Bank artistic life in 1904, after studying in 1899 under Margaret Preston, with whom she later held a joint exhibition. She lived in Paris until 1907, and then again from 1910 until her death, with short breaks back in Australia. She remained open to the new ideas and fashions that were sweeping artistic Paris during the first half of the 20th century, waiting to see what she would find when she got there. We discovered, however, that she never quite divorced herself from her early training and inclinations – from Adelaide, in other words – and never quite entered the Modernist vanguard of Parisian art.

This book would not be complete without a chapter on her, since not only did she gain awards and exhibitions, but she bridged the gap between France and her country of origin. She was one woman who, having made the journey, made a commitment to France, and chose to live and work there until her death, only returning to Adelaide in 1907 for two years, during which time she exhibited regularly with the South Australian Society of Artists and sold a portrait of Gladys Reynell – titled *Portrait of Miss G.R.* – to the Art Gallery of South Australia. During that visit, however, she did communicate what she had learnt in Paris to many friends and associates, and she did paint, often in the company of colleagues. After returning to Paris in 1910, she came back to Australia only twice, briefly.

Born and educated in Adelaide, she was, from the outset, an artist who looked to Europe – and especially France – and decided at an early age that that would be her destiny. Fortunately, her father was willing to oblige with a stipend, and thus her fate was determined relatively early on. Researching at the Musée d'Orsay Archives, we found that she was referred to as 'Scottish', but there is no doubt as to her Australian birth – though she was Scottish by heritage.

Penelope Little, in *A Studio in Montparnasse*, described Davidson as having a 'dream' of getting to Europe, and that word may suffice to encompass the multiple and complex factors that send creative artists abroad.[84] Years later she was to write to her father: 'I can sell as many pictures as I can paint, I was born under a lucky star … never worry about me'.[85]

Her emotional high on first arriving in Paris was eloquently captured by Penelope Little:

> Paris ... how to describe the effect of that first experience? Captivating, sensuous, vibrant, bewitching even – for the city casts a spell on the receptive soul that enchants its victim forever. Paris in the Belle Époque – and particularly Montparnasse – was a dazzling firmament of creativity, an explosion of stars as the two worlds of art and literature collided ... all the painters on the planet had their eyes fixed on Paris.

Years later, Marc Chagall was to recall his own arrival in 1910, as quoted by Little: 'I arrived as if borne by Fate, with all my dreams and ideas ... My every desire was fulfilled and I alighted from the train to find the light and liberty I have never encountered anywhere else'. To Bessie it seemed immediately familiar and she was certain she had lived there before in some previous life. She was enthralled, and she lost no time in sending off a telegram to her father explaining 'we are in Paris!'.

After finding her Parisian lodgings, of which some were in the rue de la Sorbonne, the rue Madame, and in the rue Léopold-Robert, all of which we faithfully sought out, she set out to find a teacher. (So many of the artists who travelled to Paris from Australia sought teachers that it seems clear they believed Australia was behind France in its artistic development – and how right they were.) She enrolled, with her close friend Margaret Preston with whom she had travelled to Europe, at the Académie de la Grande Chaumière, in the street of that name. The school was not radical, but neither was it dogmatically traditional, and Bessie seems to have been satisfied with its teaching and its facilities.

She finally found and settled in a studio apartment – a roomy first-floor atelier overlooking the street and with large windows – in the rue Boissonade. This would be her home for many years to come. We were impressed with this stylish building, well over a hundred years old. Her painting *Interior* is of this studio.[86] From the start, Davidson was an extremely social woman, entertaining and being entertained, not only by the other artists in her building but also by new friends who invited her to their homes and country retreats. Soon after her arrival at the rue Boissonade address, for example, she met 14-year-old Germaine Desgranges while helping the child find her cat, and discovered that she was the daughter of the artist Félix Desgranges who lived in the building, and he and the family were to become lifelong friends and he a colleague. This chance encounter also offered an *entrée* into French artistic and fashionable circles. She became an habitué of their apartment and it was her first experience of the warmth and generosity that she was to meet from the French. She told Edith Fry that any Australian could succeed in Paris provided she had friends and/or family to help her in the early stages. And Paris, she said, was the most truly cosmopolitan art centre in the world.[87]

She became, to use a 21st-century expression, very well networked. She was a charming woman, Little states, with a strong sense of humour, and Parisians responded to these characteristics. In time, she came to see herself less and less as Australian, and more and more as a Parisian – and part of the fabric of the French nation. From her first years in the city, through World War I and the 1920s, her life became more fruitful and her friendships more numerous.

We found no evidence that Davidson lived the bohemian lifestyle with which Montparnasse in that period is sometimes associated in the media. Yet, in Paris she felt her mind opening with exhilaration, much as she had hoped would happen. Having no domestic attachments had already liberated her as a woman, and now she was liberating herself by feeding on the art, and the sophistication, of her new city. She had experimented in Australia with Impressionist influences, but Paris displayed a much wider range of styles. Remaining aloof from many of the 'isms' that were then rising in the city, she nevertheless found herself opening up to Post-Impressionism, to which she would probably have had some exposure in Australia.

We discovered that the turning point in her development occurred when she became a student, indeed an acolyte, of René-Xavier Prinet, her teacher at La Grande Chaumière. He became the dominant artistic influence in her life. It may even be possible that, though she also showed some interest in the Fauves, from whom she may have gained her love of colour, he was the reason that she remained, in essence, a conservative painter. One thing she was determined never to do was to shock with her art, as some avant-garde artists were attempting to do. Many of her works are of French scenes. Although she did not embrace the new wholeheartedly, the fact that she was open to new influences shows that her decision to make France her home was productive for her.

It's difficult to enumerate the skills Davidson learnt from the French as there were so many. She took an interest, for example, in the current fashion of Orientalism, according to Little. Here, perhaps, was another -ism that did help to shape or at least influence her approach. Perhaps the most important lesson she learnt, from Prinet, was to capture the essential, irreducible core element of what she was painting. In her many portraits, this was the character, the inner core, of the sitter as shown in his or her face. In landscapes, it was what made that scene unique, what was at the heart of that scene and of no other. She also learnt important ideas from another teacher, American artist Richard Miller, whose light-filled interiors impressed her. Overall though,

Cézanne might have been the major influence upon her work, and perhaps, to a lesser extent, Matisse.

While her early work tends to display these influences more obviously, her later work displays the confidence and assurance of an artist who has found her place in the firmament. And it was during her middle period, after World War I, that she achieved her best work, finding the essential element in her subjects. She experimented with various techniques and materials, but took a major step forward with the discovery of egg tempera during the 1920s, which added to her ability to capture the essence of what she saw.

In other areas of her life she also leaned toward the French. Juliet Peers, in her article in *The Long Weekend*, writes: 'Georgina Downey notes how Bessie Davidson carefully identified her furniture style by reference to French, rather than English, royalty and historical periods when making a detailed inventory of her home contents. Thus she laid claim to belonging to the French community, rather than being an ignorant tourist'.[88]

Prinet was the first to congratulate her when one of her works was accepted by the Salon d'Automne not long after her arrival. He noted that this was a rare privilege for a foreigner at that time, especially one who had not been long in France. As she matured, it was sometimes remarked that she had the ability to 'bring the outside in' by linking her interiors to the landscape outside, as sunshine flooded through windows, or gardens were prominently seen.

Mother and Child (see Plate 12), painted in 1914, displays Davidson's ability to convey the inner feelings and emotions of her subjects. Using muted colours for both the two subjects and the background, save for a few highlights, such as some flowers in the garden and the object in the child's lap, Davidson leads the eye immediately to the centre of the picture where the eyes of both subjects are focused – those of the child intensely and those of the mother rather more languidly – upon a small red object, possibly a doll, which the child is holding. Despite the seriousness of the subjects, this is a joyful, light-filled painting, basically naturalistic, with only a few indications of the more colourful, Impressionistic style she was developing. The mother has put aside her book to share the child's interest. The inner feelings and emotions are suggested rather than shown – Davidson contrives to use serene expressions and relaxed bodies to make a viewer feel the closeness of the bond between these two subjects. The very fact of displaying serenity, however, implies the agitation to come when the child is no longer quiet.

In the field of interior portraiture, she was fashionable in Paris. Notwithstanding the landscapes she painted in such locations as the Luxembourg Gardens, the comfortable, middle-class, private interior was to become a recurring theme in her work.

Her career showed a steady growth in skill and confidence, a growth kept slow by her innate conservatism. For the rest of her working life she would refine her style, but by the 1920s her period of learning from the French was over. It is our opinion that the best of her paintings, completed in a city full of the world's best artists, are masterful works that stand comparison with the best.

Her social life did not change as the 1920s progressed, and she continued to enjoy Paris friendships. She adopted the French custom of having a 'day' on which she would invite some of her large circle of friends, many of them French, to her studio. Lingering in the street where she resided for so many years, so long ago, we imagined the sounds of pleasure that would have emanated from these gatherings. Penelope Little describes these social scenes: 'Her friends took tea in her studio on the rue Boissonade ... nibbled cakes ... [enjoyed] warmth and conviviality, and animated gossip about art ... presided over by her with unaffected charm and humour'.[89] Her studio was larger than most of those rented by the Australian women, and Davidson's honours included: being elected an Associate Member of the Société Nationale des Beaux-Arts; membership of the Union des Femmes Peintres et Sculpteurs; being a founding member of the Salon des Tuileries; membership of the Société des Femmes Artistes Modernes in the 1920s; and, most prestigious of all, the Légion d'honneur.[90] She received this award – normally made for service of a high order to the French State – for services to French art, and for her war service caring for wounded soldiers during World War I.

Her exhibitions were numerous and included works accepted in 1905 by the Salon des Artistes Français; works in the Société Nationale des Beaux-Arts from 1906 to 1921; group shows after World War I, too numerous to mention; a solo exhibition in the Galerie Lejuy in Rouen; an exhibition at the Galerie Ecalle in 1929, with 63 works; and an exhibition at the Salon des Tuileries in 1939.

After World War II, she was a commanding figure in the French art world, even though she was becoming increasingly frail; still, in her personal life, her friends were her salvation. She continued to serve the artistic community and the state with dignity and application, and avoided too many 'metropolitan excitements'. Today, Davidson's work is held in most major Australian galleries, including the National Gallery of Australia and several state galleries.

Paris changed the life of Bessie Davidson and validated her choices. She was, in the end, French by choice, yet Australians can be proud of her achievements.

Chapter 13

JESSIE TRAILL

A Comprehensive Vision

Jessie Constance Alicia Traill
1881–1967
In Paris 1908–1909

The Intrepid Women loved to travel, and by the time Jessie Traill was 60 she had crossed the equator twenty times, so possessed was she with a spirit of adventure. In 1911, for instance, she travelled alone by boat to Java in order to better understand the artistic vision of the East.[91] She also later flew in a flying boat up and down the eastern and southern coasts of Australia, making rapid watercolour sketches from the windows. She was an omnivore, picking up ideas and skills from wherever they came. However, Paris did exert a considerable influence upon her during her three-month study period there, an influence that was visible in her later Australian work.

One of the first women to practise etching in Australia – and her etchings were an important part of her *oeuvre* – Jessie Traill was born in the well-to-do Melbourne suburb of Brighton, of wealthy parents, and was educated, like her sisters, at an elite boarding school in Switzerland. Her family were deeply religious Anglicans, and there is a religious narrative through some of her work. She spent the years 1903 to 1906 at the National Gallery Art School in Melbourne. Before that, significantly, she had taken lessons in etching from John Mather, who ran Melbourne's Austral Art School. Her love of outdoor painting may have contributed to her desire to leave Australia, since it was not emphasised at the National Gallery Art School.

In 1906, she travelled with her family to England. Sadly, her father died while travelling. In his will, he left enough funds for Jessie to live self-sufficiently. In London, she studied with painter and printmaker Frank Brangwyn, from whom she learnt a great deal of her craft. From early on, she spent time both in Paris (1908–1909) and in London, and from 1909 she was hung both in the Old Salon in Paris and in London's Royal Academy. In those times, Paris or London schools were regarded in Australia as a necessary springboard for an ambitious art student, so Jessie was on her way. She did not, however, enrol initially in one of the better-known springboards, instead preferring Brangwyn because of his skill in printmaking and etching, which later she used as a technique to extend her pictorial vision.

At the turn of the century, French realism acquired a new dimension – images of urban life and industrial scenes started to replace country images of labour and peasants. Though she was infected with this spirit, Jessie Traill's print of a cathedral interior appears to hark back to an earlier period – we noticed this did change in her later work. Her etchings struck a note of high seriousness, recalling the traditions of the 19th century.

In 1908, Jessie Traill, then in Paris, enrolled at Colarossi's. The main influence of French art upon her work appears to have manifested itself as a result of the total Parisian experience, including her exposure to Japanese influences and the Nabis school, as well as to Art Nouveau. It was not until she had moved beyond the sphere of her English tutor Brangwyn's influence that French influences began to really show in her art. After her three months in Paris, she travelled extensively – to Italy, visiting Rome, Florence, Siena and Venice, and into Belgium – soaking up art.[92]

Throughout the rest of her career, two major themes would dominate all her work – the Australian landscape, and the growth of the new nation as manifested in large-scale construction projects, such as the Sydney Harbour Bridge.

In 1915, she won Gold and Bronze medals in the Panama–Pacific International Exposition. Lee states:

> Traill's name has since become synonymous with a body of etchings and aquatints of the Australian bush in all its poetic moods, from the extreme of dark, primordial menace on the one hand, to the mirage-shimmering desert expanses on the other ... Traill's prints bear the hallmark of a subtle and skilled technician who welcomed challenges fearlessly.

Her extraordinary aquatints, which developed from an interest in European woodcuts and lithographs, were manifestly influenced by the art of Japan.

When World War I broke out, Jessie was living in London, and, like Iso Rae, joined the Voluntary Aid Detachment, working in hospitals and in a convalescent facility, the latter a military hospital in Rouen. Jessie, Iso Rae and Evelyn Chapman were the only Australian women covered in this book who portrayed World War I in their paintings, even if they painted the aftermath of war, or men behind the front line, rather than actual battle scenes. When, in 1918, Australia first appointed official war artists, 16 men were chosen, and no women.

In 1921, Jessie Traill returned to Australia and immediately became active in the art world. It was from here that some French influences began to show in her work. She ventured into the Australian hinterland to paint the desert, followed by exhibitions of that work at Wilpena Pound in South Australia and in Alice Springs.

As a printmaker, Jessie Traill worked on zinc plates in etching and aquatint. Her biographer Mary Lee wrote that she 'worked with the largest plates that the press would take and achieved dramatic chiaroscuro'.[93] She was also a lithographer, demonstrating that she was an omnivore of artistic techniques too. Her prints of the Sydney Harbour Bridge under construction, made between 1927 and 1932, were groundbreaking for any artist in Australia, due to the degree of detailed knowledge of engineering techniques that they showed – they somewhat resemble blueprints, yet manage to convey the grandeur of a massive engineering structure. It would be appropriate to wonder if the early Futurists had any previously undetected influence upon her.

In 1921, she joined the Australian Painter-Etchers' Society and entered her etchings and aquatints in their regular exhibitions.[94] In them she experimented with unusual decorative forms including the frieze. The NGA catalogue stated that her work was vital to the evolution of post-war Modernism in Australia, and that she forged a radical path in printmaking through the duality of her vision – the natural order on the one hand, and the industrial order on the other. Her Sydney Harbour Bridge Series was shown when seven of her etchings were included in the Painter-Etchers' Society's only thematic exhibition, which was about the bridge. At the time, Arthur Streeton, writing in the Melbourne *Argus*, said:

> [Traill] has won for herself a high position by her fine sense of design and her most capable rendering of very difficult subjects.

> She dares to do a large drawing composed of enormous curves and angles, and she does it successfully. There is no other artist in Australia today who can compare with her in the fine and varied exhibition of Sydney Bridge ... her drawings of the Harbour Bridge from 1927 to 1932 form a triumphant and original record of that mighty masterpiece of steel.[95]

It is worth remembering here that Jessie Traill also painted, using broad, fluid and neo-Impressionist brushstrokes, in both oil and watercolour.

Her work *The Roadside, Flanders* (1907) (see Plate 13) displays a dark palette drawn in black pencil. Two peasant women walk toward the viewer on a dirt road flanked by a line of trees and a half-hidden farm cottage. A storm might be brewing, or night falling, and an agitated sky hangs low over an otherwise peaceful scene. The road rides away into the distance behind the women, suggesting travel and faraway places, but the women, and their cottage, seem locked forever into the darkness of a rural past.

Jessie Traill was a dedicated artist who was willing to apply herself to the hard work required to make her mark in art history. She displayed a comprehensive vision and was described by art historian Sasha Grishin as 'one of the great Australian artists of the 20th century'.[96] In 2013, when the National Gallery of Australia held a retrospective of this almost forgotten artist, it described her as 'a key figure in the history of Australian printmaking'.

Chapter 14

GLADYS REYNELL

Freedom and Dedication

Gladys Reynell
1881–1956
In Paris 1912–1913

Freedom and expressiveness are often thought of as fundamental elements of the artist's profession. To a greater or lesser degree, this is true of all the artists in this book, since they travelled a long way to achieve exactly those goals. None, however, would exemplify these traits in their work more clearly than Gladys Reynell.

Gladys Reynell was the daughter of a wealthy and established family, the granddaughter of John Reynell, who is thought to have started the first commercial winery in South Australia. She grew up on a large estate and initially studied medicine, but abandoned that for the study of art.

By 1903, she had joined the School of Design's Art Club in Adelaide and in that same year she exhibited with the South Australian Society of Art at their annual exhibition. In 1907, she joined Bessie Davidson and Margaret Preston when they established their own art school, studied with them, and became close friends, especially with Preston. In 1912, she and Margaret Preston travelled together to Paris. Her father Walter provided this gift of travel to each of his daughters.[97] He encouraged her to enjoy the freedoms offered by single life, and she worked in Paris until 1913.

By 1916, she had begun to move from painting to pottery. She taught art for a while in Ireland to raise funds, which suggests that her family background did not always provide all the funds she required. During World War I, she taught pottery to injured soldiers in a rehabilitation centre, according to *Heritage: The National Women's Art Book*.[98]

We had known of Reynell for some time, but assumed she was solely a potter. To our surprise, not only did we find that she was also a painter, but a very fine one, and, in addition, a printmaker with an original vision. This vision has been described as Post-Impressionist, but some of her works, especially her prints, have clear elements of Expressionism. According to Robert Reason, Reynell believed strongly in freedom of expression.[99] In both her painting and in her pottery, this predilection was evident. She brought to her pottery all that she had learned as a potter, painter and printmaker, and brought to all three everything that she had learned in Europe, especially in Paris, where she spent that year of intensive study. She also spent time in Brittany, painting. According to the *Australian Dictionary of Biography*, she and Margaret Preston 'enjoyed an idyllic life as artists' in France before moving to the UK in 1913.[100] While in Paris, they most likely stayed with Bessie Davidson in her atelier in rue Madame, a street we came to know well as we traversed the Left Bank seeking the milieu of the women.

According to Reason, this time in France was an intense period of study, travel and gallery-going, not to mention adventures and friendships, for both Reynell and Preston. In Paris, they met the Australian expatriate artist Rupert Bunny and visited some of Reynell's relatives, writes Reason, and hiked over the mountains to Basel in Switzerland to view the work of Hans Holbein and Brueghel.

Reynell studied with a teacher named Bernard Naudin in Paris, probably attracted by the intense expressionism of his free drawings and etchings. He had been trained at the École des Beaux-Arts as a painter and printmaker, and this latter skill may have been imparted to Reynell, to emerge much later in her career. George Oberteuffer, an American painter, was also her teacher at the Académie de la Grand Chaumière.

After her studies had been completed, her painting *Enfant Nu* was selected, in 1913, for the Salon de la Société Nationale des Beaux-Arts – the New Salon. In this and other works from around this time, it seems clear that her primary interest was not in tonalism, but in depicting the figure within the domestic interior.

In 1916, Reynell and Preston took up pottery lessons seriously in the UK and her long period of working as a potter, for which work she is best known, began at the Camberwell School of Arts and Crafts. Her original intention was to learn everything she could about pottery in order to be able to teach it to wounded soldiers as part of their recovery. With constant practice, she soon became adept, and a new direction emerged for her. A quantity of clay from South Australia's Kangaroo Island was sent to her, and this helped Reynell on her way as an inspiration. Reminiscing in 1930, she said that it was difficult to describe the impact of this clay upon her, creating as it did images and emotions associated with the earth and its exciting aromas, states Reason. She thought that it would be the 'most delightful thing on earth' using local clay … clay that 'had never before known potters' hands'.

Although she exhibited in Paris and in Britain, her influence on European art would appear to be modest – she was there to learn. This was not the case, however, in her home country, where her influence, especially on printmaking and pottery, would be difficult to overestimate. Returning to South Australia in 1919, Gladys Reynell lost no time in establishing herself as a potter. It should be remembered, however, that she did not cease to paint during this period. In the Art Gallery of South Australia's biography, it is stated that hers and Margaret Preston's paintings 'were important in exposing Adelaide's insular art scene to Modernist influences'.[101] At this time Preston and Reynell became estranged, with Preston moving to Sydney to marry, and Gladys Reynell committing herself to South Australia. She established the first commercial potter's studio in South Australia, according to Reason, but in time the labour-intensive nature of the work obliged her to bring in George Osborne as a partner, and they subsequently married.

In their pottery near McLaren Vale, Gladys Reynell developed, according to the *Australian Dictionary of Biography*, 'simple robust forms based upon early European folk pottery, and decorated them with designs inspired both by Aboriginal art and the modernists' and was probably the first Australian potter to do this.[102] She also illustrated local Australian flora and fauna. She melded Modernist symbols with Aboriginal ones, a development that alone deserves for her to be respected for her pioneering contributions to Australian art. In fact, it is possible to argue that she helped raise pottery from a craft to an art form by the power and originality of her designs.

She made several decisions that did not help her to thrive in a commercial sense. Each pot was an original and she developed no lines of pottery, for instance, preferring each pot to be unique. It seems clear to us from this that she placed her art above money. In making each pot unique, she was stating that pottery was, indeed, an art form. A decision to move to Ballarat in Victoria, possibly for the clay, did not help her either. And the lack of a network of commercial potteries made it difficult for her to market her work and gain recognition across the country. However, she deserves recognition for establishing the first commercial pottery, in the sense of making an income while remaining true to her belief in creating unique wares, and for bringing a Modernist ethos into Australian pottery, as well as for her exploration of Aboriginal motifs. Her article 'Knowledge or Feeling in Art', in *Art in Australia,* outlines her philosophy and it was widely influential in Australian pottery.[103]

In 1934, she returned to painting and to printmaking. For four years she painted and made linocuts – the latter only to be given to friends and family. She became isolated from the mainstream of Australian art, however, and was, in fact, forgotten.

Turning to her pottery, in *Beaker* (1917), a curving line of terraces in the background leads the viewer to a dog rearing up toward a cat, safely ensconced on top of a brick wall. All is ochre against a white ground, and the circular nature of the lip of the wall is respected with a circular design, the curving terraces, the curve of the dog's back, the curving roadway. Simple, almost folksy, yet Modernist in its restraint, and in its clear, simple lines.

In her paintings, Reynell used areas of flat, unmodulated colour, and maintained a commitment to realism and naturalism, modified by some Modernist influences, controlled by colour, pattern, and a pictorial construction that simplifies and flattens space. In her French paintings, she couples primary reds with primary blue-grey glazes and she consistently employs carefully considered patterned fabrics, floor coverings and furnishings.

Pensiveness (c.1913) (see Plate 14) shows a young woman nude on a fashionably striped bed, curled up and staring pensively toward the floor, perhaps contemplating her future or something outside of this room. The colours are gentle, the soft curves of her body contrasting with the straight stripes and corners of the room. Her figure is foregrounded, commanding the attention of a viewer, and contextualised within an interior that seems warm and safe, with soft tones. The flesh tones are delicate and the air of repose is complete. The compositional diagonals of the body and bed create a shallow space, and only the shadow on the wall from her back anchors her in space. The patterning of the bedspread and colourful cushions bring life and intimacy to an otherwise introspective figure. The paint surface is thinly glazed. The fleshy softness of the body is in harmony with the cool, soft tertiary colours of the bedspread and walls.

Gladys Reynell made a significant contribution to Australian art, mostly in pottery, and may be regarded as one of the flag bearers of Modernism in this country. Her love of freedom and expressiveness were displayed in her devotion to art, and it is of major benefit to Australian art that her reputation has been resurrected.

Chapter 15

VIDA LAHEY

A Pioneering Professional

Frances Vida Lahey
1882–1968
In Paris 1919–1920, 1927–1928

Vida Lahey was one of the most driven women among those in our book. Her passion to learn the best of what European and especially French art had to offer, and to keep her home state of Queensland up to date with evolving world trends in art, are the salient characteristics of her career as painter and as teacher.

Born at Pimpama in rural Queensland in 1882, the slight, quite fragile-looking woman, shy and retiring, studied at Southport's Goyte-Lea school (now St Hilda's School) before enrolling at Brisbane Central Technical College under Godfrey Rivers. From 1905 to 1906 and in 1909, she studied in Melbourne at the National Gallery Art School under Bernard Hall and Frederick McCubbin, and later with Walter Withers. Her remarkable painting *Monday Morning*, painted in 1912 before she set a foot on French soil, makes clear her degree of skill and achievement while so young. The painting launched her career. That she had been quite well developed in her art before leaving Australia is well documented.

Lahey spent four years in Europe, most of it in Paris, first in 1919, when she studied at the Académie Colarossi, and then again from 1927, when she studied art in galleries and confirmed her commitment to modern art. It was in Paris that she shaped her future style – though she did take influences from many sources. The quality of her work alone would be enough to assure her legacy, and her work in teaching and spreading the word back home cemented it. Ever present in her mind was her intention to bring home everything she learnt in Europe, and whether from her studies in Paris or her visits to galleries and exhibitions, she gave much to her fellow artists and students in Brisbane. This included administrative work and teaching, as well as proselytising the virtues of art as an educational tool.

Most of the women artists avoided Paris during the war years. Although the fighting was on the Somme to the north, Paris felt like a city under siege and was not the centre of gaiety, love and art that it had been, and would be again. Lahey's reasons for staying in London, where she arrived in 1916, as she stated in her interview with Hazel de Berg, were twofold: to learn as much as she could, and because half the commercial fleet had been sunk and the rest was required for military purposes.[104] But when she did get to Paris, in 1919, she said, in that interview, of her first few months in that city: 'I had … months of absolute heaven because it was so marvellous: Paris absolutely intoxicated me'.

When she had studied at Colarossi's, she had also taken the opportunity to travel outside of France, and was particularly impressed with 17th-century paintings that she saw in the Netherlands. When she left

Paris in 1920, at a time when she might logically have been expected to want to stay – as France began its long 'happy hour' of the 1920s – she returned to Australia. During this first visit back to Brisbane, she began her work bringing the ideas of Modernism home.

Her work then, as earlier and later, focused upon landscapes and still lifes, especially floral watercolours, which was a medium in which she excelled throughout her career. As Margaret Maynard writes in the *Australian Dictionary of Biography,* Vida Lahey is regarded as having been most successful with watercolour, and Maynard believed that Lahey's work in still life expanded the way in which this type of painting could be developed.[105] She was well regarded, says Maynard, for her treatment of light and colour and the manner in which she used light, as well as structure, to lead the eye to its ultimate destination within a painting, a technique that Maynard describes as 'vivacious' and 'sensitive'. Lahey stated, in her interview with de Berg, that she owed her love of art and of nature to her father. It therefore seems likely that the foundations for her artistic course had already been set before she left our shores.

Bettina MacAulay's *Songs of Colour* offers many useful insights into Lahey's work and life.[106] Lahey is believed to have exhibited in Sydney during 1913–14, probably with the Society of Women Painters and the Arts and Crafts Society, so it seems that her career did not follow a simple progression consisting of Oz–Paris–Oz, but rather back and forth a couple of times. An active fellow member of the Society of Women Painters was Ethel Stephens, who is likely to have provided Lahey with detailed information for her later studies in Paris. Alfreda Marcovitch recalled, as MacAulay writes, that she and Lahey stayed at the Paris *pension* that had been recommended by Stephens for Australian artists living in Paris.

'After the war,' writes MacAulay, 'there was a flood of new work for her: paintings, sketches, studies, gallery visits, and art classes'. However, she goes on to write that Lahey's 1919–1920 work shows marked points of departure from her pre-war work in Australia, so she clearly benefited from her new-found European – and especially Parisian – knowledge.

It is clear that among Vida Lahey's influences were many and varied artists, all the way from Michelangelo, Vermeer and Rembrandt in earlier times, to French Modernists including Manet, Cézanne, Monet, van Gogh, Matisse and Bonnard. Here was an artist of curiosity, open to change and eager to learn and experiment. MacAulay notes that Vida Lahey's work came to develop colour sympathies, by which she means an affinity for colour as she had seen and loved (according to her de Berg interview) in Paris. Hence, her Continental period swayed her toward French influences. This tendency, writes MacAulay, was reinforced in her studies in 1919 at Colarossi's, and in 1920 in St Ives, Cornwall (where Whistler and Walter Sickert were based at that time) and where Frances Hodgkins, who had been influenced by French and Italian painters, was her teacher. Vida Lahey's work in St Ives reveals French influences – whether through Hodgkins or directly, it is not possible to say.

In her large charcoal and watercolour *Rejoicing and Remembrance, Armistice Day, London, 1918*, probably painted in Brisbane in 1924 after her first return to Australia, she unites all of her major artistic and aesthetic concerns of the two previous decades through a language of colour, form and symbolism. A description in *Songs of Colour* states:

> ... two groups of monochromatic female figures cross the portico (of a church) between lofty pilastered columns that support a pediment roof. At left, the figures entering the church are soberly

draped, representing those experiencing grief over personal loss (in the war), as was the case with Lahey over the death at Messines Ridge of her brother. They are followed by another group in swirling attire, gesturing animatedly, the sinuous, theatrical and balletic suggestive of a joyful, sensuous return to a peaceful world ... the converging perspective of the flagged portico leads the eye to crowds of witnessing figures, and finally to a riotous profusion of flags of the victorious Allies. Inevitably they conjure up images of other forests of flags – particularly those painted in 1878 by Claude Monet (*The rue Montorgueil Decked with Flags*) and Édouard Manet (*The rue Mosnier Decked with Flags*) of the July 14 celebrations. In Lahey's painting, white doves of peace soar in the sky that is filled with light – the light which draws the eye to not only the sky and the doves, but to the hope of a peaceful future after terrible violence.

MacAulay adds, 'Everywhere in *Rejoicing and Remembrance* there are striking repetitions of strong verticals, of chromatic harmonies, of figures, of flag shapes and of forms shaped by colour contrasts (Cézanne's influence, perhaps)'.

Building the Bridge (1931) (see Plate 15) is proof that the Australian women in France did not always paint still lifes, urban landscapes and portraits. Here is a nuts-and-bolts painting of an engineering feat, accurately documented. The curving arches of the bridge, reflected in the water that it encompasses, unite engineering and Nature. This creates a rhythmic pattern leading the eye along the length (and the depth) of the bridge to the other side. Some scaffolding on the near left-hand side of the picture demonstrates that the bridge is still under construction, while the water, the sky, and the buildings on the far bank are left largely unfulfilled so as to concentrate the viewer's attention on the bridge itself. Wake-lines crossing under the bridge provide a countervailing visual narrative to the dominant line of the bridge, and shadows cast on the concrete supports offer yet another story for the viewer to follow, completing a picture that celebrates human ingenuity while emphasising the play of light.

In 1929, after returning from her second voyage to Europe, Vida Lahey, determined to get her art underway in Australia, and Daphne Mayo, her close friend, co-founded the Queensland Art Fund, through which they raised money to establish the John Darnell Bequest for the Queensland National Art Gallery, and to maintain the city's Randall Collection. From 1936, Lahey was the custodian of the Queensland Art Fund's reference library. She was a member of the gallery's Board of Advice from 1923 to 1930, and a member of the Art Advisory Committee from 1931, and also Trustee of the Godfrey Rivers Trust.

She was, therefore, a key figure in the creation and development of visual arts infrastructure in Queensland. All these executive posts, though not in themselves necessarily artistically influential, created a climate of respect for the arts that was conducive to encouraging other, younger artists, especially women and children, to follow in her professional footsteps. For example, in addition to her executive work, this tireless woman established children's art classes at the Queensland Art Gallery in 1941, looking, as always, to the future. She had developed a philosophy of the universal language of art. She published a pamphlet, 'Art for All', advocating the use of the imagination to combat what she saw as the ugliness of contemporary urban life. She brought back to Brisbane some of the techniques for teaching art to children that she had seen working in the UK, and the children's art classes she established at the Queensland Art Gallery continued after her death. A more diligent battler for the unique contribution, to human life, of art would be difficult to imagine. She was determined not to allow Queensland to lag behind art developments in Europe and North America – or, for that matter, in Sydney and Melbourne.

But this is not all of her contribution to her home country. Vida Lahey established a catalogue for the Darnell Collection in 1948, and in 1959 she published *Art in Queensland 1859–1959*, the first history of Queensland art.[107] Teacher, painter, administrator, writer, visionary – she was a core promoter of the role of art in the public life of Australians.

Nor did all this extra-curricular activity dim her desire to paint. Along with her work on the Queensland Art Fund, she was a member of the Society of Artists, and she continued painting until shortly before her death in 1968. She received the Coronation Medal in 1953 in recognition of her services to art, and an MBE for the same services in 1958.

Vida Lahey acknowledged that she was a shy person in her interview with Hazel de Berg, talking about her early love of nature. Speaking in a dry, quiet voice, with some hesitation, she recounts the high points of her life, depicting herself more as a supporter of others than as an egotistical artist seeking glory. Her voice lifts when she describes the intoxication she felt in the Paris artistic milieu – indeed, in the city itself, as noted above. One of the few mentions of her own work occurs when she describes painting *Monday Morning* while staying at a friend's house. She matter of factly compares laundry technologies, then and now: the copper tub compared to the washing machine. This matter-of-fact tone, about what is arguably one of her strongest and most striking works, seems typical of her.

Vida Lahey made clear in the interview not only her love of French art, but also that she had learnt many other techniques at the feet of the modern French masters. That she shared this knowledge with her home country contributed greatly to the advancement of art in Australia, especially in her home state, and helped to drag Australia, in those early years of the century that had been decidedly conservative, more into line with international trends and standards as they were being practised in the art capital of the world. She is still a revered figure in Queensland art circles today.

Chapter 16

MARY COCKBURN MERCER

La Vie Bohème

Mary Cockburn Mercer
1882–1963
In Paris 1899–1922

The popular imagination, fired by the media, may believe that artists live 'bohemian' lives, though this was not true for most of the Australian women artists. Mary Cockburn Mercer's lifestyle, however – though her hard work and talent were never in doubt – was certainly unusual enough to confirm this popular belief. More to our liking, though, was her concern for others and her evident love for the good life, as shown by her friendships with many artists.

Mary Cockburn Mercer seems, if the stories about her are to be believed, to have lived what many people consider to be the romantic aspect of the artistic life, as important to her, perhaps, as her actual art practice. She produced some very fine, and often innovative artworks, which alone would justify her inclusion in this book. She lived in France, mostly in Paris, for long periods between 1899 and 1922, and then in and around Europe for years after. She absorbed France's love of good living, fine food and excellent friendships. She associated with famous artists and lived in glamorous locations during the earlier part of her life.

Bohemianism, though not emphasised in these pages, was a dream entertained by several of these women artists, fired up by media stories and gossip about Parisians who smoked in public and danced in the streets (as they still do, in the rue Mouffetard and along the Seine, to mention a few spots). To combine bohemianism with the development of one's art might have been a secret desire for some, but for most it was not to be – they worked hard, with social life taking second place for many of them.

Mary Cockburn Mercer began her life of art at a young age when she ran away from school and persuaded her mother – her parents being no longer together – to allow her to study art in Italy. Her mother took her to Florence and then to London, to finish her education. Having soon had enough, however, of the strict discipline at the school to which her mother sent her, she ran away again, this time to Paris. There she followed what might be called the bohemian lifestyle of the Left Bank. She mixed with many leading artistic figures, including Pablo Picasso, Marc Chagall and Kees van Dongen, and one of her closest friends was Janet Cumbrae Stewart. It is possible to detect influences from several of her artist friends, and she collected artworks from many of them. It is clear, in fact, from our research that she cared about her friends, and some of her purchases of their work may have been designed to help them financially.

While there is no public record of her income, it might be safe to assume that her mother, having invested in her daughter's dream, continued to assist it with some kind of stipend. In 1922, however, she was working as a studio assistant for André Lhote – which may suggest a need for funds – translating his lessons into English for expatriate artists. There she was influenced by his Cubist theories of dynamic symmetry. Her *Still Life with Rose* (1922) displays his influence. He permitted a degree of realism in his students' work, provided it was within the framework of synthetic Cubism, and Mercer proved herself able to integrate his influences with her own ideas and the influences of others. By fusing a variety of influences she was, we believe, breaking new ground. Mercer was also deeply influenced by the natural environment, toward which she was extremely sensitive.

Looking at her work now, it captured our attention. Her 1940 oil painting *The Boxer*, for instance, captures the vitality and musculature of an athlete, even in defeat. A boxer lies on his back, tended by a young woman, presumably his girlfriend. His angular body, and the direction of her concerned gaze, draw our attention toward his exhausted face. There is an absence of decoration, or strong colour, forcing the viewer to enter the narrative of struggle and defeat that defines athletes' lives. Both bodies are strongly and clearly defined. This is a woman's compassionate view of the suffering of athletes, and it suggests that Mercer entertained a broad view of the world outside the narrow confines of art.

Mary Cockburn Mercer's well-known work *Ballet* (c.1939) (see Plate 16), probably painted during her Australian return though its influences hark back to her first period in France, may be considered to reflect her unconventional views, while referencing the work of several other artists, including Toulouse-Lautrec. Elena Taylor, in an article on the website of the National Gallery of Victoria, described it in these words:

Plate 1: Iso Rae, *Breton Girl with Goat*, c.1889

Plate 2: Agnes Goodsir, *Girl with Cigarette*, c.1925

Plate 3: Marie Tuck, *The Sewing Circle*, c.1910

Plate 4: Bessie Gibson, *Portrait (Woman Knitting)*, (n.d.)

Plate 5: Dora Meeson, *A Harvest Sunset*, 1888

Plate 6: Alice Muskett, *A Lost Halo*, 1897

Plate 7: Ethel Carrick, *The Fruit and Vegetable Market, Nice*, 1933

Plate 8: Ada May Plante, *Man with a Pipe*, c.1940

Plate 9: Margaret Preston, *White Gum*, 1953

Plate 10: Kathleen O'Connor, *Self Portrait*, 1928

Plate 11: Anne Alison Greene, *L'Église Saint-Étienne-du-Mont, Paris*, 1935

Plate 12: Bessie Davidson, *Mother and Child*, 1914

Plate 13: Jessie Traill, *The Roadside, Flanders*, 1907

Plate 14: Gladys Reynell, *Pensiveness*, c.1913

Plate 15: Vida Lahey, *Building the Bridge*, 1931

Plate 16: Mary Cockburn Mercer, *Ballet*, c.1939

Plate 17: Janet Cumbrae Stewart, *Studio Fairy*, 1920s

Plate 18: Hilda Rix Nicholas, *Les Fleurs Dédaignées*, 1925

Plate 19: Anne Dangar, *Pochoir Composition*, 1936

Plate 20: Evelyn Chapman, *Ruined Church, Villers-Bretonneux*, 1918–19

Plate 21: Grace Crowley, *Woman (Annunciation)*, 1939

Plate 22: Dorrit Black, *On the Rocks*, 1935

Plate 23: Stella Bowen, *Self Portrait*, c.1934

Plate 24: Madge Freeman, *Still Life*, 1926

Plate 25: Constance Stokes, *Reverie*, 1950

Plate 26: Moya Dyring, *Fishermen*, 1966

Plate 27: Betty Quelhurst, *Winter Sun – Surfers Paradise Beach*, 1961

Plate 28: Margaret Olley, *Morning Interior*, 1973

> ... painted in a decorative Cubist style, the work is based upon a complex arrangement of diagonals and verticals with forms simplified into geometric volumes after the manner of André Lhote. The painting depicts a Commedia dell'Arte scene. The central female figure is wearing full face mask, and a white-haired figure behind her is a Harlequin, identified by his mask and tunic. There is a third, younger figure wearing beach wear. The relationship between the three is enigmatic, but there are clues in the artist's choice of animals to include in the picture: the dog is a symbol of marital fidelity, the turtle doves are symbols of passionate love, and the sleeping cat may be considered to be associated with treachery. The whole work is completed with considerable skill. The dynamic interaction between the various figures is superbly suggested by the conflict between the 'restraining' diagonals and verticals and the sense of movement in the flesh of the figures, as though passion is barely held in check.[108]

She moved to Cassis in the south of France in 1922 with her partner, American artist Alexander Robinson. She painted, again with influences from Lhote, landscapes of the countryside around Cassis, subtly capturing the colour and light of that brown and yellow part of France. Her olive trees are a case in point. Later, she lived for a time on Capri. She left Robinson for a German photographer with whom she fell in love on a trip to the Canary Islands and moved with him to Spain. From there she was obliged to escape by ship during the Civil War of the late 1930s, finding herself in Tahiti.

By 1938, Mercer had returned to Australia for a time, during which she established a studio in Melbourne and exhibited with the Contemporary Art Society. Her paintings were regarded, by some contemporaries, as decadent, and on one occasion one nude study apparently hung in an exhibition behind the door – an awkward compromise, at best, between her freewheeling views and the Puritanism of her time. We imagine that there might have been more visitors to the gallery looking behind that door than at the walls. Despite her obvious love of Europe, she made her contribution to the development of art in her home country during this visit back home. As well as her exhibitions and mentoring, she ran an art school at the top of Bourke Street.

For most of her life Mary Cockburn Mercer was renowned as a hostess and her social gatherings were much talked about. This reputation, during her return visit to Australia, contributed to her influence, sometimes as a mentor to younger artists. While in Melbourne she mixed also with celebrated artists, including Ian Fairweather and her friend Janet Cumbrae Stewart, as well as such Modernist painters as William Frater and Lina Bryans. Mercer never stopped learning. For example, it was not until she was back in Melbourne that she finally mastered her figure-painting skills, partly under the mentorship of Cumbrae Stewart, who in turn had learnt her figure-painting skills in Paris.

Gallery owner Martin Browne, in an email to the authors, described her influence on Colin McCahon:

> I think it is worth noting that one of Mary Cockburn Mercer's greatest contributions to Australian art was not material but rather the encouragement and example she provided to the New Zealand artist Colin McCahon after he met her in the National Gallery of Victoria by chance during a visit to Melbourne in the early 1950s.[109]

We quote from Marja Bloem and her text for the publication *Colin McCahon: A Question of Faith*, the publication that accompanied the Stedelijk Museum's exhibition of the same name:

> For six weeks during the winter McCahon visited Melbourne, Australia. Charles Brasch sponsored him on this, his first overseas

trip. During the latter half of his stay he became a pupil of Mary Cockburn Mercer, an elderly Cubist painter who was distinguished by having been present at the famous Paris banquet given by the Cubists to honour Henri Rousseau. Her example of a life dedicated to art was something that was critically important to McCahon at this time. As a result of their conversations his interest in the Cubists was revived.[110]

Colin McCahon was then quoted in Browne's email:

In 1951 I visited Australia and became a pupil of Mary Cockburn Mercer in Melbourne. Mary was old … she had a broken leg and no money. She charged me three shillings an hour for 'tuition' for two hours in the afternoons – painting – and nothing for the mornings at the National Gallery [of Victoria] – and nothing at all for the late afternoon conversations. I was taught how to be a painter, and all the implications, the solitary confinement which makes a painter's life. I remember her with great affection and gratitude.

This 'solitary confinement' of which McCahon speaks might help to explain the love of social life that was a part of many artists' lives, including Mercer's.

Bearing in mind the number of her students, one can well imagine her mentoring and assisting a great many artists with their skills and their sense of vocation. Mercer's fellow teacher at George Bell's art school during the early 1950s, Jack Courier, remembered her in Melbourne as an exciting and forceful woman.

Her work was well received by the media during her Australian return sojourn, especially when reviewing her works included in exhibitions by the Contemporary Art Society. In 1972, Victorian art dealer Russell Davis came upon some of her works, and spent three years tracking more until, in 1975, he staged her first retrospective show in Melbourne. In doing so he rescued her from oblivion as an artist.

Mary Cockburn Mercer was a complex person, able to enjoy the delights of Paris and the South of France, but also to work hard to achieve goals as an artist. Her career may epitomise for some the supposed 'bohemian' elements of a typical artist's life, but she knew only too well the loneliness and isolation, the ups and downs, the struggle to perfect one's work that actually typified the life of an artist, then as now. An artist's work reflects their life, and the discipline and commitment of Mercer show through in her paintings, and in her kind and intelligent mentoring of younger artists. She has deservedly been brought back to public attention.

Chapter 17

JANET CUMBRAE STEWART

Trailblazer

Janet Agnes Cumbrae Stewart
1883–1960
In Paris 1924–1931, Europe until 1939

Many women have painted sensuously in colour, and many have painted the human form. Janet Cumbrae Stewart combined these styles, working mainly in pastels, and did so in a way that had a major impact on Australian art.

She combined sensuousness with delicacy and charm and, it should be added, respect for her beautiful young female subjects, depicted nude, and for the female body in general, though she did also depict some male nudes. She brought out the delicacy of their features and the softness of their skin tones, never once treating any of them as sexual objects. She did not idealise them, but she contrived to display their inner as well as outer beauty.

What attracted us most to Janet Cumbrae Stewart, and prompted the subtitle 'Trailblazer', was her courage in facing potential disapproval for her choice of subject matter. We were also impressed with those of her paintings that were not of nudes, many of which, such as *Wagon Train on the Murray* (1916), were oils on canvas. Despite her reputation in some quarters for pandering to male objectification of the female body, there was obviously much more to this woman, as a painter and as a person, than met the eye.

If anyone imagines that an artist who depicts, in a large part of her *oeuvre*, naked young women could not be a feminist, they would be mistaken. In her day, Cumbrae Stewart was a trailblazer. She did sell paintings – then, as now, nudity is intrinsically commercial – but she associated with reputable artists who respected her for the quality of her work. We believe she painted nudes because she believed they were beautiful, because men were allowed to do so, and because she wanted to blaze a trail by making it more acceptable for women to do so, too. She was, therefore, we believe, an artist who wanted to break the bonds of Puritanism. In an age when it was easy to shock, and shocking for women to do so, Cumbrae Stewart shocked. She did so by showing her models relaxed, beautiful, and comfortable with their bodies.

She later studied under Bernard Hall at the National Gallery Art School in Melbourne, winning student prizes and second place in a travelling scholarship, which became her highway to France, and she exhibited with the Victorian Artists' Society between 1909 and 1919. It was while studying in Melbourne, according to *Heritage: The National Women's Art Book*, that she developed the belief that sensuality is decorative and began to concentrate on her nudes, though she also continued with landscapes and still lifes.[111] It had become clear to her that she had a special gift for depicting the nude human body. So she was well on her way as a skilled artist before heading to Paris.

In 1907, Janet Cumbrae Stewart was invited to show her work in the first Australian Exhibition of Women's Work at the Melbourne Exhibition Building, a move that represented an important development in her career and in her confidence. In fact, her fame developed quickly prior to World War I, a fact that contradicts the claim that women artists only came to the fore because so many men were lost in that conflict.[112] She had her first solo exhibition at the Coles Book Arcade in 1911, as reported in the catalogue for the exhibition *Janet Cumbrae Stewart: The Perfect Touch*, where it was written: 'It was a resounding success with many works purchased by prominent collectors as well as by Rupert Bunny and other artists and lecturers such as Bernard Hall'.[113] From 1916 to 1922, she was a full member of the Australian Artists' Association, a prestige usually conferred on male artists. Cumbrae Stewart won a Silver Medal at the 1915 Panama-Pacific International Exposition.

She was welcomed by the Parisian artistic community, where she exhibited at the Société des Artistes Français (the Old Salon), receiving an honourable mention from them in 1923. She continued to send works back to Australia for solo exhibitions at the Athenaeum Gallery in Melbourne, thus continuing her connection to her native land. With her female companion 'Bill' Bellairs, she travelled extensively in Europe, particularly in France and Italy. She continued to exhibit, notably at the Beaux-Arts Gallery in London between 1924 and 1931.

According to *Heritage: The National Women's Art Book*, Janet Cumbrae Stewart's success in Europe was limited to 'circles of late Victorian taste. On Radio National in 2003 it was stated that Queen Mary bought and commissioned work from her.'[114] John Shirlow, in *The Pastels of*

Cumbrae Stewart, writes of her pastels: 'that dainty, fragile, beautiful method whereby dry colours are worked on a suitable surface' and 'there is no conscious forcing effect'. And further: 'These luscious figures are usually conceived as items in general colour schemes where textures and brocades of various kinds play an important part', admiring also her 'impeccable drawing'.[115]

Pamela Gerrish Nunn, writing in the *Australian and New Zealand Journal of Art*, uses Shirlow's glowing accounts of Cumbrae Stewart's work as a launch pad to investigate her choice of the nude.[116] Shirlow had argued that the example of Australian forthrightness contested the hypocritical prudishness of the English. Nunn argues that Cumbrae Stewart did nothing to advance our vision of the nude, preferring to imitate a long tradition of the sexualisation of the female body, which is tantamount, in Nunn's view, to pandering to male taste, when she could have depicted the female nude in such a way as to establish a uniquely feminine, and indeed feminist, vision of the female. Instead, she adopted a policy, or strategy, of seeking acceptance and sales, at the expense, according to Nunn, of advancing a feminist cause by re-imagining the female nude from a truly female perspective. While recognising that the search for sales and acceptance is true enough of most artists, and perfectly natural for artists who were professional, we believe that Janet Cumbrae Stewart's work was indeed striving to present a non-sexualised, though sensual, view of the female body, as demonstrated by the soft, pastel nudes she produced.

Her search for acceptance and sales, whatever its motivation, was successful. She was included in exhibitions in the UK and France, as well as in Australia, throughout her 51-year career.

It is our belief that Cumbrae Stewart did, indeed, have a feminist vision of the female nude, and that the fact this vision was essentially sensual did not prevent it from being, still, a feminist vision. Perhaps there is some truth in the assertion that the British, while buying nudes and enjoying their sexual potential, were fond of making pronouncements of a moralistic nature about how un-artistic sensual art could be. There appears not to have been a corresponding moralism among the Parisian art-buying public, conservative though the French *bourgeoisie* could be.

There was, of course, a long history of the nude in art, from Greek and Roman times and throughout the late medieval and early modern periods, sometimes cloaked as religious images of angels or cherubim, and in later modern times as exercises in painting the human anatomy. Cumbrae Stewart's contribution, in our view, was to find the beauty in the human body, which was a humanist vision, and an honest one because she was not asserting that these young women were anything else but ordinary young women. Moreover, we do not believe that she enhanced their beauty, merely that she chose women with naturally beautiful bodies, thus bringing back the Classical ideal of the unadorned human form.

Her work received considerable attention in Australia as well as Europe.

When the Mornington Peninsula Regional Gallery mounted their retrospective of Cumbrae Stewart's work in June of 2003, Susan McCulloch, reviewing the exhibition for the *Weekend Australian* wrote: 'The type of pastel study [of] Janet Cumbrae Stewart, while perfectly normal in its humanity, is curiously free of any sex sensationalism'.[117] McCulloch goes on to write: '[She] offers a ... somewhat idealised, view of the female form'. McCulloch, unlike some other reviewers, pays some attention to Cumbrae Stewart's streetscapes, calling them 'rather formal' and saying that they are 'fresh and competent if not especially memorable', and that her still lifes of flowers show a fluidity of line. She reviews one work, *Model Disrobing*, in the following terms:

> There is great depth to these pastels. Through multi-layering she built a unique surface with a solidity akin to paint, yet retaining the translucence of chalk. *Model Disrobing* shows these qualities well – the curves and fold of shoulder blade and buttock shine with the smoothness of a softly buffed stone. Faces seemed almost immaterial to Janet Cumbrae Stewart, perhaps because they distracted from her intention to capture texture and shape. Back views of nameless nude models predominate throughout her work. In the more formal portraits the sitter is often captured side on or glancing backwards. In the narrative nudes such as *Bereaved*, *The Breton Oil Bottle*, and *Bird of Night*, faces are dropped into shadow or masked by an upheld arm. There is an anonymous quality about many of these pictures.

In an article for *The Perfect Touch* catalogue, Juliet Peers urges us to 'appreciate the rich, voluptuous surfaces and the intense, Venetian colour of her pastel works'.[118] She also refers to the streetscapes: 'Her view of the Pont Neuf suggests that the artist could take on one of the most clichéd and over-exposed views of 20th-century art and still say something that is fresh and sincere'. Indeed, 'fresh' is a word that occurs not infrequently in appraisals of Cumbrae Stewart's work.

Janet Cumbrae Stewart references the traditional worlds of Australian middle-class women in domestic situations, which have arguably been undervalued. Perhaps, argues Peers, her traditional, commonplace, mostly unsexual nudes could be read as validating, and valuing, women's lives, which have been thought not worthy of artistic attention. If this argument is to be accepted, then she was actually quite a radical painter, one who challenged, albeit within the parameters of traditional modes of visual communication, the ways in which women are seen, especially by women, and, if so, it might not be unrealistic to call her work 'revolutionary', though we will stick with 'trailblazing'.

We are particularly taken with one of Janet Cumbrae Stewart's works that does not feature a nude, *Studio Fairy* (see Plate 17), a pastel thought to have been made prior to 1930. A young woman, perhaps early teens, sits on a window ledge in a high-ceilinged room, largely in shadow though the window behind her highlights her figure. She wears ballet costume and adopts a thoughtful, introspective pose, head lowered toward her upraised knee. The artist contrives here to probe the mind of the girl, suggesting she may be about to enter a dance contest, or that she might be facing some limitation to her dancing abilities. The filmy, almost other-worldly atmosphere of the work, utilising to the full the delicacy of pastel, conveys the – perhaps unrealistic – hopes and dreams of a young woman temporarily escaping into a world of magic and art.

For an artist who helped open up new areas for women artists, Cumbrae Stewart enjoyed a respectable career and advanced, through her work, the cause of the liberation of women by her sensitive portrayal of the nude female body as a thing of beauty, thus showing that nudity need not be the same thing as nakedness.

Chapter 18

HILDA RIX NICHOLAS

An Open-minded Traditionalist

Emily Hilda Rix Nicholas
1884–1961
In Paris 1907–1918, 1924–1926

When Ballarat woman Hilda Rix (later Hilda Rix Nicholas) arrived back in Paris after her second trip to Morocco in 1914, her work from her time there was met with critical acclaim by the French, and that, together with her subsequent work utilising Australian subjects, earned her the respect of the Paris art world and the position of Associate of the Société Nationale des Beaux-Arts. Such was the respect in which she was held.

In 1919, Grace Cossington Smith, another major Australian female artist, who, however, did not study in Paris, viewed an exhibition of Nicholas's in Sydney (which included her famous *Defiance*) and wrote:

> I met (my Fate) the other day in the ART line! There has been a very stunning exhibition here, which created quite a furore …
> I went to see it three or four times and any other picture seems

very dull after seeing these … a huge room at Anthony Hordern's full of them – very coloured – scenes of Morocco – and people, dresses – all sunny – but the most astonishing thing was the life in them: the people really had expressions, not just a painted thing.[119]

Hilda Rix Nicholas studied others' work, but she was always her own woman. While she learnt techniques in Paris, especially Impressionism and the Japonaise fashion, she continued her development of line, form and structure that she had learnt before leaving Australia. Her style, however, never fully crossed the line from traditional painting into Modernism though her subject matter, as for example in her painting *The Chinese Robe* (1913), sometimes reflected current Parisian fashion. The National Gallery of Australia describes the painting in these words in its entry for this work:

> *La robe Chinoise* depicted Nicholas' sister, Elsie, enjoying the fun of 'dressing up' and acting the role of a haughty belle-dame. By creating an image of a European model clothed in a rich blue and red costume of oriental design and placing it in an ornamental frame Rix playfully exploited the exoticism of the East and its cultural difference.[120]

Her reason for going to Paris was not to find herself as an artist, but rather to find the technique to fully develop the artist she already was. Gérard-Austin, in 'The Greatest Voyage' refers to Nicholas's talent, which needed to be brought to its full potential by study of the great European masters.[121] Speck, in 'The "Frontier" Speaks Back', states in her opening paragraph that it was 'almost obligatory' for young artists to go to Paris.[122] And as John Pigot makes clear in *Hilda Rix Nicholas: Her Life and Art*, Paris was the hub of the international arts world, the goal of every artist who wanted to build a professional career.[123]

Her mother Elizabeth Rix was a painter who had studied at the National Gallery Art School in Melbourne. When the family moved to Melbourne, her mother became a member of the Austral Salon, which had been set up in 1890 in Melbourne to encourage the arts, and Hilda and her sister, both of whom played at least one musical instrument, sometimes performed there. She studied painting at school, Merton Hall, and between 1902 and 1905 studied at the National Gallery Art School. After the death of her father in 1906, she and her family prepared a joint exhibition of work that was held at the Flinders Buildings in December. This, together with Elizabeth's savings, enabled Hilda, her mother and her sister to travel to Europe in 1907. They left Australia on 22 March aboard the *S.S. Runic*, first to London and then to Paris.

In their *pension* in Paris in 1908 their life was congenial, with evenings of singing and dancing, no less *gai* than 'Gai Paris' – if somewhat less risqué. Hilda played the violin and her mother the piano. The *pension* was inexpensive and, it seems, pretty basic. Like many expatriates, Hilda soon noticed, according to Gérard-Austin, that Paris was pretty free and open and one could do more or less whatever one wanted, as long as one did not do it in the street and frighten the horses. She had mixed feelings about the French, loving their impulsiveness but distrusting what she sensed, as a true Anglo-Celt, was a kind of louche undercurrent. But then she was possibly painting the whole of France with a Left Bank brush. Be that as it may, she settled into the *pension* at 7 rue Joseph Barra, just south of the Luxembourg Gardens and right in the heart of the artistic district. She was not the only artist to live and work there. She wrote: 'Our pension is – ugh! – At present – several there whom we hate! So work all day, and am just there for meals – and go straight to bed after dinner (we are too poor to go away from there for it's cheap!)'.[124]

Life for Hilda Rix Nicholas consisted mostly of the work she loved doing. When not painting, she explored galleries, acquainting herself with the new movements and all that had gone before. The funds she and her family had brought with them seem to have gone a long way. Clearly they were very careful. Expatriation was, as Speck writes, a liberating time for women and Nicholas had some adjustments to make to the sophistication of Paris, most of which she contrived to avoid, although some of her work acutely observed the finer elements of the Parisian lifestyle of the period.

Before leaving Australia, Arthur Streeton had advised her not to remain too long with any one teacher. Accordingly, Hilda studied with a number of well-known Paris masters. Auguste Delécluse and American Impressionist Richard Miller taught her for a time at the Académie Delécluse. There she learnt to use a brightly coloured palette, but she complained that Auguste's colour was 'too drab', although his corrections of her drawing were excellent. She had, it might be remembered, arrived in Paris, in northern Europe, with Australian colours in her head. Later, she studied at the Académie de la Grande Chaumière under Théophile Steinlen and, in 1908, under Claudio Castelucho. She enjoyed painting her fellow students, and completed her first oil painting from a live model.

In July 1910, the family moved to Étaples, where they found a large international community of artists. The internationalism of this community may have influenced the formation of Hilda Rix Nicholas's work, establishing the style and character of her forceful imagery. She travelled to Morocco in 1912, and later that year exhibited a number of paintings of life in Tangier at the Galerie Chaîne et Simonson. The critics liked the liveliness of the scenes, and the French Government purchased one of the works, *Grand Marché, Tanger*. In 1913 and 1914, she exhibited a group of Moroccan paintings at the Société des Peintres Orientalistes Français in Paris.

Hilda Rix Nicholas was 'fearful' of modern trends, stated Pigot, but this stands oddly with the fact she loved the exotic and sometimes explored non-naturalism. She certainly learnt, in Paris and Étaples, a sure and precise mode of drawing, suggesting form, texture and subject matter with few strokes of the pencil. She learnt from her teachers, especially Richard Miller, to create 'evanescent images of light and atmosphere', writes Pigot. She avoided political statements and instead painted street life and strongly coloured exotica, including much sketching in the Luxembourg Gardens. Yet Speck writes that Nicholas 'immersed herself in cosmopolitanism', which was a central tenet of turn of the century Modernism – an early form, perhaps, of globalism.

Hilda Rix Nicholas had a love of masquerade and fancy dress, but, masks and dresses aside, she remained, in France, what she had been brought up to be – remembering that her family was always with her – a decent, provincial Australian, let loose among the sophisticates of a great and ancient city.

However, she made her mark in that city. In 1911 and 1914, she exhibited with the New Salon. In 1912, she was made a member of the Société des Peintres Orientalistes. In 1914, her work was hung at the 'Orientalist' annual exhibition in the Palais-Royal. Her work in Morocco had led to her first international acclaim, and it is interesting that some of her Moroccan works displayed some Post-Impressionist influences. Gérard-Austin claimed that her work at the Old Salon,

Retour de la Chasse, in 1911, led to her being hailed in the Paris art world as a brilliant newcomer. A review of an exhibition she mounted in Paris 1914 stated: 'her work is singing with a feeling of decorative youthfulness of spirit, freshness of inspiration … with a sense of movement and a knowledge of design and colour that characterises our Orientalist painters'.[125]

Personal disaster was, however, waiting for her. During 1914, her sister Elsie died of typhoid fever. Her mother, already in shock because of the German invasion of France – according to Gérard-Austin – and living in a nursing home in Australia, died eighteen months later, possibly due to the further shock of her daughter's demise. She had written in her diary that she had lost the will to live. Then, in 1916, more misfortune. Hilda met an Australian officer, Major George Nicholas, after he was posted to Étaples and admired her work, and then sought her out in London, where they met. They married in October of that year and she took his surname. After three days together he returned to the front, where he died three days later. She was again devastated, and stated that she could barely put one foot after another. During this period of mourning she painted *Desolation*, a study of a woman, in a wasteland setting, withdrawn within herself in sorrow. There are few more powerful depictions of loss, in the canon, than this work.

Pigot gives the impression that Hilda Rix Nicholas was conservative, and she did display her work in non-Modernist venues. But like many mainstream conservatives, she appeared to believe 'if it ain't broke, don't fix it'. With her love of Orientalism she would have found common ground with modern Japan, which forged its post-World War II society on the basis of its traditional values, but was open to Modernism in technology and politics. And if the Salons were places where expatriate careers were created or shattered, she used them to her advantage. If there was a time when she appeared to flirt with the possibility of crossing that line into Modernism, it was after her return to Australia, when French influences had seeped more thoroughly into her work. Nicholas was one of the more successful Australian women artists in France, but she also had great success in Australia. She returned to Australia for the first time in 1918 and soon held an exhibition of more than a hundred works in Melbourne's Guild Hall, many of which were sold. Although, as with the other women, it is often difficult to determine how much artistic success leads to influence, there can be little doubt of the connection between the two.

After World War I, she made her second trip to Europe in 1925. In that year she had an exhibition at the Galerie Georges Petit in Paris. A work was sold to the French Government for the Musée du Luxembourg, making her the only Australian woman to have more than one work there. In 1926, she was elected an Associate of the Société Nationale des Beaux-Arts. That same year, she returned to Australia.

Her portraits of Breton peasants display an attitude of kindness and empathy toward them: she is not judging them for their poverty or their prematurely aged faces. She paints them as she sees them, without any attempt to introduce into the picture any of the trends then raging through fashion-conscious Paris.

Hilda Rix Nicholas held more exhibitions, and in 1925, having returned to Paris, she painted *Les Fleurs Dédaignées* (1925) (see Plate 18), often regarded as one of her masterpieces. It displays dramatic technique in the depiction of the model's nervous tension, as well as confident mastery of flesh tones and of the cold, selfish face of the subject. Several times, both in France and in Australia, she was praised for painting 'like a man' – directly, in clear, vivid, strong terms.

Despite some forays over the border into Modernism, an unattributed article in the *Sydney Morning Herald* in 1926 stated, inter alia, that 'Mrs. Nicholas deprecated the ultra-modern tendencies in art as decadent, savage and primitive, though this kind of art had become fashionable among certain patrons, who were without taste. Leading artists, however, had made a firm stand against these tendencies, and should do much towards making art sane again'.[126] Reading this, it is not difficult to see why so many of these women felt they had to get out of Australia and go to Europe.

Perhaps what most distinguishes Nicholas's work overall are two things: Orientalism (by which is meant also Morocco, which is actually not east of Paris; perhaps 'exoticism' would be a better word) and Australian pastoral values. Two polar opposites, one might think, displaying the love of adventure and the curiosity that characterised this remarkable woman. A cosmopolitan she was, even if by choice she was no sophisticate. As Speck says in 'The "Frontier" Speaks Back', she responded with openness to new ways.

Following her second marriage, to a New South Wales pastoralist, Edgar Wright, she began painting scenes of Australian pastoral life, embodying the then-fashionable values of Australian ruggedness and rural life, in opposition to a perceived corruption in European life – which mirrored her own, paradoxical, views of Europe. This marriage brought her the joy of a child, at age 46, and she concentrated on motherhood while continuing to paint, many of her works being portraits of her husband and child. Perhaps she had never fully embraced Europeanism, and perhaps her Moroccan pictures, and these later pastoral idylls, epitomised a belief in the purity of non-urban existence. Be that as it may, she remained commercially viable. Her entry in *Heritage: The National Women's Art Book*, states that the Australian critics were amazed at the range and versatility of her work.[127]

However, her adoption of rural values, containing her idealised view of pastoral life – the rugged stockman, the noble rancher – led her to slowly fall out of step with current art world fashions in Sydney and Melbourne, which were in favour of Modernism from the 1920s on. It would be hard not to imagine an influence from her husband in all this. She remained hostile to Modernism, despite dabbling in it, and her reviews became less and less positive. Nevertheless, her work is held in several major Australian galleries.

Her work is vivid, naturalistic and relatively straightforward, with technique submerged in the picture frame and never intruding. Describing *Morocco: Market Place with Pile of Oranges*, the same writer states: '[The work] is a small, on-the-spot painting which depicts a group of figures against a backdrop of low buildings. The work is extraordinarily modern in its tight compression of space and interest in decorative patterning, as well as the loose and expressive application of bright, unmodulated colour'.

Although she was always certain to be included in this book, and our attention was always drawn to her work, after reading about the death of her family and her first husband and the way she recovered and worked on with courage and grace, she sealed her place like so many of the other courageous women. We found in this she was typical of the strength manifested by so many of these women in their struggles to fulfil themselves.

Speck, in 'The "Frontier" Speaks Back', says that Hilda Rix Nicholas was one of a small group of women artists who introduced Modernism to Australia. This was true of others, such as Anne Dangar, Dorrit Black, Grace Crowley and Marie Tuck, but it may be less easy to make this claim for Hilda Rix Nicholas. Although she had experimented with some elements of Post-Impressionism, by 1930 she had summarily rejected all Modernism. Her reasons can only be guessed at, but her embrace of a nationalistic, rural ethos after her marriage to Edgar Wright is clearly evident in the later work. What can be known, however, with some certainty, is that she was one of the most talented of the Australian women artists who graced the French art world.

Chapter 19

ANNE DANGAR

Communard and Theorist

Anne Garvin Dangar
1885–1951
In Paris 1926–28

Anne Dangar was a complex person, but her art was simple and clear. Her ideals, and strongly held beliefs – communalism, spirituality, closeness to the earth, Cubism, to make art that was useful and practical, to help others, and Catholicism in her later years – informed both her art and her way of life. Her art was a product of her beliefs. She suffered for her art, in poverty and isolation, yet never wavered.

Anne Dangar was born in 1885 in Kempsey, on the New South Wales mid-North Coast, daughter of a member of the Legislative Council, Otho Dangar. The Dangars were an influential family in the State. She studied art in Sydney under Horace Moore-Jones, then at Julian Ashton's school in The Rocks. She taught at Ashton's from 1920, and in 1926 sailed for France with her close companion Grace Crowley. She studied with André Lhote in Paris, then joined his summer school at Mirmande. Returning to Australia in 1929, she became frustrated with what she considered the parochial attitudes toward modern art, and returned to France in 1930.

She came to our attention when we discovered Helen Topliss's book *Earth, Fire, Water, Air*, which was a collection of Anne Dangar's letters home from France, mainly to her great friend and the person she held in most esteem and loved, Grace Crowley, who had returned to Australia.[128] The book, which was full of serious tips on painting and pottery, theory, and personal episodes, was a remarkable and valuable contribution to Australian visual arts, and should be widely read for what it has given to Modernism in Australia. Dangar has been widely credited – by Gérard-Austin among others – as being one of the women, along with Dorrit Black, Grace Crowley and others, who brought a more detailed knowledge of modern art, its techniques and its theories, home to Australia.

It may not have been well known at the time that her letters were imparting useful information to Australian artists. Helen Topliss, in her book *Modernism and Feminism*, states:

> When Humphrey McQueen wrote that Margaret Preston was the only Australian woman to express a clearly defined account of her art, he might have been ignoring the fact that Anne Dangar conducted a regular correspondence with Grace Crowley over a period of twenty-one years, and that these letters are a rich repository about her art practice, and her theories about art.[129]

Dangar may seem to have been unduly obsessed with theory, but so were many artists in those days, and in amongst the theory is a lot of practical common sense.

Anne Dangar lived in Paris between 1926 and 1928, then in 1930, after a brief visit home, chose to remove herself from the cultural hothouse of Paris to an artists' commune at Moly-Sabata, on the Rhône in southern France, where she could follow her ideals of agrarian communalism, traditional pottery, and Catholicism, and where she lived until her death there in 1951, apart from short trips to Morocco and Paris, and partially abandoned painting for pottery. She revered her mentor there, Albert Gleizes, whose theories of Cubism she readily adopted, berating herself in her letters when she felt inadequate to realise them. Despite her admiration of him, they had many disagreements, according to her letters home. Apart from that one visit home, she remained in France, living in poverty but obsessed with her art and theory, influencing Australian art from abroad through her letters to Grace Crowley, which spoke of continuing developments in French art.

Anne, like many of these women, had studied art before leaving Australia, and when she made her first visit to France in 1921 she already knew what she wanted: modern art. There was no need for her to convert. Her time in Paris was therefore a time of intense learning. On arriving in France, before settling in Paris, she first visited the home of Cézanne in Aix-en-Provence, her eyes set firmly upon one of the major inspirers of Modernism, at the beginning of what was to be a long exile from Australia. In 1928 she saw an exhibition at the Grand Palais, which included some of Albert Gleizes's paintings. This event is described in the NGA biography of Dangar as having been an epiphany for her, as though she had suddenly, yet finally, found her true path.[130]

Anne Dangar turned to pottery, and this again may have been because of her spiritual belief in the close relationship between art and the earth, or it may have been at least partly because the clay at Moly-Sabata was good, plentiful and inexpensive. Although she complained often in her letters about some of the people there – and about Albert Gleizes himself, and his wife – and about her poverty (despite her spiritual belief in it), she seems to have found her ideal place in the world. She had accommodation, food (provided she worked in the garden, which again accorded with her beliefs in the peasant way of life) and the use of the local clay. There she also found companionship, ready-made among her fellow communards, and with monks in a nearby monastery, which was something that had eluded her in Paris.

Life at Moly-Sabata was hard. The National Gallery of Australia's online profile on Dangar states:

> The artists were expected to earn their living by practicing various crafts. The locals often took pity on Dangar and brought her produce from their farms ... Dangar slaved like a labourer to extract her livelihood from the earth but produced art as if she were a more privileged urban artist. Dangar's letters are full of descriptions of her horticultural activities as well as her agricultural struggles, such as her combats with the beehives.

And again: 'The gruelling physical labour made her scornful of artists in major cities such as Paris or Sydney'.

At Moly-Sabata she became fully conversant with Gleizes's theories on art, at least on paper. His theories originated from Cubism's initiation of a new pictorial space – the representation of reality solely as something the artist perceived. The Cubists reduced the pictorial space to a two-dimensional plane, eliminating illusionism and representing objects as geometric solids. They argued that a painting was a self-sufficient entity independent of the external world. To this Gleizes added his spiritual view of culture. He 'established a system based on a series of shifting planes, known as translation, which were activated by a dynamic, circular rhythm known as rotation'. And: 'The two-dimensional painting partakes of the same scheme of proportion as the three-dimensional shape which it decorates, and the mysterious rhythm which controlled the whirling circles of clay on the potter's wheel, shaping them into a thing of beauty, penetrated also into the design of the vase-painter', wrote Helen Topliss.

She struggled to get across the master's theories and seems sometimes to have foundered a little in deciphering them, even though she was intent upon translating his theories into the world of ceramics.

At Moly-Sabata, Anne Dangar saw herself, according to Helen Topliss in her Introduction to the collection of Dangar's letters home, 'as someone who had seen the light at a late stage of her life (40) and who was, therefore, impatient with those who did not share her values'. Moly-Sabata was her Holy Land – there, she came into her own. In her letters to Grace Crowley, she espoused Cubism and, with the zeal of a proselyte, lectured the recipient on her adopted point of view.

It may be argued that Gleizes's typically French love of theory melded awkwardly with a life dedicated to the four medieval elements, or that Dangar substituted provincial Australia for provincial France. Yet, the NGA profile argues that at Moly-Sabata, immersing herself in the soil of peasants, she was able to develop an art form that she could never have created in Australia. She revitalised peasant pottery. Her communistic and Catholic-agrarian views, as happens so often with gifted artists, did not, in the end, impact unduly upon the hard graft of her work and the beauty of her art.

A few quotes and references from her letters home to Grace Crowley may serve to show the useful information on Modernism that she sent home in her letters, and which influenced the small band of Modernists in Sydney.[131] The letters show that, although based at Moly-Sabata, she travelled extensively – to Lyon, to Paris, to Morocco, and elsewhere. The letters have been drawn from *Earth, Fire, Water, Air*:[132]

- 1930, undated, p.47: 'Fornichon teaches artists to obtain light <u>through</u> colour.'

- c.1930, undated, p.48: 'I don't know if I will ever return to Australia.'

- January 1931, undated, p.53: 'I feel ... free ... to paint landscape or still life ... but constructed to my outside shape ... and this construction of moving, living form made <u>with</u> colour, and not made with drawn forms filled with colour.'

- January 30, 1931, p.53: 'This method of building in pure colours instead of ... safe greys ... already I know I have gained power.'

- February 10, 1931, p.55: 'painting must be free: to arrive at rhythm one must be unhindered. (Gleizes) speaks of 'cadence' a great deal ... the dictionary describes it as applied to music.'

- January 2, 1932, p.65: (Dangar refers to some differences between Black, herself and Crowley): 'I know Dorrit chokes me, but I thought you had a real affection for her and ... I was wrong and perhaps unconsciously spiteful and jealous and that was why I didn't get on with her.'

- March 17, 1932, p.71: She talks about the way colour balance may inform the composition of a work.

- January 26, 1932, pp.68–69: This letter contains advice from Gleizes and Lhote about Cubism; thoughts on Cézanne's lonely struggle to reconstruct art; art as something that can only be found after a long search of the inner man.

- April 13, 1934, p.121: 'Cubism is pure joy for it is light and life. If one lives in the life one fulfils man's destiny to be made in the image of God.'

- May 17, 1936, p.149: She relates how Gleizes told her to find the architectural forms inherent in her work.

Later in her life, changes in her thinking are evidenced by her letters. On 24 March 1935, Anne Dangar wrote: 'Oh Smudge [her nickname for Crowley] may I come home? I'm longing to return to you and to my people but I am ashamed to return without money'. So she may have wanted to end her exile, but it had become her destiny. In her last year of life, she converted to the Catholic faith.

Her *Pochoir Composition* (1936) (see Plate 19) in gouache illustrates many of the fundamental ideas of Cubism as enunciated by Albert Gleizes and André Lhote. Her surface is flat with no depth or perspective, and true to the Cubist belief in circular structure, the work consists almost entirely of circles, framed within a square background, rather in the manner of a Buddhist mandala, which itself offers no illusion of depth. The colours are bright and flat, mostly primary, with little subtlety or shading.

Anne Dangar struggled, physically, mentally and spiritually, with her art and with herself. She never settled, despite remaining at Moly-Sabata. The Dangar family, rooted in the history of New South Wales, was extremely wealthy, yet appears to have helped her little. Her place in Australian history, and among the Wild Geese who brought Modernism back to Australia as books never could, secures her place in the exalted company of this book. Though it may, as always, be difficult to precisely quantify her contribution to Australian art, it must be considered substantial, and she will rightly be remembered among the pioneers of Australian Modernism despite never returning permanently to her country of origin.

Chapter 20

EVELYN CHAPMAN

A Pioneer War Artist

*Grace Evelyn Chapman
1888–1961
In Paris 1911–1914, Villers–Bretonneux 1919–1920*

Evelyn Chapman's *Ruined Church with Poppies* (1919) graces a cover of *Look* magazine published by the New South Wales Art Gallery Society.[133] The painting stops one in one's tracks it is so arresting, as is the work shown with the article, *Interior of a Ruined Church, France* (c.1919). She drew attention in some of her best-known work not only to the heroism of soldiers, but to the terrible human and cultural cost of war. She painted the ruins of churches and other buildings on the battlefields of the Somme – the two works mentioned in the opening paragraph of the article were near Villers-Bretonneux, 1919, shortly after the cessation of hostilities. The dead bodies of German soldiers were all around her. She helped establish a tradition of wartime and immediate post-wartime art that stands proudly beside art that depicts the actual fighting, or the lines of blind, gassed soldiers with their hands on the shoulders of the man ahead of them, as painted by the American artist of World War I, John Singer Sargent. This work must surely have had an influence on Australian and other artists following her. 'Chapman went to war by setting up her easel in situ and physically working in the battlefields', writes Anne Gérard-Austin.

Born in Sydney in 1888 of New Zealand parents, Chapman lived a typically sheltered middle-class life, and studied under Antonio Dattilo-Rubbo in Sydney, one of the teachers who helped start the careers of several of the Australian women artists. She moved to Paris with her family in 1911, continuing her studies at the Académie Julian until 1914. She stayed in London, which was to be her base for the rest of her life, during World War I, returning to the Continent in 1919 with her father, an officer with the New Zealand War Graves Commission, who took her with him onto the former battlefields in Normandy, where she painted the scenes she saw until 1920. From 1920, and in the years that followed, she exhibited with the Salon de la Société Nationale des Beaux-Arts and with other Salons, though, sadly, most of the works she exhibited during that time appear to have been lost.

When brought face-to-face with the grim reality of human cruelty and suffering, of which she could have had little prior awareness, Evelyn Chapman's paintings of these blasted battlefields created her legend. Her deep compassion for the suffering and useless destructiveness of modern warfare shines out through these paintings, and her rendering of poppies, growing up like fresh life emerging from grim death, somehow finding sustenance in the torn soil and symbolising hope, were her enduring motif.

When she travelled to Europe with her family, she brought with her a developing skill in painting, acquired from Dattilo-Rubbo, which she further developed and refined at the Académie Julian, especially within the style of Post-Impressionism.

Even before we had seen the evocative quality of her work, with its lucidity and vibrancy in the face of devastation, we were impressed with her devotion to her art and with her technique. During her time studying in Paris, from 1911 to 1914, she had absorbed Modernist influences, notably from Cézanne, Gauguin and van Gogh, using tempera on paper, light colours layered on top of dark, high keys with low, to striking effect. This technique was, as it turned out, uniquely suited to the representation of her sombre battlefield subject matter. Her daughter, Pamela Thalben-Ball, wrote in 2004: 'My mother, who was a far better painter than I shall ever be, said that one should always do some painting every day, but use as few colours as possible. In fact, you can do an extremely colourful portrait using ivory black, titanium white, yellow ochre and cadmium red'.[134]

Although not officially appointed to record the war in images, she accompanied her father to Villers-Bretonneux, on the Somme, in 1919, shortly after the Armistice. There, following in his footsteps as he recorded the dead of his country, she saw at first hand the sheer scale of the destruction, and rather than turn away in horror, she began to paint what she saw. She painted intelligently, using motifs and symbols, revelling in the quality of light, and recording scenes that perhaps were painted by no other artist.

In 'The Greatest Voyage', Anne Gérard-Austin argues that Evelyn Chapman revealed an unexpected lyricism, for example in *Interior of a Ruined Church, France*.[135] A vibrant, bright palette of orange and yellow in, and reflected from, the stone of the ruin, the bright blue of the sky through the open roof, deep purple against olive and brown – all displayed, she says, a real talent in the colour and light of Post-Impressionism.

As well as her studies, she frequented the art museums of Paris and nearby cities, absorbing a strong influence from the artistic narratives of Europe. When the outbreak of war necessitated a retreat to London, it is easy to understand why she would want to return to continental Europe: a task unfinished. This is despite the fact that in one of her letters home to Australia she stated that she disliked Paris and Parisian life, claiming that all the people of that city cared about was pleasure.[136] Researching her papers at the archives of the Art Gallery of New South Wales, we were informed by staff that we were the first researchers to open her file and set eyes on the gathered memorabilia, and study her collected correspondence.

Although Evelyn Chapman was not one of the artists who travelled to Europe on her own, the fact that she did take advantage of her family's trips to Europe, and did remain in London for the rest of her life, returning only briefly to Australia in 1960, indicates that she was a committed artist who would probably have gone to Europe even if her family had not made that journey a lot easier for her – because the lure of the French art world, if not Paris itself, was too great to resist.

Did the scenes she saw on the former battlefields mature her as an artist? Certainly it is true that, unlike some official war artists, Evelyn Chapman's paintings did not glorify war – quite the opposite. Hers was an art of humanism, of the tears of mothers and wives whose sons and husbands would never return to them, of the ultimate futility of such institutionalised violence. It is also true, however, that she saw beauty in the shattered remnants of Villers-Bretonneux, a village that we have visited on several occasions. We have seen the museum dedicated to Australian troops who, on a hill outside the town where the official war memorial now stands, were the first, in 1918, to stop the apparently irresistible advance of the German Army, losing thousands of men in one day to do so. Somehow, she was able to paint these scenes of man's inhumanity, and yet retain a certain optimism.

In *Old Trench, French Battlefield* (1918–19), she suggests, as Gérard-Austin puts it, the resilience and rejuvenation of the landscape. Colourful poppies, the natural symbol of both remembrance and resurrection, are already sprouting around the shattered building and among the corpses and shell holes.

In *Ruined Church, Villers-Bretonneux* (1918–19) (see Plate 20), Evelyn Chapman also shows the resilience of a rejuvenated nature as grass reclaims part of the site. The corpses of German soldiers are not evident, but they must have been, to her. The gaunt outline of the desecrated church, once a symbol of hope, foregrounded against a dark and ominous sky, displays her subtle use of muted colour and, in particular, her command of the play of light.

There is another aspect of Chapman's career, one that was quite likely shared by at least some of the other women artists in Europe. According to her letters at the Art Gallery of New South Wales, she sent money home on numerous occasions to her bank in Sydney, asking that it be deposited and invested in bonds and shares of her choosing. The bank manager, however, was slow and disrespectful of her instructions, causing her considerable frustration, which a male artist in that era would likely not have had to endure. In one letter to her bank manager at the Bank of Australasia, remitted to its Australian branch through its office in London's Threadneedle Street, she writes: 'I seem to be always doomed to disappointment – I have no word from you'. On another occasion, in a letter of 14 June 1912, she uses the words 'I beg you', to the manager, imploring him to obey her instructions regarding the best ways of investing the money she was making from her art in France. She wanted him to invest in shares of the Union Bank of Australia, and he was simply refusing to even reply to her. In a letter to her daughter written in September 1943, and contained in her papers at the Gallery, in the midst of yet another military catastrophe, she writes: 'Never let a solicitor, or a person at a bank, act for you on his own, trust no one'.

Evelyn Chapman's career was in some ways contradictory. A woman from a wealthy background in a quiet, complacent country, who was exposed to the horrors of a brutal European war, a woman with no background in the military and no history of anti-war activism, painting battlefields and joining a long Western tradition of humanist outrage at war itself. We only know some of the details of her life and beliefs, but she quite possibly paved the way for other women, such as Stella Bowen, to work as official war artists, and she contributed in no small measure to the gifts Australian women artists made to French art.

Chapter 21

GRACE CROWLEY

A Major Australian Modernist

Grace Adela Williams Crowley
1890–1979
In Paris 1926–1930

If art exists to uplift the human spirit, in our view Grace Crowley was one of the most uplifting Australian artists of her time. The critical factor in the life of Crowley is her search for the new, the iconoclastic, the revolutionary. The search, alone, by an artist for some possibly unattainable ideal of beauty or of truth about the human condition is itself uplifting regardless of whether the artist's goal is fully achieved.

Although educated in classical, traditional art, Grace Crowley seems to have wanted something more, something she thought could only be found 'out there', in the wide world. This gave her the strongest reason to head for the world capital of art. In her case, there was also a desire to escape her rural and family background, hating the hold her past had on her, and sensing strongly that there was something 'out there' that she needed to find. And find it, she did.

Her mother was proud of Grace's art – until it began to look like a career choice. When Grace was 14, her mother sent one of Grace's drawings to *New Idea* magazine; and when Grace was sent to boarding school in Sydney for her final year, she was allowed to attend Julian Ashton's Art School for one lesson a week. However, on Grace's return to the family home at Glen Riddle, near Barraba in New England in northern NSW, her mother sacked the maid, expecting that Grace would take on the household duties. One imagines the frustration Grace might have felt, with the talent she had simmering. In 1910, Julian Ashton made a *plein air* expedition to Glen Riddle and persuaded Grace's family to allow her to return to Sydney to continue her lessons, and after three years, she became a teacher at Ashton's school. If proof were needed of her talent, this would surely be it.

Like her close friend and artistic co-adventurer Anne Dangar, Grace Crowley was on a mission to seek out the best painter she could be, within the context of the new, according to her notebooks.[137] That she succeeded is demonstrated substantially in the work she did back home in Australia, after her Paris sojourn, which broke new ground for her and advanced the cause of modern art in her home country. As an artist and as an innovator, she was a major figure, and a major influence in the Australian art world of her time, as confirmed by Anne Gérard-Austin.[138] For this reason alone, it is important that her work and life be studied. However, her early success in the salons and in a commercial gallery, as will be discussed later in this chapter, confirms that in Paris she was also regarded as an artist of major talent.

We need to bear in mind that Grace Crowley was born at tiny Cobbadah in rural New South Wales, with a population of barely a hundred people, to a grazier family. We authors both came from small country towns, though nowhere near as tiny as Cobbadah, and although life can be idyllic during childhood, the town soon starts to seem small and stifling, especially if one does not want to go on the land, perhaps by taking over the family property, or run a shop. Cities beckon for their supposed excitement and, perhaps even more, their choices. When she was studying with Ashton, Crowley was already dedicated to her art, but faced resistance, states Janine Burke in *Australian Women Artists, 1840–1940*, from her parents until they finally relented and gave her a fare to Europe after she failed to win a travelling scholarship.[139]

Grace's four years in Paris, from 1926 to 1930 were, according to Daniel Thomas in the *Australian Dictionary of Biography*, the most enjoyable of her life.[140] Gérard-Austin writes that, before leaving Australia, and despite her Modernist aspirations, she adhered to less radical forms of art until she was fully competent in them – perhaps because she did not want to be dismissed as 'choosing Modernism because it did not require as much skill', which was a common misapprehension at the time, although she did experiment with Impressionism. It was Anne Dangar, states Gérard-Austin, who helped inspire her to follow her dreams into Modernism.

Her diary notes on her time in Paris reveal a woman entranced by everything she experiences.[141] She moved first into premises on the Boulevard Saint-Michel, near the Luxembourg Gardens, with Anne Dangar. As with most of the women, we imagined her walking around the neighbourhood, getting to know the geography of the area, taking everything in. She writes that she spent a week searching for the Latin Quarter before realising she was in the midst of it. Later she was to write in her notebooks: '1927, 1928 and 1929 were the happiest years of my life, why? Because they were productive ... there was a joy in discovering Paris in our own way. We soon learned more about Paris than the rich people who took guided tours'. As evident in the archives of the Art Gallery of New South Wales, however, on her arrival in Paris, Grace Crowley meticulously documented every penny spent daily – the funds she received from her family, it seems, were conditional on strict accounting.

After a time at Académie Colarossi without a tutor, and then privately with portrait painter Louis Roger, Grace Crowley and Anne Dangar moved to the Académie André Lhote on the rue d'Odessa. She wrote of the school: 'sometimes it seemed alive – a feeling of expectancy permeated the place'.[142] Janine Burke wrote that 'Lhote brought the work of Crowley ... alive in a way that Australian art teaching never could'.

André Lhote's Cubism may have formed a bridge for her between her past work and Modernism, since she states in her notebooks that she never regretted her early Australian training in Impressionism. Janine Burke states that Crowley went to Europe opposed to at least the more radical forms of Modernism, but if so, she soon began to change her opinions. In Lhote's teaching, the human form remained intact while the composition was considered in open, shifting, interconnected planes of light. She was able to hold on to the figure, while moving into the new realm of Cubism, but not straight into its extreme fringe – it therefore suited Crowley that André Lhote's teaching was on the conservative side of the principles earlier enunciated by Paul Cézanne. Many of Lhote's own figures were almost classically naturalistic with only a slight suggestion of geometric structure to suggest the underlying principles of Cubism. Elena Taylor, in *Grace Crowley: Being Modern*, agrees with Gérard-Austin that it was Anne Dangar who led Crowley to Modernism.[143] After that she did not deviate from the path set out by Lhote.

At first, André Lhote was dismissive of her work. This may have been his method with all new students. However, under his influence her landscapes began to take on a geometric form. Her work was 'difficult', and not in the easy, decorative Modernist style. She acknowledged in her notebooks that she had learnt everything that mattered to her about art in Paris from her two teachers, André Lhote and Albert Gleizes. Although she had only limited contact with Gleizes in 1929, after she approached him asking for lessons, her correspondence with Anne Dangar, who returned to Moly-Sabata while Crowley returned to Australia, was the major source of Gleizes's influence upon her, growing over the years as she worked back home in Australia.

In 1929, Albert Gleizes invited Grace Crowley to visit his newly established artist colony at Moly-Sabata, on the Rhône. Gleizes's work made a major impression on her, including two large religious works of his in a nearby church, which inspired her to make a drawing, *Study for a Religious Mural* (1929). In another drawing on tracing paper, she analysed the underlying pictorial structure of her drawing into a series of translated and rotated rectangles within a circular composition. This influence came to the fore in her next major work, *Portrait of Gwen Ridley* (1930). But it would be some years before she would move so far as to explore painting fully abstract Cubist pictures.

Grace Crowley soon learned, according to *Modernism and Feminism*, that there was more to Modernism than she had expected.[144] In her notebooks she wrote: '... for the first time I heard about dynamic symmetry and the section d'or – that it was necessary to make a PLAN for a painting of many figures ... and then construct your personages on it. It was a revelation'. To André Lhote, she said, she owed the realisation that there were abstract elements that were a vital necessity to be considered in constructing a solid piece of painting. She further stated, perhaps surprisingly, that she remained indebted to Julian Ashton of Sydney for the study of 'The Momentary Effect of Light'. Everything she had learned, from Julian Ashton to André Lhote and Albert Gleizes, she put to good effect in her work, but there was nowhere other than Paris where she could begin to master Cubism.

Anne Gérard-Austin maintained that André Lhote was the main influence upon Grace Crowley's work, though others have argued that this honour belongs to Albert Gleizes. It is true that from Lhote she absorbed all of the theory and, particularly during her short stay at Mirmande with Dorrit Black and Anne Dangar, she began to be able to put that into practice. This was indeed a conversion from Impressionism.

Grace Crowley's use of Lhote's ideas is well demonstrated in *Sailors and Models* (c.1927), a large work in which, because it was unfinished, and a drawing, its underlying structure is revealed – the pictorial space broken into prismatic forms that intersect the figures. She soon began, like Dorrit Black, to move beyond the mere exposition of her teachers' theories, little by little leaving behind her figurative style of the late 1930s in favour of a more abstract approach, though some remnants of Impressionism may yet have remained. She began laying out each flat plane against another and rendering the objects in the picture frame non-naturalistically. Always, though, for Grace Crowley painting was 'an essentially rational and objective act, undertaken according to a set of pictorial principles. The artist's individuality was expressed in their sensitivity to the placement of form and colour rather than the work's subject matter', as she states in her notebooks. So, she would always be a Cubist in the final analysis.

Grace Crowley abandoned what had been offered her – security, a life on the land, family. She chose freedom, an unconventional relationship with Anne Dangar, others and art. Alison Carroll, in *Moral Censorship and the Visual Arts in Australia*, states that this moral censorship may have been a major reason for women such as Grace Crowley, who preferred women's company, to live in the Latin Quarter of Paris, where they would have heard there was less moral censorship, at least in artistic circles.[145]

One of the most impressive facets of Crowley's personal life was her generosity and compassion for other artists. This was notable in her relationship with her close friend and former companion Anne Dangar, after Crowley had returned to Australia. In *Earth, Fire, Water, Air*, Dangar's letters contain many references to receiving gifts by mail from Crowley, no doubt sometimes crossing with Dangar's information and helpful letters to Crowley about technique, fashions and her struggle to flourish as an artist on Albert Gleizes's commune. She writes, for instance, on 16 January 1946: 'Three packets have arrived from you at the same time. You spoil me utterly'. These packets contained mostly food. On 26 May of that year she writes, 'Six more packets ... !' On 12 August, more parcels are acknowledged, and on 20 October, a 'multitude' of packages, and there are more such acknowledgments of Grace's care.[146] She often sent desperately needed money, large amounts, presumably drawn from her teaching income, and she was widely respected also for the help, advice, and teaching she gave freely to fellow artists in Australia.

Having escaped, with Julian Ashton's help, to achieve her desired lifestyle, she lived it to the full. She and Anne Dangar dived into the heart of Left Bank bohemia, which she identified in her notebooks as centring around three sites: Le Dôme, La Rotonde and La Coupole. She speaks lovingly about the lifestyle of herself and her fellow art students in this area, while also bewailing the lack of bathrooms, and enjoying the variety of cheap restaurants. One wonders if the Latin

Quarter of those days was perhaps the template for artistic and intellectual urban districts around the world.

Grace Crowley's work clearly reflected her Parisian environment. For example, her grasp of Cubist theory was cemented into her DNA and became her life's work. In *Modernism and Feminism* it is stated, 'those foreign artists who took the time to make such pilgrimages [to Paris] were better able to understand the theories that French artists had developed'. Unfortunately for Grace, but fortunately for Australia, her artistic career in her host city was just getting started when she was forced to return to Australia for family reasons – a problem that bedevilled the female Australian artists perhaps more than the men. It is possible to speculate that her family told her to return, or else no more allowance was provided, since it was not easy for a developing Modernist to make a living just from painting. She exhibited her André Lhote-influenced paintings at the Salon des Artistes Français and the Salon des Artistes Indépendants. Following this, she was invited to exhibit at the Galerie Bernheim-Jeune, but she had already been ordered by her family to return home, although the family illness that was given to her as the reason for her urgent return turned out, on arrival, not to be as serious as she had been led to believe.

She must have been less than delighted, but she nevertheless plunged herself into the art world of Australia, just as she had into the art world of Paris. It was to be in Australia that she would strive to make a difference. She appears to have made an effort to overcome her feelings of bitterness for the sake of what she could contribute to Australian art. Cubism was a new development in Australian art and when she, along with Dorrit Black and the influence of Anne Dangar, returned to Australia, she helped spearhead its growth and encouraged artists and critics to take it more seriously.

In 1930, Grace Crowley was one of the so-called 'Group of Seven' artists who exhibited at the Macquarie Galleries in Sydney. In 1932 she held her only solo exhibition, in Margaret Street, Sydney. Anne Dangar wrote to her, saying she hoped Grace had sold some pictures, but if not, take heart – Picasso had held a show earlier that year and did not sell a single picture. In 'Grace Crowley: Being Modern', Elena Taylor refers to the 'generally unenthusiastic reception of her work' at her solo exhibition. The exhibition was seen by only a handful of people. Stung, she kept apart from the art world, with her close friends Ralph Balson and Rah Fizelle. In 1939, she exhibited with a group that included Balson and Fizelle at the David Jones' Art Gallery in Sydney. In the 1940s and 50s, according to Daniel Thomas in the *Australian Dictionary of Biography*, her, by now abstract, Cubist work was 'unique in Australia'.

Although she did a lot to bring modern art to Australia in the 1930s and beyond, Grace Crowley's ideas at first made little impression on the Australian art scene, where they were often regarded as bizarre, or just a passing fad. Very little non-figurative art was exhibited in Australia prior to the 1950s, as noted by Robert Hughes, and modern art gained acceptance among artists rather than among the art-loving public.[147] This does not mean that her contribution to Australian art was insubstantial. From a small core of followers, she helped establish a strong support base, over time, for modern art. She also helped to fix the gaze of many young Australian artists on what was happening in Europe, and in doing so she helped overcome the nationalistic parochialism that characterised so much of the Australian art scene in the early part of last century. She helped also to set up the Modern Art Centre in Grosvenor Street, Sydney, the city's first gallery to present only modernist art, near The Rocks – Sydney's 'art district' at that time – with Rah Fizelle and Dorrit Black.

Throughout the 1930s she continued to move toward, and then into, abstraction, and in this area she was undoubtedly a major influence upon many younger artists. In the late 1940s and early 1950s, her work became more hard-edged and geometric, balanced by her move toward more naturalistic curves and the use of colour and form to create a sense of movement. She never ceased challenging herself. She made a number of paintings of city life, some from her family home at Glen Riddle, in which she applied her Paris training to quintessentially Australian projects. And it may have been at least partly her influence that saw some female artists being more open to Modernism than their male counterparts.

The work itself tells the tale of her growth and development. *Les Baigneuses* (1928), for instance, an oil on canvas at the National Gallery of Australia, shows Cubist influences with naturalistic characteristics. She creates a sense of motion in several ways – the figure on the right, as the viewer faces, leans away from the centre of the picture frame, while the model on the left leans toward the centre, thus creating a tension suggesting movement from left to right. The bridge in the background has two curved arches suggesting circular motion. Each of the two figures in the picture constitutes a plane, but their bodies are broken into smaller geometric planes. Pale flesh tones contrast with cool, pale greens and blues on either side of the picture, and in the background mostly greys. That there are figures shows that, in 1928, when André Lhote's influence was still fresh, she has not yet exploited all of the technique she has learned. The green bush on the left behind a model leans toward the centre of the picture while the green bush behind the right-side model leans sharply away from the centre, again creating a tension suggesting movement, though not necessarily a complete circular movement. The background looks like a wall hanging close behind the figures, which creates a feeling of flatness, a lack of depth. She has not yet begun to create her own take on Cubism, so it would be more like an exercise, except for the extreme delicacy with which she handles the figures and the colours and forms, making this an exceptional artwork despite being in some ways a demonstration of Lhote's ideas.

Woman (Annunciation) (1939) (see Plate 21) uses a model, but it is not a portrait in the sense of an attempt to bring out the innate character and sensibility of the sitter. Here the sitter, a young woman, is used solely as a way of organising the coloured planes into which the sitter's figure has been divided into an ordered whole, where the order is imposed by the artist, and not by observed nature. The model's face has a blank expression and the structure is based upon a circle using the model's figure and her clothing as its perimeter.

We admire Grace Crowley's spirit of exploration and adventure, her refusal to settle for what had always been done, instead trying to push the boundaries, grow and challenge herself and the world of art. This spirit is what makes art remain relevant in a constantly changing world. Her life changed as a result of her Paris sojourn. Her decisive move into Modernism, from which she never deviated subsequently, might have made it more difficult for her to sell her work in Australia, but she made up for this by teaching and by exhibiting, thus bringing her influence to bear.

Grace Crowley was a major Australian artist who, like many major artists, blended the best of the old with the best of the new. She helped bring modern art, and a European consciousness, to Australia at a time when it was steeped in a somewhat habitual adherence to all things English. Hers was a life of exploration of the inner spirit, and kinesis of art.

Chapter 22

DORRIT BLACK

An Influential Convert to Modernism

Dorothea Foster Black
1891–1951
In Europe 1911–1914, Paris 1928–1929

Dorrit Black's art and character were game changers. She took Modernism by the horns and reshaped it to her own design, and not content with that, she worked hard to sell it to a rather uncertain Australian public.

A modest and somewhat shy person, she rarely spoke about herself, and it may be that her state of mind, and her inner, visceral reasons for converting to Modernism may never be known. All that can be said is that, having gone to Paris to study art without, perhaps, any fixed idea of where the journey would take her, she needed only to see modern art to become curious about it, and subsequently to fall under its spell – and then to bring her new passion back home.

Artists benefit the society that produces and nurtures them in two ways – one by creating art that excites the imagination and uplifts the human spirit, and two by teaching or mentoring others to do so. Most of the women in this book have done both, but Dorrit Black is arguably the most notable one, who not only created culturally enriching art, but who also taught and mentored many others to carry on the Modernist tradition she had espoused. In both these ways, she made a significant contribution to the culture of her country.

She was one of a small band of pioneer Australian Modernists, most of them women, who embraced, in her case, Cubism both in theory and in practice, and is rightly regarded as one of those who brought the intimate knowledge of Cubism home to Australia from France.[148,149] Most of her mentors in the development of her art were European – first Claude Flight in London, and later the great French teachers André Lhote and Albert Gleizes. Yet she did not initially set out to create in the Modernist tradition.

She grew up, like so many of the women in this book, in a wealthy suburb – Adelaide's Burnside. She attended the Adelaide School of Arts and Crafts, and later, in Sydney, at Julian Ashton's art school in The Rocks, Sydney. Her training in Australia had been in oils and watercolours. She had not, at home, been influenced by Modernism – her early work in Australia, such as *Heat Haze*, painted in 1919, displays little if any of the influences that would later shape her artistic life. Using naturalistic colour and light, it is a landscape of a farmhouse with wooded hills beyond.

Her first adventure to Europe ran from 1911, when she travelled there with her family, to 1914. She returned to France in 1927 at the age of 35, and at first travelled to London to study under Claude Flight at the Grosvenor School. Influences of Flight's teaching show in her work, but much more, we suggest, of André Lhote and Albert Gleizes, from 1928 to 1929. She returned to Australia in 1929.

Ian North states that Black needed to return to Australia in order to find her true inner voice.[150] While that may be true of her relationship with her subject matter, her technique and style quite clearly seem to have been absorbed in Paris.

From Claude Flight she learned the power of curved and sweeping movement across a canvas, and from André Lhote the technical fundamentals of that style, which she was to modify later in life – perhaps this is what North is referring to? She was an artist who always believed in change and growth, and this was also a key element of her teaching.

Albert Gleizes taught Black to relate all the forms in the picture to the frame by making use over and over again of some of the proportions of the frame – he achieved this by dividing the frame into eighths and further subdivisions. He also emphasised the natural properties of the surface, thus acknowledging that a painter really works on a flat surface of only two dimensions, and it is the filling and animation of this surface that is the primary fact of all painting.

Anne Dangar, through her letters to Dorrit Black's close associate Grace Crowley in Australia, also helped by keeping Black and her little circle of Modernists *au fait* with the latest developments in French art.

It has been suggested that Dorrit Black's parents offered her no emotional support for her decision to live and work as an artist. Yet the fact that she was able to travel extensively in Europe, and appears never to have had to work there, such as cleaning studios, strongly implies that she took substantial funds with her to France. When she began to sell her work, she became independent in a truer sense, an enviable achievement for any female artist of her generation.

Dorrit Black reported that she took time to settle into Parisian life, and that she found some of their ways a little strange, but that is to be expected of any stranger in a strange land. It is known that she moved in a circle of emerging Australian artists, including Grace Crowley and Anne Dangar, fellow converts to Modernism. It may well be that the social circles available to her were small and on the outside, as the French did not, on the whole, engage socially with foreigners in their city, who largely mixed among themselves. She lived mostly on the Left Bank, but later moved to the suburbs.

In her journal, *Account of Travel and Work, 1927–29*, Dorrit describes 'crossing over' from London to Paris to gain a definite understanding of the aims and methods of the Modern movement, and of the Cubists in particular.[151] A bolder aim it would be difficult to imagine for an artist of that period when, in Paris as well as in an outpost such as Adelaide, art mostly meant landscapes, portraits and still lifes, naturalistic or, at most, Impressionist.

Her studies with André Lhote at his academy on the rue d'Odessa were her turning point. He taught his students to draw sketches, and then to alter them to fit an assumed underlying grid, owing much to the golden mean, which he had first drawn on the picture plane. Then geometric crossed lines linked objects, applying passages of tonal colour between them, sometimes overlapping. He was concerned with the inherent conflict between the desire to achieve depth (an illusion) on a flat surface. Dorrit Black's work in *Composition Study – Sailors and Girls* (1928) demonstrates these theories. She achieves a flattened look with the use of lines to outline some figures. From Lhote she learned to emphasise form, line and colour.

In 1927, Dorrit Black moved for a time to the art colony near the village of Mirmande in south-eastern France. It was there that she mastered the Cubist technique of pyramidal landscape. It was quite likely there that she began to move beyond the rather rigid ideas of Lhote to explore Cubism her own way. She was developing a style that emphasised the flowing curves inherent in Cubism, with its belief in a sense of circular movement around the picture plane, rather than seeking to conform to an assumed underlying structure.

The warmth and humanity of her work was greatly enhanced by what she learned and practised at Mirmande. Her work began to be more dynamic in its sense of flowing movements and rhythms, and her later work from here reflects this growth in her potential. In growing beyond the latent limitations of geometric Cubism, she was finally discovering the inner voice of which North had spoken. Yet, she never abandoned the respect for design that Lhote had so impressed upon her.

After André Lhote, Black spent a short time learning from Albert Gleizes, who in later years expressed admiration for her work. He was both a theorist and a considerable artist, one who 'never sought to create a visual reality' according to Tracey Lock-Weir.[152] Though Black appears not to have merely imitated Albert Gleizes's approach, her own notes indicate her interest in his beliefs. From him, as from André Lhote, she had fully absorbed the importance of drawing as a basis for art.

That Dorrit Black took some time to find her feet as an artist in Paris, working her way through the fashionable theories, indicates the seriousness of her commitment to her art. Believing in the necessity of constant growth and change as the basis for improvement, she embraced the influences that Paris had to offer, before transcending them into her own style. As this happened, she was able to enjoy her painting more, growing in confidence and maturity.

In Paris at that time, fashions swept through the capital, wave after wave. That these fashions were often based, as with Cubism, on academic theories, which some might feel inhibit rather than channel the creative impulse, could be seen, and was seen by Dorrit Black, as a challenge rather than as a call to conformity – her way, perhaps, of saying that she felt she had found what she had come to Paris seeking.

Mirmande (1928) and *On the Rocks* (1935) seem to epitomise the achievement of this artist. *Mirmande* is a landscape featuring the village of that name, and was painted on the same site, on the same day, though from a different viewpoint, as similar works by Anne Dangar and Grace Crowley. The wedge shape of the village seems to draw the eye skyward, but, in fact, our vision rests on the town itself, drawn to its church, which rises slightly above the other buildings, and to the life we imagine going on within the village walls. The tones, typically of Dorrit Black, are contrasting – lighter tones for sky and foreground fields, darker for vegetation, and sunlit for buildings. Resisting the temptation to draw the viewer into a perspective, she uses flat planes and yet imbues the scene with vibrancy and a sense of the dynamic, creating a sense of movement in an otherwise static scene.

On the Rocks (1935) (see Plate 22), a little known work, deserves more attention than it has received. True to her Cubist vision, Dorrit Black has contrived to make the rocks, which step down a shallow drop to the sea or perhaps a river, seem flat, and yet they curve laterally, forming an enclosed circle and creating a sense of movement that conforms to that of some of the people clambering over them, whereas the rocks, though contrasting, are in subdued earth colours. A linocut on white woven tissue, its circular structure draws the eye into the centre of the circle, to an orange figure, apparently enjoying a game, perhaps of chasing or of hiding, or perhaps merely walking carefully around the inner section of the restrictive rocks. The emphasis is not on the subject matter – figures, humans, having fun by the water – but on the paint, the lines, the colour, the structure, and the flattened planes.

At Mirmande, she quickly became part of the local life. She was hosted there by the wife of a businessman, and painted with groups around the surrounding countryside. At night the resident artists would all gather at the Bert, where a meal was followed by entertainment arranged by Lhote, and staged in his studio nearby. Later in 1929, she sadly left the village and returned to Paris.[153]

At around this time she began to have the confidence to contribute to the city of her adoption, Sydney. It was with 'confidence and enthusiasm', according to Shirley Cameron Wilson in *From Shadow into Light*, that she set forth later that year to return home.[154] Wilson also credits Dorrit Black as being partly responsible, through her teaching, for bringing Modernism and Post-Impressionism to Australia – the latter, no doubt, through her observations of the work of others. Although Australian artists knew about Modernism, little was known in Australia about its techniques and theories. The level of Black's confidence after her European sojourn may be gauged to some extent from her letter home to Graham Young at Sydney's Macquarie Galleries in 1929.[155] She writes: 'I think it is about time I wrote to ask whether you … are willing to let me hold [an exhibition] in your gallery. You may remember that you said something about such a possibility before I left'. This led to an offer of an exhibition at the Macquarie.

After her return to Sydney she began to exert an influence over a small cohort of artists who were attracted to Modernism. 'Influence' is notoriously difficult to quantify. Some of Dorrit Black's work clearly owes a lot to André Lhote, but her later work suggests that she has taken control of her art and owes allegiance to no mentor.

The Art Gallery of South Australia's Education Resource on Dorrit Black states that she 'had a passion to promote modern art in Australia, becoming the first woman to open an art gallery, the Modern Art

Centre in Margaret Street, where works by Australian modern artists were shown'.[156] She held her first one-woman show at the Centre, and Roy de Maistre, Roland Wakelin and Grace Crowley also exhibited there. According to an article in *Art and Australia*, Crowley, her partner in the Modern Art Centre, 'taught drawing and Black taught the other classes'.[157]

We admire Dorrit Black's sense of adventure, and her openness to change, which allowed her to convert to Cubism. We also respect the fact that South Australia, so tiny and so isolated during the first half of last century, produced so many fine artists. Dorrit Black made her own way and was her own woman. Living away from family, she created her own family of artistic acolytes and peers in the world of art. Her life was cut short in 1951, and it may be speculated that she still had interesting and vibrant work to create, as she seems to us to have been an artist who challenged herself.

Chapter 23

STELLA BOWEN

The Symbiosis of Art and Life

Esther Gwendolyn Bowen
1893–1947
In Paris 1919–1921, 1923–1928

One of the more significant features of the short life of Adelaide-born artist Stella Bowen is the manner in which her troubled private life was intertwined with her life as an artist and her art work. From her earliest days, she states in her 1941 autobiography *Drawn from Life*, she desired to experience both the life of an artist and the life of a bohemian. For her, as for many others in those days, this meant the Left Bank of Paris, which was at that time the world centre of the visual arts. She later lived there with English novelist Ford Madox Ford, on the rue de Fleurus.[158]

Born into a comfortable Adelaide family in 1893, Stella Bowen initially trained as an artist in that city with Margaret Preston, by whom, according to Lola Wilkins, she was initially inspired to become an artist.[159] Her desire to travel to Europe led her into conflict with her mother, but after the death of her mother in 1914 the family eventually relented and paid her fare, at first to London, where she met Ford Madox Ford, with whom she began a relationship. The poet Ezra Pound, whom she met in London, introduced her to Ford and to many other famous artistic personalities of the time. In 1919, she moved to Paris with Ford. Their daughter Esther Julia Ford, known as Julie, was born in November 1920.

In 1922, she was living with Ford at Cap Ferrat in rural France, with the Duke of Connaught on one side and the Rothschild family on the other, though their own circumstances were decidedly less affluent. In 1923, they moved to Paris, where she thrived in the Left Bank atmosphere of unconventionality – her dream of what Paris ought to be like.

Wisely or not, all of her inheritance was invested in Ford's *Transatlantic Review*, a literary magazine. It was during this period that Ford and Jean Rhys began their affair. In 1925, Bowen rented a studio of her own in rue Notre-Dame-des-Champs. There she had freedom to paint as she wished, and it was a fruitful time for her, with their daughter Julie living with a nanny. In the winter of 1925/26, she and Ford and Julie lived in Toulon, where she painted one of her best works, *Bridge at Avignon* (1926), done in the Italian style she had learnt while travelling in that country. At the end of 1926, Ford went to America for a time.

In authoring the Introduction to Stella's autobiography, Julie discusses the efforts Stella made to realise her European dream, and the extent to which she may have succeeded.[160] What attracted us initially to this artist was her determination, a quality also found in others, such as Marie Tuck. Stella overcame obstacles throughout her life, and they were not few in number. Had she been freer to focus on her work, and not just in short bursts, she would, in our view, have achieved significantly more. She was already well known before our research began, but for some of the wrong reasons – her difficult partnership with Ford Madox Ford, for instance – and we felt she needed to be appraised predominantly on the basis of her best work. Ford was very demanding and dependent, and his presence may have frustrated her artistic spirit.

On a personal level, Stella Bowen exhibited some of the qualities that might be associated with the naive Colonial transplanted into the world's most sophisticated metropolis – a desire to immerse herself in what she imagined was an exotic world of 'sophistication' and metropolitan excitement. There seems not to have been a strong political aspect to her private life. Julie mentions that Bowen was not an activist, as many artists are, and did not regard herself as a feminist. She was a pacifist in World War I, but never joined a demonstration as far as is known. She struggled to realise her ideal – the life of a free woman. That she was waylaid while on this path, that she, for example, devoted herself for years to the comfort and career of Ford and others, did not diminish her longer-term goal of reaching the ideal that she had set herself.

Alan Judd, in his biography of Ford Madox Ford, refers to her as 'a generous and open-hearted woman with that naiveté that is temperamental rather than intellectual, more a matter of trusting than not seeing, a quality that in time matured into shrewdness and realism'.[161] But Judd wonders if she was unable, in the final analysis, to escape her bourgeois Adelaide upbringing that trained women to be helpers to men.

In Chapter Four of her autobiography, Stella Bowen states: 'The Luxembourg Gardens was one place where the travails of ordinary

people hang in the air' – presumably, available to be experienced.¹⁶²
Indeed, she characterises Paris in that chapter as a city where lives are lived in public, which was one of the reasons, she says, that she felt at home there. Art is a very public manifestation and every artist puts his or her heart on display when they sing, dance, act or paint. It is therefore interesting, if somewhat paradoxical, that this self-confessed shy person should find the courage and the enthusiasm to display herself both in her art and in her social life in public places in this most public of cities.

Influenced by artists of the past such as Hans Holbein, and by the Italian masters, she declared her admiration for their 'formal and pellucid serenity'.¹⁶³ She claims that she learnt from them clearly defined edges, and a certain thin quality of the paint. By contrast, her distaste for what she sees as the ugliness of much modern art is palpable. Later still, she discovered El Greco and started trying to paint recession and space and a third dimension, something she never stopped attempting. There was, thus, demonstrated growth in her work.

Stella Bowen was also, in her private life, deeply influenced by those with whom she came into contact. Ford made perhaps the greatest impact upon her. He was her mentor, he introduced her to many concepts of art, philosophy, politics and life with which she had never dealt, and by the sheer power of his personality he corralled her, for a time, under his wing. Much has been made of her failed relationship with Ford. She lived with him for nine years and he was Julie's father. He broke faith with Bowen, however, by covertly inviting Jean Rhys into their home and then commencing their secret affair. Although she speaks of the joys of falling out of love, it is difficult not to see subtext in her daughter's comment that it was with sadness that she later returned to England without Ford.¹⁶⁴

Her pain-filled relationship with Ford, and with Jean Rhys, whom she initially, perhaps naively, welcomed into their home, did, according to *Drawn from Life*, impact negatively upon her work. She complains about how Ford's incessant demands for her attention made it difficult for her to concentrate on painting, and about how his affair with Jean Rhys distracted her mightily from it.

She does seem to have felt that *La Vie Bohème* fell somehow short of what she had imagined it to be. She enjoyed the parties, she states in her autobiography, but it is difficult to see her as other than a very serious young woman, wanting Life with a capital L. Yet, with friends like Ezra Pound, Edith Sitwell, Ernest Hemingway, Paul Valéry and Gertrude Stein, life could hardly have been humdrum. These friends were drawn into her life through her relationship with Ford, and in her autobiography she relates her enjoyment of their company, but one gets the impression, reading it, that these famous people were not close to her, but rather moved around and through her life on a superficial plane.

In the turbulent flux that was the Left Bank in the 1920s, a home, a permanent base from which she could not be dislodged, was a constant goal, never achieved. Her efforts to find a home, including making offers on properties outside Paris, kept her from her easel almost as much as did Ford's selfish demands upon her.

After her decision to end the nine-year relationship with Ford, she painted one of the saddest works of her career – *Ford's Chair* (c.1928). The empty chair, the thin paint, the leafless tree, the overcast sky, the brown palette display a deep grief, from which she may never completely have recovered – despite the problems he had brought her.

In another poignant work, her *Self Portrait* (c.1934) (see Plate 23), Stella Bowen paints her own face without any attempt at beautification or falsification. Her hair is greying, at 41, intimations of mortality, and her eyes are steely and her jaw set tight. The skin tones are delicately rendered, and all colours in the picture are warm – but this is a very honest picture. Soft drapes behind her converge toward her figure. There is strength in that face, perhaps the face of a woman who has had to grow up fast. When one thinks of her life, this portrait is almost a narrative of it.

Throughout her Paris sojourn she worked hard at advancing her art, despite her self-description as a sluggard. She exhibited fairly widely there, more so than many of the other Australian women artists who made that pilgrimage. A number of her works were shown in group exhibitions, too, though her Paris debut was at the Salon d'Automne in November 1923. *Villefranche* was exhibited in the Salon des Tuileries in August 1924, her portrait of Madame Serruys at the Société Nationale des Beaux-Arts in 1925, and *Ford Playing Solitaire* at the Salon d'Automne in 1927. In addition, she had a solo exhibition in a private gallery in the rue de Seine, selling almost half of the works.

As her work developed, her lines became more sharply etched and the character of her sitters was more boldly exhibited. It is also possible that there was some small influence from the Fauves – some of whom she associated with – in both the colouring and the backgrounds of some of her portraits, and indeed in some of her interiors, in many of which she is looking outward through windows. She was a truthful painter and never 'gilded the lily', despite pleas from some of her sitters to do so, she states. She gives her sitters strong, firm expressions, however, which must have pleased them. In the *Bulletin* in 1944, an unnamed reviewer wrote of *Embankment Gardens*: 'The artist achieves a remarkable effect of atmospheric envelopment by means of a subtle appreciation for tonal values, but at the same time formal and linear qualities are preserved'.¹⁶⁵ The same reviewer also states: 'Bowen refused to be absorbed by the prevailing artistic isms; she was determined to retain her integrity and follow her own path'.¹⁶⁶

Stella Bowen died in London, of breast and liver cancer, in 1947. She may perhaps be seen as a Colonial who brought a provincial simplicity of nature to the heart of Europe. She had always believed in self-sufficiency and Paris was, for her, perhaps its crucible. It was there that she matured and lived the life of a professional artist, learning from her mistakes and working as a war artist with the Royal Air Force during World War II, showing that in her work, as in her private life, she was resourceful and willing to embrace change.

Chapter 24

MADGE FREEMAN

A Steady Achiever

Frances Margot Freeman
1895–1977
In Paris 1925–1926, Europe 1930–1934

In Bendigo, before Madge Freeman left to study art in Melbourne, her students at Bendigo High said of her, 'her good looks combined with her charm had all the boys enchanted'. One student, George Speirs, later said: 'The tall willowy girl with the proverbial "peaches and cream" complexion … was more than sufficient inducement for boys of our class … to pass over the head of our Mistress, and ask ever so kindly from Madge the methods of correction necessary for our drawing mistakes'.[167]

Madge Freeman displayed, in her work and in her life, many fine qualities such a perseverance and determination, and an unwillingness to draw attention to herself personally. Nonetheless, her sociable nature saw her speaking in public when necessary to advance the cause of art, and administrating art organisations. As an artist she did not seek the limelight, yet her work was respected, as was she, and her contribution to the visual arts in Victoria was significant. An energetic and controlled painter, she worked hard and gave of herself, always ready to help or to put in some extra effort throughout her career. Although she exhibited in France, England and Australia, she was not widely known during her life, but her achievements have been recognised posthumously.

Madge Freeman experienced Paris from 1925 to 1926. But like most of the Australian women who studied and painted in Europe, she brought back something from the world centre of art, though it is not always easy to describe what that was. Technique, certainly; a broader understanding of European art that can only be gained from looking at the paintings themselves and not merely reproductions; a better understanding of colour and its use to structure the picture plane; and a better knowledge of line. Freeman herself said, in a letter home, that it was necessary to visit Europe and its galleries in order to mature as an artist. Yet it is hard not to feel that there is something else that a sensitive artist can bring home from Europe, even if it cannot easily be articulated in sensory terms. It is not merely sophistication, literally understood; nor is it just a blasé worldliness, or the ability to drop the names of famous French artists one has briefly met at private salons – those invitation-only social gatherings where wealthy patrons bring artists into contact with those who may help their careers. It is indefinable and yet it seems to have motivated quite a few of the Australian women who sailed to France.

According to Joan Kerr's biography of her in *Design & Art Australia Online*, Madge was determined, from her youth, to study abroad.[168] Before leaving she studied at the National Gallery Art School in Melbourne, where she would have become aware at least of the less radical forms of Impressionism as practised by some Australian artists – an English tradition that was rigidly copied by some teachers. It was from Melbourne that she left for Europe in 1924, having raised funds for this trip by holding joint exhibitions with her close friend and fellow student Elma Roach, who travelled with her. So it seems clear that her family did not supply her with funds for her foreign sojourn. In which case, her determination – like that of Marie Tuck – deserves respect.

After time studying at the Slade School in London, she moved to Paris in 1925, studying with Post-Impressionist Adolphe Milich and exhibiting. Life in Paris was not easy for her. A friend, Justin Gill, told a reporter that Madge Freeman achieved her best work when she was 'poor and starving' in Paris. However, according to her biography at Australian Art Gallery online, her work was exhibited in 1925 at the Salon des Tuileries, though it is not known which paintings were hung.[169] She painted largely in watercolour.[170]

Her work at this time demonstrated her new passion for French Post-Impressionism, melded with a somewhat traditionalist vision, though with some influences from Paul Cézanne. Her first solo show, and the first by a woman artist by Bendigo Art Gallery, was held in 1928, while she was overseas, at the Bendigo Memorial Hall (details of this show are difficult to locate).

Madge Freeman left Paris in April 1926 with her first husband, and friend from Bendigo, Lanfear Thompson, an engineer, and travelled with him to West Africa's Gold Coast, where he contracted malaria. Madge and her friend Elma took him back to London, where they nursed him till his death in 1929. She had nursed him for three years prior to his demise, but no doubt felt grief when his life finally ended. After he died, she returned home to Australia. However, 1930 found her back in Paris, and she toured the great galleries of Europe with Elma Roach, reinforcing her knowledge by studying great art in the flesh, so to speak. In her descriptions of what she saw, contained in letters home, colour looms large – although in her own work colour was mostly subdued.

In 1934 she returned to Bendigo, where she set up a studio in Barkly Street and gave lessons. She also spent time in Melbourne, where she was associated with various contemporary art societies, possibly commuting between the two cities. She had a new sub-career as an administrator, acting as Convenor of the Art Circle at Melbourne's Lyceum Club for 15 years, as well as her work with the Melbourne Society of Women Painters and Sculptors, and was part of the Post-Impressionist movement in Melbourne.[171] She was represented in the exhibition by the Independent Group in Melbourne in 1940. Women predominated in this group and a good many of the better things in this show were contributed by them. Here can be seen Freeman's use of colour, albeit often sparingly applied. Erif Vincent states: 'Her paintings have been constructed with extreme constraint. Her impressions in watercolour have all been translated in fresh, free ... style, in which colour has a leading role'.

The catalogue of the exhibition of her work at the Bendigo Art Gallery in 1981 states:

> Madge Freeman was certainly eclectic and it is difficult to find a consistent stylistic pattern throughout her work. Her subject matter shows a preoccupation with still life and landscape with a vast amount of this work being done abroad... [In 1938–39] she began exhibiting with the Melbourne Society of Women Painters and Sculptors (she later became President of the Society), continuing until 1971. In 1938 she met George Bell which was to become a lasting friendship: she attended Bell's classes for many years.[172]

In her work, the theory of colour modulation, as developed by Paul Cézanne, was sometimes used. She blended warm reds and yellows with mid-tones of orange and violet and cool shades of green and grey. A wide colour range often indicates a strong light source.

Still Life (1926) (see Plate 24) was the first work by a local Bendigo artist to be purchased by the Bendigo Art Gallery according to the Australian Art Gallery.[173] Fruit in warm tones in the foreground lead the eye in a graceful line to two decorated white jugs, against a dark ground suggesting walls and drapes, as though the fruit and jugs are not merely utilitarian, but decorative and on display.

Melbourne's *Herald* of 9 July 1934 said her exhibition at the Sedon Gallery contained 'Oils and watercolours carried out in flat and simple tones with a tendency toward modern methods'.[174] In *River Boats in a Mediterranean Town* (1936), a building in flat, warm colours dominates the right-hand side of the picture, guiding the eye to the river, where coloured buildings in warm to grey tones form a contrast to the rounded blue-green trees. The whole painting is in a high colour key of reds, oranges, yellows, olive greens and bright browns. *Boats on the Yarra* (1936) shows four wooden fishing boats from left to right, with wharves forming the top of a semi-circle. Warm colours with white highlights display ripples, while violets and cool blues show shadows along the wharves.

Madge Freeman was not afraid of controversy. When the Contemporary Art Society experienced internal political struggles in the 1940s, George Bell and his followers walked out, Madge Freeman with them, and she severed her ties with CAS, joining the Melbourne Contemporary Artists Group with Bell. Her exhibitions and her administrative roles in Australia testify to the respect and determination she had with regard to the artistic scene in her home country.

Madge Freeman married again in 1940 and moved to Longwarry in Victoria's Gippsland region, with her grazier husband Basil Davies, who bred Ayrshire cattle. She commuted to Melbourne, continuing to paint and maintaining a studio in South Yarra at her family's home. In 1953, she again travelled to Europe, this time with her husband, he to research 'cows and bulls', she to look at galleries. After Madge's death in 1977, her husband left funds for the Madge Freeman prize, which was administered by the Bendigo Art Gallery.

Madge Freeman was never famous, yet was influential behind the scenes and with a not inconsiderable reputation as an artist. What she brought back from France was more than merely a charisma that may be perceived to exist in an artist who has lived and worked there. Her teaching, her art, and her administrative work have contributed significantly to the Australian art world. The contribution of 'minor' artists should not be underestimated. It is a loss to Australian art that more is not known about Madge Freeman and others like her.

Chapter 25

CONSTANCE STOKES

A Determined Career

Constance Stokes (nee Parkin)
1906–1991
In Paris 1931–1933

Constance Stokes achieved what comparatively few artists of her generation did – she successfully adopted much of the new while remaining within a tradition of naturalism. Her work demonstrated a fine skill at drafting, yet she remained, until recently, little known and less appreciated, despite a stellar career during which her works sold for very high figures.

She is something of an exception among the Australian women artists, although, in another way, she exemplifies them. She was an exception in that she married, and accepted, albeit grudgingly, what that meant in terms of the reduction in her painting output, but was exemplary in that she grew and changed, adopting a good deal of Modernism into her work, as a result of her time studying in Paris, until what emerged was a style of her own. By melding Modernism and Classicism into something new that was uniquely hers – on the face of it a difficult if not impossible assignment – she showed courage and intelligence. A shy woman, she was often regarded as an 'artist's artist' and lived quietly for a time in Paris, avoiding even the café life, yet she returned to Australia exuberant and began incorporating into her art all that she had learned there.

Constance Parkin was born in western Victoria's Wimmera region in 1906, into a Catholic family, her father a prosperous farmer. In 1920, he moved the family to Melbourne and it was there that her talents began to blossom. Susan Cochrane, a teacher at the school to which she was sent, who was the first to detect Stokes's strong talent for drawing, persuaded her parents that their daughter would be better off home-schooled while studying part-time at the National Gallery Art School, which she did from 1925 under Bernard Hall, who was impressed with her.[175] She flourished under his tutelage and he had great respect for her. She won a number of awards, culminating in winning the Travelling Scholarship in 1929, which guaranteed her two years of study in Europe. Bernard Hall encouraged his students to go to Europe to see great art for themselves, and through her study of the great works of the past, particularly the Italian Renaissance painters, she began developing her own style. The important point is that, not willing merely to learn and imitate, she thought about how to create something new, something uniquely her own.

Before going, she exhibited with the Australian Art Association at the Athenaeum Art Gallery in Collins Street, selling much of her work there. Then, in 1930, she set sail for the Old World. Gérard-Austin states that Stokes was an extremely determined woman, committed to doing everything in her power to become a fully professional artist.[176]

After some time in London, Stokes went on to Paris, and she appears to have learnt more from André Lhote and some other influences, not all of them French, than she did anywhere else. According to Lucilla d'Abrera, her daughter and biographer, she sought in Paris to become what she termed an 'international' artist. She stayed in Paris from 1931 to 1933. Her apartment in Montparnasse was extremely elegant and belonged to an Italian publisher and his wife. The paintings on the walls were original Henri Matisse and André Derain, and the house was full of books that Stokes lamented she could not read, nor could she understand the French.

The major French influence upon her work was André Lhote, although she never adopted his Cubism, preferring to try to absorb his teachings into her own modus operandi and combine what he taught with her earlier Classical influences. Under Lhote's influence, she began to re-arrange pictorial elements in order to achieve a balanced composition, no longer aiming at accurate resemblance. She referred to this as her 'Free Style', according to Andrea Lloyd in *Constance Stokes, Her Life and Art* in 1991, concerning herself less with the 'gross sin of resemblance' (Lhote's words) than with an impression or an idea.[177] Andrea Lloyd writes:

> ... the rhythmic design evident in *The Village* shows the influence of André Lhote, and Stokes' developing style. Equal importance is given to both the foreground figure and the background design in her new and successful approach to the total picture plane. The lines of each form continue into the next shape, unifying the self-consciously Madonna like, contemplative figure with the background. The soft and muted colours of the restricted palette used to portray the foreground figure are used again in the background, adding to this effect of a unified whole.

The Paris interlude under André Lhote was also the beginning of Constance Stokes's experiments with the vitality of colour. Lucilla d'Abrera quotes from Stokes's diary on page 44 of her autobiography of her mother, 'A world of colour and form ... as opposed to surface painting which I had known before ... [Lhote] made me see colour independently from subject. This opened my eyes to real creativity ... he had a brush and pulled everything together'.[178] D'Abrera is convinced that 'Stokes's brief period under the tutelage of André Lhote was to prove a pivotal influence, if not immediately, then more so as her style developed and changed later in life'.

She also learnt to emphasise the form and structure of a work and a formal and intellectual approach to the work, rather than the 'mere act of visual seeing'. And, finally: drawing as the basis for all art.

To combine what she learnt from André Lhote with the illusionism she had learnt from Bernard Hall at the National Gallery Art School was a bold and innovative step, which stands out among the Australian women artists. Stokes retained from more traditional modes a sense of monumentality, according to Lucilla d'Abrera, and the influence of some major Italian painters, including Fra Angelico, Giotto and Botticelli. So it would be possible to argue, as does d'Abrera, that she remained in many ways a Classical artist while importing many elements of Modernism. Nor did she compromise to achieve her fusion of two great traditions, but rather melded them both into a strong and vibrant style of her own.

Lucilla d'Abrera states that Stokes's subjects were often passive, with expressionless faces, whereas their costumes and background have colour and movement. She 'had a natural tendency to describe rather than suggest form in a way that flattened ... their two dimensionality'. This also 'drew attention to the decorative side of her art'. Some of her figures were 'elongated' and 'slightly distorted', suggesting Modernism, while her use of colour and form suggested the influence of Henri Matisse as well as that of André Lhote.

Although she reconciled the two sides of her artistic work, she never quite reconciled the two sides of herself: career artist and mother. Lucilla d'Abrera states:

> When asked about her life as a wife, mother, and artist, Stokes wryly observed: 'Any creative work is a difficult life for a woman if she is a wife and mother. Painting requires so much concentration. Inspiration does not come unless you can brood over it. Art cannot be conducted coldly and methodically like a business'.

Constance Stokes had in common with Stella Bowen and Ethel Carrick that the men in their lives, to varying degrees, restricted their ability to develop their art as consistently as they may have wished. Dora Meeson and Carrick worked hard on furthering the careers of their husbands; Bowen tended to the needs of hers. However, to be balanced, we, as well as Anne Summers[179] and Lucilla d'Abrera, make clear that Constance Stokes was devoted to her husband Eric Stokes, whom she married in August 1933, and he to her. Marriage was not thrust upon her, she chose it, although, as Andrea Lloyd makes clear, at the beginning of her career she had delayed marriage in order to make the most of her career opportunities.

Anne Summers, in *The Lost Mother*, described how Constance Stokes painted her mother, twice, when her mother was ten, firstly as 'Alice' – innocent and childlike – and later as 'Madonna' – independent, assertive, and free. Summers theorises that the first may have expressed Stokes's desire to escape, like Alice, into a rabbit hole to a fantasy world of freedom – because at the time of the painting Stokes was to be married in two weeks. Summers puts forward the idea that the second painting was one of the early paintings of the New Woman, one who was free, self-determining, and equal in all respects to men (despite the fact that it was of a child).[180]

While it is true that Constance Stokes worried about the constraints on her work that motherhood might bring, it is only fair to add that until she became pregnant she and her husband shared a studio in Collins Street and she continued painting. It was the advent of children into their lives, later on, that arguably restricted Stokes's freedom to paint as she wished. During the early child-rearing period of her life, however, Anne Summers opines she actually painted more than is commonly supposed, and reports that many of Stokes's finest paintings were created then, so the widespread belief that she only drew while bringing up her family is, she believes, untrue. It was during this period that she and her husband moved to suburban Elwood.

She did, however, experience some bitterness at the drag on her creativity caused by child-rearing. In her interview with Hazel de Berg she said: 'Often I'd be painting and carried right away, and I'd feel someone tugging at my skirt, and my instinct was to turn around and say something brutal, and then I'd think, no, this is my little daughter, I can't, I've got to behave myself!'[181] She did maintain her lessons with George Bell, taking three trams and buses to get from her home in Elwood to his studio in Toorak.

Lucilla d'Abrera states that Constance Stokes's husband at first believed that her art was 'a phase she was going through', but was forced to change his mind when, travelling to Europe with his wife, he saw at first hand the respect in which she was held. In the 1950s, d'Abrera remembers, he stood up in a public meeting and stoutly defended her and her art.

When she came home, she began a long period of putting what she had studied into practice, developing and refining her work as she went. In 1933, she held her first solo exhibition. This was no longer, says Andrea Lloyd, the work of a student but of a mature artist who demonstrated a new individuality. The show 'elicited strong reactions, both positive and negative, from the critics'. From the late 1930s she did exhibit fairly regularly in group shows.

Upon her husband's early death in 1962, from which she never really recovered, she returned to painting full-time, out of necessity to service their debts, and created some more of her finest work, no doubt executing more ideas that had been germinating in her mind through the long years in suburbia of listening to the hiss of sprinklers. In 1964, she exhibited this work at the Leveson Street Gallery.

There were some negatives in her life. As an associate of George Bell, she was drawn into the bitter divisions within the Contemporary Art Society in 1940. She also suffered from being classified as a 'woman artist', a label that she despised, wanting only to be judged by the quality of her work. She chose, in fact, not to associate with women's art groups in order to try to avoid the stigma of being so derided.

From the 1940s, however, she did start to become better known, especially after the National Gallery of Victoria purchased *Yacht Club* (1942), and it is the opinion of d'Abrera that she influenced buyers as much as she did her fellow artists. Well regarded by critics, d'Abrera believes that, with her European influences, Stokes is as much an international as an Australian artist. A number of artists were said to have admired her work, among them Fred Williams, Russell Drysdale and George Bell. When she and Drysdale exhibited together during the 1940s and '50s, her work, according to Summers, was higher priced, and attracted more attention, than his. She and Drysdale both perfected the use of powerful red colours and a thick glaze, possibly as a joint exercise, although it was to Drysdale that the credit went for these developments.

Again and again we discovered admirers of her work. In 1947, Joseph Burke, Professor of Fine Art at Melbourne University, was asked, according to Summers, by an American art magazine to nominate the Australian artists he most admired – one of his six was Constance Stokes.[182] The London *Times* critic stated in 1948 that *Girl in Red Tights* was 'the best picture in London that week', writes Lucilla d'Abrera, and a Dr Ellis met Stokes at the London opera and told her the *Times* critic had that day said to him it was the one painting in London that he must see.

Ursula Hoff, in the quarterly *Bulletin* of the National Gallery of Victoria, wrote in relation to *The Baptism*: 'Stokes avoids the classical pose, the dignity of bearing. She subdues the animation of her figures but her composition achieves the solidity associated with the classical ideal … a rich and unearthly colour scheme accentuates the solemn mood of the scene'.[183]

In 1974, Charles Bush of the Leveson Street Gallery wrote that 'she happens to be one of the finest contemporary painters Australia has ever produced', noted d'Abrera.

In the *Weekend Australian* for 23 August 2015, critic Patricia Anderson wrote: 'Stokes's style … veers dramatically … as academic tradition gives way to flattened picture planes, electric colours, agitated brushstrokes and abbreviated form'.[184] Summers comments: '[A] portrait of Mrs Turner … owes much to Rembrandt in its use of contrasts; in this case the light on Mrs Turner's face is matched by the light on a scarf falling onto her chest'.

After the Leveson Street exhibition she continued to exhibit in Melbourne through the 1960s and 70s. Her work fell into disregard, however, only to 'come out' again in the 1980s through a series of retrospectives, and she is held in some major Australian galleries, including the National Gallery of Victoria, the S.H. Ervin Gallery, and the Queensland Art Gallery, as well as several regional galleries.

In her *Road to Ballarat* (1944), a powerful, disturbing work, Stokes displayed her ability to explore the alienation of her subjects.[185] The strong red colours and the thick glazes were characteristic touches. She used this painting to give expression to the mood of her characters. The windswept, empty landscape is given added human and social significance, writes Lloyd, by 'the faceless men in a buggy who both avoid looking at each other or the changing scenery. The men are also indifferent to the isolation of the woman on the verandah of a cottage who is condemned to her own static view of the landscape'.

Many of her drawings and paintings are of the female figure, which she regarded as the central element of her art, often women in private, contemplative or intimate moments in domestic settings, or large nudes. Her ability to convey a sense of the inner life of her subjects allows her to explore their alienation and isolation. Her subversion of the nude as a sexually available woman was a characteristic she shared with some of the other Australian women artists.

Reverie (1950) (see Plate 25) painted in oil on Masonite, features a luxuriating nude young woman sitting in a large chair, her small breasts and ample thighs and torso partly cloaked in what appears to be a silk wrap. Her figure dominates the picture plane, and is flanked by a vase of colourful flowers and background planes suggestive of affluence. Her face is angled and her eyes stare distantly into some private vision. Her pose is passive, almost melancholy. Stokes's command of the figure is evident, and the bright blue of the vase highlights the lush, warm colours.

Constance Stokes appealed to us for this book because, in contriving to combine Modernist and Classical influences in her work, she showed an intelligent and, more importantly, an independent approach to her career. It was not easy, then as now, to do something new in the world of art, but Stokes could be described as having achieved it. Had she not studied in Paris, it could be argued that she wouldn't have felt sufficiently confident in her use of Modernism. It would be fair to say that Paris made her the artist she became, whose work has been so respected.

Few of the women in this book made the decision to balance career and marriage. She is therefore a worthy role model for any woman who wants to have both. Her insistence upon forging a pathway of her own, all the while enriching our vision of women as they really are, divorced from the male gaze, makes her a powerful advocate and a woman, and artist, of principle.

Chapter 26

MOYA DYRING

Artist, and Artist's Friend

Moya Claire Dyring
1909–1967
In Paris 1928, 1938–1939, 1949–1967

From the start, after graduating from Victoria's National Gallery Art School, Melbourne-born Moya Dyring was the centre of the art party set in her home city. Stories abound of friends visiting her gatherings and vividly remembering bodies all over the floor in various stages of lovemaking. Artists are sometimes supposed, in the popular imagination, to lead lives as bohemian rebels, exploring alternative lifestyles, and generally living exciting lives as mythic outsiders. Moya Dyring is one artist who did live the imagined, mythic life of a bohemian artist.

Her early life in Victoria showed the signs of both of the major narratives of her life. She first entered the world of art as a student at the National Gallery Art School in Melbourne under Bernard Hall, who taught her the massing and grouping of light and shade, based upon the perceived standards of excellence of the Paris salons.

According to *Travels with My Art: Moya Dyring and Margaret Olley*, the school taught a specific British tradition of art.[186] There, however, she met her future husband, Sam Atyeo, and became part of a rather self-conscious group of students of whom George Johnston, in his book *My Brother Jack*, wrote: 'They were living according to some constantly changing creed of noisy controversy. They would dress extravagantly ... they would be forever flinging their prejudices and beliefs and opinions at each other. They would plagiarise their own gods, and defile the gods of anyone else'.[187] Moya's love of the group life was surfacing early.

She graduated in 1931, having demonstrated a growing interest in classical Modernism, following encouragement in that direction from George Bell, with whom she studied at the Bourke Street Studio School in 1932, and who influenced more than one of the Melbourne women artists. She later studied also under Rah Fizelle – another Modernist – in Sydney. Later, she lived for a time at Heide, located at Bulleen, on the outskirts of Melbourne. Heide, the home of John and Sunday Reed, was a centre known for its camaraderie and social life as well as for its art. By the time she was ready to travel overseas she was already a well-trained artist with some experience, though her training would have been behind developments in Europe.

In her book *Paintings from Paris*, Gaynor Cuthbert writes, 'Various clans were situated around the foothills of Melbourne, including the Boyds at Murrumbeena, Adrian Lawlor and Danila Vassilieff at Warrandyte, Justus Jorgensen and his extended family at Montsalvat in Eltham and the Reeds at Heide in Bulleen'.[188] On the one hand, these disparate groups shared a common goal of finding a new Australian cultural aesthetic and identity; on the other, there were different ideologies as to how this could be achieved. And while there was a constant exchange between most of the communities, families, cliques and cohorts, the Reeds generally kept their distance, though later on in the 1940s, the artists associated with Heide, such as Joy Hester, Albert Tucker, Arthur Boyd and John Perceval, who had also been somewhat separate, would mix freely between the different artistic clans. Moya was a keen gardener and environmentalist, and shared a love of the garden at Heide with John Reed, with whom she spent many hours working to make it better. However, all was not work and gardening.

Considering her extravagant bohemianism at art school, and her later involvement in the sometimes idiosyncratic Melbourne art scene, it could almost seem as if Moya Dyring was rehearsing for her future life in Paris. She first went with her sister Rosa, in 1928. Cuthbert states that Dyring fell in love with Paris and said: 'I will return', stating: '[Paris] is the only place for a painter to live, everything is so accessible, and one can find so much beauty'. Presumably, the 'everything' referred to was galleries, schools, ateliers and artistic social life.

Before Moya Dyring left for Paris for her second visit she had a solo exhibition at the Riddell Gallery in Little Collins Street. The outstanding painting was *Melanctha*, discussed later in this chapter and which John Reed purchased for the Heide Gallery.

Having decided at 19 years of age that Paris was to be her home and having later realised that dream, her home in Paris became the hub for a great many Australian artists, between 1938 and 1939, and after World War II for the rest of her life. Russell Drysdale recalls how the first thing one did on arrival in Paris was 'ring Moya'. John Olsen, who also visited her apartment, appreciated her work and remembers her as 'vibrant, energetic, disciplined, with a strong work ethic: an important linkage figure and connector who understood Paris and had an earthy affection for it'.[189]

Despite her brief time in Paris during 1928, it was not until 1938 that the Paris dream finally came to pass, and apart from a few years away from that city during and immediately after World War II, Moya Dyring lived the rest of her life beside the Seine, with occasional forays back home to Australia to exhibit. She went with Sam Atyeo, whom she married the following year, and Gaynor Cuthbert writes that their life was harmonious, shopping and cooking together, and learning French as they went. To begin with, work meant study as much as actually painting. She began in 1938, after a short but unhappy time in America. She initially studied at the Académie Colarossi, where she drew three days a week with no tuition. Cuthbert says that Dyring must have been among the last to study there.

Later, she studied at l'Académie de la Grande Chaumière, and also with André Lhote, who had been a major influence on a slightly earlier generation of Modernists, including Dorrit Black. On top of the not inconsiderable study she had completed in Melbourne, this must now have set her up to paint confidently in whatever style she chose, knowing she had the knowledge and the technique to succeed.

Also, according to the exhibition catalogue of *Travels with My Art: Moya Dyring and Margaret Olley*, European artists frequented Chez Moya, her Paris home on the Île Saint-Louis, including her close friend English artist Sir Francis Rose, Spanish painter Antoni Clavé, and Eugène Baboulène.[190] Dyring had purchased a long lease on an apartment in a 17th-century building and also hosted a transient coterie of some of the best-known Australian artists of their generation, including Margaret Olley, Donald Friend, Russell Drysdale, Lloyd Rees and John Olsen, all visiting her in what was, in effect, a private salon, in the long French tradition of salons run by women.

Regardless of her love of social life, she was a dedicated artist who worked very hard at her craft. We have criss-crossed by her place on the Seine many times, imagining those heady days, those talented frequenters, calling to mind, as we walked, images of that place produced by her, and by Margaret Olley also, as well as other depictions in and around that area, such as her *View from the Studio* (1952). Moya Dyring was working intensively throughout this period, developing what she termed her Post-Impressionist style, starting with *plein air* using an abstract base of undercolour, so that when she returned to her studio she could paint her pictures direct in a few hours. The Tweed Regional Gallery catalogue notes quote Juliet Peers saying that Dyring also gained a considerable reputation among French regionalist and nationalist artists for her sympathetic appreciation of provincial scenes and life. It is for her art, rather than her social life, that she will be remembered. In fact, Dyring reminds us a little of Mary Cockburn Mercer in her ability to combine hard work with fun, or indeed her close friend, Margaret Olley. The world of art is extremely competitive and, even with talent and hard work, luck is also necessary. She combined all three, and for this, as well as the quality of her work, she deserves inclusion in this book.

Apart from her studies at art schools, Moya Dyring – like so many other Australian women in Paris – spent a lot of time at galleries, studying the masters. She loved the importance Parisians placed on art, and the atmosphere of the city with its architectural beauty and rich history. Cuthbert writes that Dyring wrote to John and Sunday Reed telling them she had seen a 'brilliant' exhibition of Picasso's at the Petit Palais and also some interesting works by Amedeo Modigliani and Georges Braque. Nearly every Sunday she went to the Louvre, enjoying the early Greek sculpture and the early 'primitive' painting from Italy. She told the Reeds also about a Surrealist exhibition she and Atyeo had seen in Paris, although it was obvious from her letters that she was not in love with Surrealism.[191] She described in her letters the 'appalling' technique and what she seemed to feel was the use of extreme images to shock rather than to stimulate in any aesthetic sense.

In 1938, Dyring and Atyeo purchased land in the Alpes-Maritimes region, at Vence, a village beside a rushing stream surrounded by spectacular mountain scenery. There, they hoped, they could find peace to work, away from the intense and inward-looking bustle of the city. There also they could garden, as Dyring had at Heide. She worked hard at Vence, as she always had, and found it a very congenial location. However, the events in Germany were frightening her, and she sensed Europe was in for something terrible. During 1938, she painted a great many studies, but was never really satisfied with them and destroyed a lot. She continued her zest for friendship, making friends among the locals, and entertaining them with her cooking, using vegetables from her garden.

After the war, in 1949, Moya Dyring had her first one-woman show, at the London Gallery in Brook Street, Mayfair, London.[192] Cuthbert writes that the paintings of nudes, shells and landscapes were well received by the critics – the consensus being that her work was fresh and vigorous, unlike much British painting at that time – and by the public, and she sold paintings.

During all of this, both before and during the war, her love of sociability did not flag. Her apartment after the war, her hospitality not having waned, remained famous in Australian art circles for its welcome to Australian artists visiting Paris, and it was during this time that Dyring began her well-known friendship with Margaret Olley. With her artist friends, as stated in *Travels with My Art*, she would often set out on an excursion into the French countryside to paint and to enjoy conviviality, as well as to record ways of peasant life that were slowly disappearing.

In 1948, Atyeo ended their marriage for another woman. Although she was shocked and hurt, she got her life together, relied on friends, and continued work. The friends who helped her out during this time of emotional recovery included Donald Friend; Margaret Olley, of course; Jean Bellette; Russell Drysdale and a few others. It may well be that her painting also helped to see her through a difficult time.

Moya Dyring's work shows strong Modernist influences, adventurousness and a willingness to seek challenges and variety, from Cubism to an almost naturalistic style. Her undated charcoal and pastel drawing *Old Mill the Aveyron* reveals a very sure technique together with a beautiful appreciation of light, which seems to permeate the work almost without needing, so to speak, a source. It is a river view, with what one assumes is a mill in the middle distance on its bank. The river and a line of straight-trunked trees lead the eye along both sides of a wedge to the mill. The colours, except for small parts of the river, are warm browns, rusts, and a colour that resembles burnt sienna. The grove of trees on the left of the picture, and the river, form a dominant shoulder of muted colour, through which can be seen a distant line of hills. It is not clear that the building is a mill as its wheel cannot be seen, nor is the river turbulent. Colour is used to segment the picture and delineate areas of interest. The quality of light is translucent, like the view of the hills through the trees, and this is the real achievement of the drawing. The landscape seems insubstantial, evanescent, almost liquid, and the air seems almost to be a visible part of the scene.

Her *Melanctha* (1937), now at the Heide Museum of Modern Art, displays flat panes that nevertheless conspire to produce a sense of depth around, and to, the central asexual figure who alone captures the viewer's attention. Perhaps the background is drapes, or furniture, or some of both, or just a fantasy painted array of coloured planes because, after all, a figure has to have some kind of background against which to stand, but it hardly matters because there are no objects to be discerned, however segmented. The frame of the nude central figure, slightly menacing in its stance, leads the eye upward to the face, which possesses a quiet strength and sense of self, unmoving because it is where it needs to be, still yet surrounded by a chaos of colour and revolving planes. Partitioned by colour, or rather in some areas of the painting by shades, the figure commands its personal space, and its feet are firmly planted as if chaos were the last thing on its mind. The colours, mostly warm but with cool patches of greens and blues close to and behind the figure, create a sequence that circles it. The figure has one eye closed and gazes slightly downward as if meditating. There is no eroticism in the figure, but rather a sense that its colours are its clothing. One may choose to see in the picture an 'inner woman' of strength whom Moya Dyring wishes to present to us.

With *Notre Dame* (c.1950), the first thing the viewer notices is that the light, coming from the left and a little behind the viewer, makes the cathedral seem to dance as the light plays on its complex interior. The plain, light-etched bridge in the foreground – the one that has more recently been covered with lovers' locks – stretches square across the picture plane, framing the church and drawing our attention to it. Around the cathedral, small buildings and trees also dance, darkly and raggedly, indistinct beside the clarity of the dominant structure, simultaneously in harmony with it, and in contrast to its permanence and solidity. Notre Dame itself, however, is foreshortened – the real edifice is much longer and its metal spire nowhere near as high – but its squat presence unifies the picture frame and the light on its front wall suggests uplift and hope. Hope, indeed, is what all lovers of great architecture now hold for the rebuilding of the spire and roof after the terrible fire of April 2019. The French Government has pledged to restore the Cathedral to is original state and with modern technology, that should not be impossible.

Fishermen (1966) (see Plate 26) shows three shadowy men, their faces obscured, holding fishing rods at almost the same angle and in the same direction, from a small boat over tranquil, shining waters. There is much of Modernism in this picture, yet she retains the figure at the centre of it. The men seem identical in their dark coats and caps, their faces downturned to the water that has drawn them to this place. Only the rods – yellow – and the upper edge of the boat – warm orange and brown – are bright. Anonymous, timeless figures, performing a ritual as old as humanity, passively posed in an engagement with nature, more active than their poses suggest. To us, this picture honours these men.

Moya Dyring returned to Australia several times from 1950, mounting exhibitions in 1953, 1956, 1960 and 1963. The *Australian Women's Weekly* ran an article on her return to Australia, focusing on the delights and the difficulties of an artist's life in Paris.[193] Some of these exhibitions travelled to more than one Australian city. French artist Claude Bonin-Pissarro, grandson of Camille Pissarro, opened her 1953 exhibition at Sydney's Macquarie Galleries. Her final exhibitions in Australia were in 1963 at the Barry Stern Gallery in Sydney, opened by Mary Alice Evatt and Brisbane's Johnstone Gallery, at which she exhibited many more paintings of children than she had shown in previous exhibitions.[194]

Moya Dyring contributed a great deal to the success of many Australian artists of her generation in France, not by serving on committees of organisations or by teaching, but by providing a temporary home, and moral support, to the many Australian artists who passed through her apartment on Île Saint-Louis and other homes. She has graced the Australian art world with her work, and her life, and she will be remembered and respected for her contributions in both spheres.

Chapter 27

BETTY QUELHURST

A Dedicated Artist and Teacher

Betty Pauline Quelhurst
1919–2008
In Paris and Europe 1952–1953

Betty Quelhurst created art, and served art, for decades. She was a thoroughly modern 20th-century woman, in her appearance, thought, and painting. She epitomised the Australian myth of the dauntless individualist, assertive and adventurous.

She absorbed the study and fashions that had preceded her era, yet she was a painter very much of the late 20th century, in that some of her work can be said to contain influences from Impressionism and Post-Impressionism – work she did in her late years was of that time. When she painted *The Topless Bather* in 1984, the colours she used, and the sense of motion and enjoyment she depicted, are a well-observed expression of the Australian lifestyle.

In a review in the *Australian* of an exhibition of Quelhurst's work at the Gold Coast City Gallery in 2012, Bronwyn Watson quotes curator

Virginia Rigney: 'Betty Quelhurst lived virtually all her life on the Gold Coast, but she was absolutely sure of herself as an artist. She is a very formal artist dealing with a difficult composition'.[195] Quelhurst said of *Topless Bather*: 'At the time everyone was bathing topless ... so I chose that as the title, and I set it on the beach ...'.

Betty Quelhurst was one artist who achieved as much recognition, success and influence through her teaching as she did through her painting, although she was a very talented artist who never ceased to explore and grow. Like so many unsung heroes, she worked silently and effectively at her art, developing her love for the human figure and for portraiture, and at her teaching and administration – a quiet achiever who did a lot to advance the cause of art in her native Queensland.

She went late to Paris, held up in Australia by World War II, during which she served in the Australian Air Force. After the war she attempted to make up for lost time by studying, from 1948, with William Dargie at the National Gallery Art School in Melbourne. She financed this partly with a scholarship from the Half Dozen Group of Artists, who clearly saw her potential. She was awarded the Hugh Ramsay Portrait Prize, and the Sara Levi Prize for most outstanding student. During this time, she absorbed a sense of strong tones in her work, and the precision that naturalistic painting requires.

From her savings, she financed her trip to Paris – still pretty much obligatory during this period for developing artists who wanted to catch up with world trends. An artist of such talent, already rewarded and trained, might have felt it necessary to 'finish' her development in the rich fields of the European art world. Based in Paris from 1952 to 1953, she demonstrated in the work she did there that she understood the mood and spirit of that city, its colours, its light, its architecture, and its people. She is a clear example of the gains that could be made, during that period, by an artist who studied in Paris, in her case, at the Académie de la Grande Chaumière. During her period there she painted a number of watercolours and some oils, capturing much of the city's architectural beauties. In her trips around Europe she studied the great masters in major galleries.

After her studies in Paris she backpacked around Europe, demonstrating the 'can do', determined spirit of Australian women – something that earlier generations of women artists in Europe in the pre-World War I period, or even in the 1920s, might not always have felt able, or safe, to do. She used this time, like other women before her, to study the rich heritage of European art, and also some of the emerging trends of the 20th century. As part of her mission to absorb the best of French and European art, she visited many major galleries across Europe.

Betty Quelhurst's style was unique, and she continued throughout her life to explore and develop her vision and her technique, yet she painted within the broad parameters of the traditions she had imbibed, a vibrant naturalism, with only modest nods in the direction of Modernism. Her time in Europe had polished her technique and her knowledge of her craft, and perhaps it this that was the source of the confidence referred to by Rigney. The forms of her work were often of the human figure, which was embodied largely in her portraiture and in beachscapes, though not always naturalistically portrayed. In *Boulevard, Paris* (1952), however, she created a semi-naturalist urbanscape of the city using warm earth colours, with indistinct figures on the street, rather like those figures that are included in architects' drawings of proposed urban developments. Soft tones and a lack of sharpness give an air of mystery, as though these buildings, which were not old enough in her day to hide secrets as medieval or ancient edifices can do, were sheltering exciting mysteries, or at the very least a Continental sophistication, as an Australian might have sensed it.

She was a highly skilled portraitist, but much of her work consisted of landscapes, of which *Winter Sun – Surfers Paradise Beach* (1961) (see Plate 27) is a prime example. The scene is shown in clear, sharp detail, etched by the sun that drenches the beach, immobilising the figures on the sand – again, seen as anonymous characters whose faces are either hidden or barely sketched. Bright, vibrant colours, contrasting with the more muted tones of some of her Parisian work, add to a sense of somnolence and slow self-indulgence under a permissive sun. Although she clearly loved her Parisian subjects, it was to the bright subtropical sunlight of her native Queensland to which she reacted most strongly.

In her portraits, Betty Quelhurst was respected for her detail, especially the textural effects and the colourisation achieved by a very skilful application of paint. She had always shown, even before leaving Australia, a strong concern for the development of technique.

After her return from Europe, she set out to create a career path, based mainly in Brisbane. She established a private teaching facility, a wise move that guaranteed her an income whatever the fate of her painting might be. She also taught at secondary schools in the Brisbane area, as well as providing adult education courses throughout regional Queensland. She obtained numerous commissions, mostly for portraiture. She demonstrated her control of the technique of portraiture in her study of the *Reverend Mervyn Henderson*, Principal of Emmanuel College at the University of Queensland, before his retirement. (The commissioning of portraits of outgoing Principals is a tradition at Emmanuel College.) This portrait was accepted for the 1954 Archibald Prize.

Despite never mounting a solo exhibition, she maintained a strong presence in group exhibitions and contests over the years. She exhibited with the Half Dozen Group of artists from 1949 to 1967, and entered the Redcliffe Art Prize in 1957, in which she won first prize for *The Pier, Woody Point*. She was awarded the first Johnsonian Club Art Prize in 1961 for her work *Anzac Park*. She was a founding member of the Gold Coast Branch of the Royal Queensland Art Society in 1957.[196] Her work *Winter Sun – Surfers Paradise Beach* was included in an exhibition titled 'A Time Remembered: Art in Brisbane 1950 to 1975', and in a book of that name published the same year.[197]

Her contribution to Australian art was significant. Her reputation in Queensland continued to grow as she applied to her work what she had learned in Paris and in Europe. She was not an innovative or daring artist but she earned a place in the cohort of fine Queensland painters. Perhaps, as with so many female artists, her work was undervalued because she was a woman.

Betty Quelhurst was perhaps one of this country's most generous artists, and embarking on that exciting journey to travel to Paris and Europe certainly paid off in what she contributed to her homeland. Despite her steady success as a painter, she gave of her time and energy to students and to the visual arts community, and helped lift Brisbane to a stronger position as a major centre of art.

Chapter 28

MARGARET OLLEY

A Lover of Life and Art

Margaret Hannah Olley
1923–2011
In Paris 1949–1953

In her earlier days, Margaret Olley was the very model of the free-living artist, loving life, friends, art and social life, and enjoying a drink. She was, during those years, perhaps almost a caricature of the 'Bohemian' artist, one whose life is as much play, and personal freedom, as work.

Throughout her career, she concentrated mostly on still life, but in her case this was not a limitation on her as an artist. She learnt most of what she needed in Paris and continued from there, not exploring new ways of painting, but adding to her already formidable skills. She loved Paris, living there between 1949 and 1953 and was a close friend there of Moya Dyring. She became, in her lifetime, perhaps our best-loved artist, and she is a prime example of the benefits to artists of living and working in the great capitals of art.

Olley was, by all accounts, always fun to be with, and throughout her life, more importantly, she was a giver – to her friends, to her art and, in later life, to the Australian community. She ranks as one of our finest painters of interiors and still lifes.

Olley was born in Lismore, so New South Wales can rightly claim her – and indeed the Tweed Regional Gallery has claimed her, creating a Margaret Olley Art Centre, from where some of this information has been gleaned. She grew up on farms as a child, later moving with her family to Brisbane where she first studied at Somerville House, a girl's boarding school. There, her art teacher Caroline Barker noticed her talent and encouraged it. After study at Brisbane Central Technical College from 1941, Olley moved to Sydney to study at the East Sydney Technical College, graduating in 1945 with first-class honours.

After graduating, she became part of the thriving Sydney art scene, becoming friends with William Dobell, Russell Drysdale, Justin O'Brien, Sydney Nolan and, most closely, Donald Friend, with whom she painted at Hill End – one of the first to do so. In 1948, she held her first solo show at the Macquarie Galleries, and this was also the year in which Dobell painted his famous portrait of her. (Her face had an attraction for artists, for in 2011 Ben Quilty also painted her portrait, both painters winning the Archibald with their respective works.)

In 1949, she took the major step – as had so many other artists before her – of departing for France. Barry Pearce, in his book titled *Margaret Olley*, writes that, once settled in, Margaret Olley came to regard the banks of the Seine as her spiritual home.[198] Settling on the Île Saint-Louis, where she shared an apartment with friends, she attended the Académie de la Grande Chaumière and, again, found a lively social scene. According to Christine France, she enjoyed playing the clown to amuse her friends, and was also influenced philosophically by Jean-Paul Sartre and Simone de Beauvoir, in particular adopting their love of freedom and of self-determination.[199]

In *Far from a Still Life*, Meg Stewart quotes a bold statement by Brisbane reviewer Paul Grano, reviewing Margaret Olley's exhibition in Brisbane in July 1950:

> The first [observation] is the impressive advance [Olley] has made in technique since leaving Australia to study abroad. The second – how surer, freer and fresher is her work in pen and wash than it is in oils. The third is her sensitivity to immediate influences. Practically all indications of the impact of certain Australian artists apparent in her earlier work are gone. She has been studying in France, and French influences now dominate her brush.[200]

Margaret Olley enjoyed a close friendship with Moya Dyring, and Meg Stewart reports that Olley and Dyring painted fast, recalling to mind the *plein air* technique of some of the earlier Australian women in France, in particular Kathleen O'Connor. Stewart wrote that though Margaret Olley loved living in Paris, she did not forget to show some works in exhibitions in Australia. But Stewart also indicates that Olley had money worries, as is not uncommon with artists, so all was not plain sailing in her life.

In 1952, Margaret Olley was invited to exhibit at the Paul Morihien Gallery at the Palais-Royal in Paris, her first overseas exhibition according to *Design & Art Australia Online*, and received favourable reviews from three Paris journals, all of which commented on her sense of poetry. In 1953, she travelled to Brittany – like many of the Australian women she liked to travel around France and the rest of Europe, visiting galleries, painting the local scenes and seeing places where famous artists had lived. She enjoyed a very fulfilling stay in Paris, peopled by the likes of Jean Cocteau; the eccentric baronet Sir

Francis Rose; Alice B. Toklas, the lover of Gertrude Stein; Stein herself; and other famous individuals. Then, in 1953, she received news of her father's death and she was obliged to return to Australia.

In her interview with Barry Pearce in 2009 for his book on her, she cited Edgar Degas, Édouard Manet and Paul Gauguin as her major influences. The influence of the last named can be seen in her use of vivid, almost tropical colour. She also told Pearce that Paris had changed her life. In the period after her return she won the Finney's Centenary Art Prize and the Helena Rubinstein Portrait Prize as well as the Redcliffe Art Prize.

Margaret Olley's influence in Australia was considerable. Having studied in France, she contributed considerably to Australian art by the sheer quality and subtlety of her work. Although she travelled extensively in Europe and Asia while based in Paris, she was always committed to Australia, and in 1990 she established the Margaret Olley Art Trust to acquire paintings for public collections. Had she done no more than this she would have made a major contribution to the development of art in this country, and it was typical of her generosity of spirit.

Margaret Olley had approximately 80 solo exhibitions in her lifetime, most of them in Australia.[201] Her 1955 exhibition at the Macquarie Galleries cemented her reputation and brought her major recognition. In 1959, she gave up alcohol, which had been a big problem for her, and this was the beginning of major commercial success, giving her financial independence and the opportunity to buy real estate, including a home in Sydney's Paddington, with a former hat factory behind it for a studio. All this time, still life was her mainstay.

The first retrospective of her work was held at the S.H. Ervin Gallery in Sydney in 1990. Olley was appointed an Officer of the Order of

Australia (AO) in 1991. The Art Gallery of New South Wales also held a retrospective, curated by Barry Pearce, in 1996. She was made a Life Governor of the Art Gallery of New South Wales in 1997. She became a Companion of the Order of Australia (AC) in 2006. She also received honorary doctorates from a number of universities. She opened Stage Two of the Margaret Olley Art Centre at the Tweed Regional Gallery in 2006. She had completed a body of work for an exhibition at the Philip Bacon Galleries when she died suddenly in July 2011.

Her work speaks for itself. Her many still lifes are not forced or laboured, but seem intimate and full of rich, full-bodied colour. At its best, her painting was luminous. Barry Pearce reviewed one of her watercolour landscapes, *Institut de France* (1950), in these words:

> The eye is led from the river across a bridge to nineteenth century neoclassical buildings. It is winter, cold and spare. She painted quickly, and somehow created the impression of cold water with greys and soft whites under the spindly metal bridge which looks as though it might crack with the cold. In the hands of a lesser artist, the buildings, domed and classical with Southern European associations might have seemed out of place in this Northern European cityscape. Her feeling for place makes one wish that she had done more landscapes alongside her wondrous interiors.[202]

In *Morning Interior* (see Plate 28), painted in 1973, it is as if the light from outside the room is being drawn into it by the objects that it illuminates, making it seem as if they have a life of their own. The table with its scattered fruit is the centre of attention in a mostly low-key interior, where the light strikes most brightly upon the table. The room is connected to a wider world by the view of another house, not far away, outside the French doors. A door is open, suggesting that the wider world, like the light, is welcome in this room. Flowers are present on a sideboard but not imposing, in the background for decorative effect. A corner of the room is shown, and its two sides seem to draw the eye first to the table, and then to the world seen through glass, at one remove. The painting is at once prosaic, and worldly.

It could be said that Paris made Margaret Olley, as it has many artists. Certainly her time there was a turning point, and both the city and its art made a tremendous impression on her. With Olley, fun and sociability always ranked alongside single-minded seriousness, and it is open to argument that this facility for seeing the lighter side gave her a more flexible and relaxed vision, which can be seen in all her work. She never ceased to soak up images and influences, learning technique while enjoying life, and there is much to admire and, as an Australian, to be proud of in this way of living a life in art.

AFTERWORD

Our original mission was to honour these women who undertook a perilous and often lonely expedition to Paris to further their art and to grow both personally and creatively. We started out with seven, but we kept adding another, and another, and another, each with a claim to be a pioneer, a seeker after the Holy Grail of art, until in the end we undertook to write about twenty eight of them, who might represent the cohort of an estimated three hundred who made the voyage.

We were determined to honour the sheer talent of these women, and the mighty contribution they made to Australian art – and, not inconsiderably, to French art. Finally we wanted it to be more widely known that some of our women were the ones who carried the torch of Modernism to Australian shores. And while doing this, we hoped to bring back into the fold of public attention those wonderful artists who had fallen into obscurity despite their talent and success.

While it is something of a truism that women have always experienced unnecessary difficulties in pursuing their careers, or even being able to follow one, and while this may not end any time soon, it is also a truth that hit home forcibly when we were planning and researching this book.

We have been impressed by the tenacity of these women who not only gained, but maintained their freedom – even allowing for the fact that some of them had financial help from their families – using it to produce art that would justify their struggle. It is worth observing that it was often their fathers who gave them the funds to travel to Paris to become professional artists, and who encouraged them and believed in them, a fact that was brought to our attention by the artist Wendy Sharpe, who wrote the Foreword to this book.

Compared with the volume of work they would have produced during their lifetimes, and taking into account that which has been lost or discarded, we had seen little of their art, and that only occasionally. But now, seeing their *oeuvre* en masse, we realised that here was talent, innovation and sheer beauty, on a scale and of a standard that could not be dismissed, and was easily the equal of work being produced by male artists in that period.

We felt, also, that these artists had somehow let us into their lives, taciturn though many were about anything personal. We found ourselves holding imaginary conversations with them in their studios, holding our breath for them when they exhibited in the salons and galleries as they picked their paths between the safety of tradition and the dangerous excitement of Modernism. They became our pathfinders as they explored the international art world, and we came to feel as if they were our friends as they struggled up flights of stairs to rheumy ateliers, carrying their canvases, their paints, their brushes, their groceries and, of course, their *vins rouge*.

As we came to know them, we resolved to write about them, to pull together various strands of excellent research that had already been completed, and to help show the world that here, among our own Australian women, were significant artists with initiative and curiosity.

We soon came up against the question of 'women artists'. To treat them only as women artists would be to marginalise them, to see them as some sort of oppressed minority and to suggest that their art was somehow intrinsically different from that of men.

While it may be true that many of them manifested strength in painting interiors, portraits and still lifes, it is also true that many of

Afterword

them excelled in landscapes and abstracts. We decided not to write about them as women, but as artists. Artists who happened to be female. While it was only because of their gender that some of them experienced difficulties that a male artist might not, their gender is not, we feel, in the end, decisive in the making of our decision to write about them. In any case, in Paris they found a climate in which they could be themselves, artistically and personally. However long or short was their stay in Paris, for all of them it was a dramatic revelation, and the start of a process of growth that made them the mature and exciting artists they became.

We made the decision to include artists such as Gladys Reynell of South Australia, and Anne Dangar of New South Wales, who were best known for their pottery, because in both their painting and their pottery they created art that we considered to be of the highest level.

Deciding on the images was not easy. We chose in the end to try to find a balance between displaying paintings that were better known, at least within art circles, such as *Girl with Cigarette* by Agnes Goodsir, and some that are not normally associated with particular artists, such as *Studio Fairy* by Janet Cumbrae Stewart, better known for her beautiful pastel nudes. By the same token we sought to balance featuring well-known artists side-by-side with some who have been almost forgotten. In doing this, we sought to show that some lesser known artists – and lesser known artworks – could stand comparison with their better known compatriots and works.

Surveying the images now, we are struck by the fact that most of these women strongly emphasised colour, whether using it to delineate space as with the Cubists, or for decorative power.

We were also surprised to see, while correcting the manuscript, how many of them were taught at the National Gallery Art School in Melbourne before going to Europe. Again, the disproportionate number of women from South Australia was noticeable.

The research, too, offered challenges, spread as it was across a number of gallery archives in at least four states and the ACT. We undertook a motoring trip around the capital cities, soaking up obscure but often significant pieces of information that would add substance to the narrative. It was this trip that drove home to us just how much influence some of these women – especially the Modernists like Dorrit Black and Grace Crowley – had had on Australian art when they returned.

Of the several hundred Australian women artists who were reputed to have travelled to Paris, a few others, apart from those included here, deserve mention, even though the paucity of information about them precludes their inclusion. Among these are Eveline Syme, Christina Asquith Baker, Nancy Goldfinch and Ethel Spowers. Brief outlines of their careers and a few examples of their work may be found in such online sources as the *Australian Dictionary of Biography*, *Design & Art Australia Online*, and Wikipedia, or by application to the authors.

Finally, the joy that any researcher feels when discovering something new and exciting was ours, again and again. Our journeys to Paris to research the women bore fruit. The pluck of Adelaide's Marie Tuck, who worked in a shop for ten years to raise the money for her trip, and the generosity of Dora Meeson, who praised her husband's work while producing such outstanding paintings of her own, show some of the qualities that many of these women demonstrated – one of the criteria we used in choosing them as exemplars from the hundreds who made the pilgrimage to Paris. It was not easy deciding who to include and who not to. In other cases, an artist might spend a year in London and only a couple of weeks in Paris, neither exhibiting nor studying there.

Afterword

We hope that we have managed to achieve the right balance. We hope this book will help inform generations of young Australians about the heritage they inherit from women who displayed a strong Australian spirit of adventure and can-do, and who were dismayed by nothing.

Clem and Therese Gorman, January 2020

APPENDIX

Featured Australian Women Artists in Australian Art Schools, 1880s to 1940s

Adelaide School of Arts and Crafts
Black, Dorrit: 1909–1911

Bendigo School of Mines
Goodsir, Agnes: 1898–99

Brisbane Central Technical College
Gibson, Bessie: 1889–1905
Greene, Anne Alison: 1898–1900
Lahey, Vida: early 1900s
Olley, Margaret: 1941–1942

Dattilo-Rubbo School of Art, Sydney
Chapman, Evelyn: early 1900s

East Sydney Technical College, Sydney
Olley, Margaret: 1942–1945

George Bell School, Melbourne
Mercer, Mary Cockburn: 1938

National Gallery Art School, Melbourne
Cumbrae Stewart, Janet: 1901–1907
Dyring, Moya: 1929–1932
Freeman, Madge: 1916–21
Lahey, Vida: 1905–1906, 1910
Meeson, Dora: 1895–96

Nicholas, Hilda Rix: 1902–1905
Plante, Ada May: 1894–95
Quelhurst, Betty: 1948–1949
Rae, Iso: 1880s
Stokes, Constance: 1920s
Traill, Jessie: early 1900s

Norwood School of Art, Adelaide
Tuck, Marie: 1886–96, as student and as teacher

Perth Technical College
O'Connor, Kathleen: early 1900s

School of Reynell, Davidson and Preston
Bowen, Stella: early 1900s

The Sydney Art School (Julian Ashton), Sydney
Black, Dorrit: 1915
Crowley, Grace: early 1900s
Dangar, Anne: early 1900s
Muskett, Alice: 1886–1895

NOTES

1. Lucilla Wyborn d'Abrera, *Constance Stokes: Art & Life*. Melbourne, Hill House Publishers, 2015, p.43.
2. Anne Gérard-Austin, 'The Greatest Voyage: Australian painters in the Paris salons, 1885–1939' (postgraduate thesis, University of Sydney, 2014).
3. Elizabeth Butel, *Margaret Preston: the art of constant rearrangement*. Melbourne, ETT, 1985.
4. Joan Kerr (ed.), *Heritage: the national women's art book, 500 works by 500 Australian women artists from colonial times to 1955*. Sydney, Craftsman House, 1995.
5. Hazel de Berg, Kathleen O'Connor interviewed by Hazel de Berg, 28 May 1965. Canberra, National Library of Australia, Hazel de Berg Collection, http://nla.gov.au/nla.obj-214365783.
6. Grace Crowley papers, Art Gallery of NSW Library, CY 1284.
7. Anne Gérard-Austin, 'The Greatest Voyage: Australian painters in the Paris salons, 1885–1939'.
8. Helen Topliss (ed.), *Earth, Fire, Water, Air: Anne Dangar's letters to Grace Crowley, 1930–1951*. Sydney, Allen and Unwin, 2000, pp. 6, 47, 55, 65.
9. Sebastian Smee, *The Art of Rivalry: Four friendships, betrayals, and breakthroughs in modern art*. New York, Random House, 2016.
10. Kathleen Calderwood, 'Frenemies: how Friendship and Rivalry Defined Modern Art', Radio National 'Books and Arts', 20 September 2016.
11. Jane Jacobs, *The Economy of Cities*. New York, Vintage, 1970.
12. James Panero, 'Why Paris?', *Humanities* 31:6, Nov–Dec 2010.
13. Helen Topliss, *Modernism and Feminism: Australian Women Artists, 1900–1940*. Sydney, Craftsman House, 1996.
14. Hazel de Berg, Kathleen O'Connor interviewed by Hazel de Berg.
15. Joan Kerr (ed.), *Heritage: the national women's art book, 500 works by 500 Australian women artists from colonial times to 1955*.
16. Betty Snowden, 'Iso Rae'. *Wartime*, Australian War Memorial, Issue 8, Summer 1999.
17. Grace Joel, 'Iso Rae'. *Art and Architecture Australia*, 19 May 1906.
18. From https://en.wikipedia.org/wiki/Iso_Rae.

19 Terry Ingram, 'Whatever happened to Isobel Rae?'. The *Age*, Arts Page, 12 November 2002.
20 *The Art Student in Paris*. Boston, Boston Art Students' Association, 1887.
21 Anne Gérard-Austin, 'The Greatest Voyage: Australian painters in the Paris salons, 1885–1939', p.5.
22 The *British Australasian (London)*, 6 December 1906, p.11, quoted in *In a Picture Land over the Sea: Agnes Goodsir 1864–1939*, Edited by Karen Quinlan (Bendigo: Bendigo Art Gallery, 1998), Exhibition catalogue, p.28.
23 *In a Picture Land over the Sea: Agnes Goodsir 1864–1939*, Exhibition catalogue, p.28.
24 A.T. Woodward, Letter to President of Bendigo Art Gallery, 2 October 1929, in The Goodsir Archive, Bendigo Art Gallery.
25 On winning the medal, see The Goodsir Archives, letter from Arthur T. Woodward to A. Abbott, 1931. Her exhibiting details are recorded in the Musée d'Orsay Salon Archives.
26 *In a Picture Land over the Sea: Agnes Goodsir 1864–1939*, Exhibition catalogue, p.50.
27 Joan Kerr (ed.), *Heritage: the national women's art book, 500 works by 500 Australian women artists from colonial times to 1955*.
28 Karen Quinlan (curator), Curator's Report. Agnes Goodsir exhibition. Bendigo, Bendigo Art Gallery, 1998.
29 Muriel Segal, 'Exhibits by Australians at Paris Salon'. The *Herald*, 3 July 1930, p.24.
30 Ruth Tuck, 'Marie Tuck', *Kalori* magazine, Vol. 2, No. 14, March 1964.
31 Shirley Cameron Wilson, *From Shadow into Light: South Australian women artists since colonisation*. Adelaide, Delmont Pty Ltd, 1988.
32 Elizabeth Young, *Marie Tuck*. Adelaide, The *Advertiser*, Arts Page, 9 December 1972, p.41.
33 *Bessie Gibson: An Artistic Life*. (Murwillumbah: Tweed River Art Gallery, 2012), Exhibition notes.
34 *The Long Weekend: Australian artists in France 1918–1939*, Edited by Karen Quinlan (Bendigo: Bendigo Art Gallery, 2008), Exhibition catalogue.
35 Nancy Underhill, *Art and Australia*, 1979, Vol. 17, No. 1.

36 Anne Gérard-Austin, 'The Greatest Voyage: Australian painters in the Paris salons, 1885–1939', p.62.
37 Dora Meeson Coates, *George Coates, His Art and His Life*. London, J.M. Dent, 1937.
38 Myra Scott and Joan Kerr, 'Dora Meeson Coates'. *Design & Art Australia Online*, 1992 and 1995 respectively.
39 Dora Meeson Coates, *George Coates, His Art and His Life*, p.12.
40 Clare Wright, *You Daughters of Freedom*. Melbourne, Text Publishing, October 2018.
41 Hels, 'Dora Meeson, an Australian expat artist in London". Melbourne, *Art and Architecture, Mainly*, online blog, 5 Nov 2013, http://melbourneblogger.blogspot.com/.
42 Christopher Allen, 'Heart of the River', *Weekend Australian*, 2–3 November 2013, p.13.
43 Joan Kerr, 'Alice Muskett, Biography'. *Design & Art Australia Online*, accessed November 2019.
44 Joan Kerr (ed.), *Heritage: the national women's art book, 500 works by 500 Australian women artists from colonial times to 1955.*
45 Unnamed correspondent, 'The Art of the Year'. Sydney, *Lone Hand* magazine, 1 April 1910.
46 Susanna de Vries, *Ethel Carrick Fox: Triumphs and Travels of a Post-Impressionist*. Brisbane, Pandanus Press, 1997.
47 *Painted Women: Australian artists in Europe at the turn of the century*, Edited by Anne Gray, (Nedlands, Lawrence Wilson Art Gallery, UWA, 1998), Exhibition catalogue.
48 Anne Gérard-Austin, 'The Greatest Voyage: Australian painters in the Paris salons, 1885–1939'.
49 ibid.
50 *Art, Love and Life: Ethel Carrick and E Phillips Fox*. Edited by Angela Goddard (curator) (Brisbane, Queensland Art Gallery, April 2011), Exhibition catalogue.
51 Katherine Feeney, 'A partnership in love and art'. *Sydney Morning Herald*, 12 April 2011.
52 John McDonald, 'Fine art of a happy marriage'. *Sydney Morning Herald*, 30 April 2011.
53 Juliet Peers in *The Melbourne Modernists*, Edited by Nathan Paramanathan (Melbourne: Victorian Artists' Society, 1990), Exhibition catalogue.

54 Anne Gérard-Austin, 'The Greatest Voyage: Australian painters in the Paris salons, 1885–1939'.

55 Jennifer Phipps, 'Plante, Ada May'. *Australian Dictionary of Biography*, Vol. 11, (MUP), 1988.

56 Jennifer Phipps, quoting Arnold Shore, 'Plante, Ada May'. *Australian Dictionary of Biography*, Vol. 11, (MUP), 1988.

57 *Margaret Preston*, Edited by Deborah Edwards & Rose Peel (Sydney: Art Gallery of NSW, 2005), Exhibition catalogue.

58 Margaret Preston, 'From Eggs to Electrolux', *Art in Australia* 3, No. 22, December 1927.

59 *The Art of Margaret Preston*, Edited by Ian North (Adelaide: Art Gallery of South Australia, 1980), Exhibition catalogue.

60 Margaret Preston, 'Why I Became a Convert to Modern Art', *The Home*, Australia, Vol. 4, No. 2, 1 June 1923.

61 *Margaret Preston*, Exhibition catalogue.

62 Helen Topliss, *Modernism and Feminism: Australian Women Artists, 1900–1940*.

63 *The Art of Margaret Preston*, Exhibition catalogue, p.76.

64 Elizabeth Butel, *Margaret Preston: the art of constant rearrangement*.

65 Margaret Preston papers, Sydney, Art Gallery of NSW, MS1963.1.

66 Notes on Margaret Preston. Musée d'Orsay Archives, Paris, sourced 2015.

67 Janine Burke, *Australian Women Artists, 1840–1940*. Melbourne, Greenhouse Publications, 1980.

68 ibid.

69 Janda Gooding, *Chasing Shadows: The Art of Kathleen O'Connor*. Sydney, Craftsman House, 1996.

70 *Painted Women: Australian artists in Europe at the turn of the century*, Exhibition catalogue, p.27. And Papers of Kathleen O'Connor, State Library of Western Australia. Call no. MN1405, ACC. 4417A.

71 *Painted Women: Australian artists in Europe at the turn of the century*, Exhibition catalogue.

72 Anne Gérard-Austin, 'The Greatest Voyage: Australian painters in the Paris salons, 1885–1939'.

73 ibid, p.114

74 Hazel de Berg, Kathleen O'Connor interviewed by Hazel de Berg.

75 Kathleen O'Connor, 'Paris', The *West Australian*, 7 January 1910, p.5.

76 Kathleen O'Connor, Correspondence. Perth, AGWA Archives. Call no. MN1403, Stacks AU4417A.
77 Robert Hughes, quoted in 'The Australian National Gallery building; the collection'. *Art and Australia*, Sydney, The Fine Art Press, Vol. 14, Nos. 3 & 4, Summer–Autumn January and April, 1977, p.263.
78 James Watson, 'O'Connor, Kathleen'. *Australian Dictionary of Biography*, Vol. 11, (MUP), 1988.
79 Julie Lewis & P.A.E. Hutchings, *Kathleen O'Connor: Artist in Exile*. Fremantle, Fremantle Arts Centre Press, 1987.
80 K.G.T. Walker, 'Greene, Anne Eliza'. *Australian Dictionary of Biography*, Vol. 14, (MUP), 1996.
81 'Anne Alison Greene, Biography', *Design & Art Australia Online*, 1999.
82 Radio 4QR, 'The Founders Speak'. Brisbane, Queensland State Library, 11 December 1945.
83 Tansy Curtin in *The Long Weekend: Australian artists in France 1918–1939*, Edited by Karen Quinlan (Bendigo: Bendigo Art Gallery, 2007), Exhibition catalogue.
84 Penelope Little, *A Studio in Montparnasse: Bessie Davidson: an Australian artist in Paris*. Melbourne, Craftsman House, 2003.
85 Jane Hylton, 'Davidson, Bessie Ellen'. *Australian Dictionary of Biography*, Vol. 13, (MUP), 1993.
86 Bessie Davidson, *Interior*. Oil on panel. Edinburgh, City Art Centre, Accession No. CAC160/1964.
87 Edith Fry, 'The Work of Bessie Davidson', *Drawing and Design*, September 1922, pp.147–48.
88 Georgina Downey, 'Reading Rooms: Domesticity, Identity and Belonging in the Paintings of Bessie Davidson, Margaret Preston and Stella Bowen in Paris and London 1910s–1930s'. (PhD thesis, supervisor Professor Catherine Speck, University of Adelaide, 2004), as quoted in Peers, Juliet, 'I Love Paris Every Moment', in *The Long Weekend: Australian artists in France 1918–1939*. Exhibition catalogue, p.38.
89 Penelope Little, *A Studio in Montparnasse: Bessie Davidson: an Australian artist in Paris*, p.82.
90 ibid, p.101.
91 Mary Alice Lee, 'An Australian student of Frank Brangwyn: Jessie C.A. Traill in London and Belgium, 1907–1908', Melbourne, NGV, *Art Journal*, No. 30, 2014.

92 Jessie Traill, papers, State Library of Victoria, MS 7975, Box 795.
93 Mary Alice Lee, 'Traill, Jessie Constance Alice'. *Australian Dictionary of Biography*, Vol. 12, (MUP), 1990.
94 Biography of Jessie Traill', *Stars in the River: the prints of Jessie Traill*, Edited by Roger Butler (Canberra: National Gallery of Australia, 2013), Exhibition catalogue.
95 Arthur Streeton, 'Art Exhibitions: Miss Jessie Traill's Works'. Melbourne, The *Argus*, 3 May 1932, p.10.
96 Sasha Grishin, in 'Jessie Traill'. *Wikipedia*, 2015, p.1.
97 Art Gallery of South Australia, 'Biography of Gladys Reynell'. Art Gallery of SA Outreach Education Program, 2004.
98 Joan Kerr (ed.), *Heritage: the national women's art book, 500 works by 500 Australian women artists from colonial times to 1955*.
99 *Gladys Reynell: the most delightful thing on earth*, Edited by Robert Reason (Adelaide: Art Gallery of South Australia, 2006), Exhibition catalogue.
100 Noris Ioannau, 'Reynell, Gladys'. *Australian Dictionary of Biography*, Vol. 11, (MUP), 1988.
101 *Gladys Reynell: the most delightful thing on earth*, Edited by Robert Reason (Adelaide: Art Gallery of South Australia, 2006), Education Kit and Biography.
102 Noris Ioannou, 'Reynell, Gladys'. *Australian Dictionary of Biography*.
103 Gladys Osborne, 'Knowledge or Feeling in Art', *Art in Australia*, 15 August 1935.
104 Hazel de Berg, Vida Lahey interviewed by Hazel de Berg, 26 November 1965. Canberra, National Library of Australia, Hazel de Berg Collection, http://nla.gov.au/nla.obj-214438572.
105 Margaret Maynard, 'Lahey, Frances Vida'. *Australian Dictionary of Biography*, Vol. 9, (MUP), 1983.
106 *Songs of Colour: The art of Vida Lahey*, Edited by Bettina MacAulay (Brisbane: Queensland Art Gallery, 1989), Exhibition catalogue, pp.40–45.
107 Vida Lahey, *Art in Queensland 1859–1959*. Brisbane, Jacaranda Press for Queensland Art Gallery, 1959.
108 Elena Taylor, 'Cockburn Mercer's "Ballet"'. Melbourne, *Art Journal* 49, National Gallery of Victoria, 2010.
109 Martin Browne, owner, former Yellow House gallery, Email to the authors re Mary Cockburn Mercer, 8 August 2015.

110 Marja Bloem and Martin Browne (eds), *Colin McCahon: A Question of Faith*. Nelson, New Zealand, Craig Potton Publishing; Amsterdam, Stedelijk Museum, 2002.

111 Joan Kerr (ed.), *Heritage: the national women's art book, 500 works by 500 Australian women artists from colonial times to 1955*.

112 Juliet Peers, 'May I re-introduce Miss Cumbrae Stewart?', in *Janet Cumbrae Stewart; The Perfect Touch*, Edited by Rodney B. James (curator) (Victoria, Mornington Peninsula Regional Gallery, May 2003), Exhibition catalogue.

113 S.M. Quinlan, in *Janet Cumbrae Stewart: The Perfect Touch*. Edited by Rodney B. James (curator) (Victoria, Mornington Peninsula Regional Gallery, May 2003), Exhibition catalogue.

114 Amanda Smith, *Deep End: A Review of The Perfect Touch*. Exhibition of Janet Cumbrae Stewart, Mornington Peninsula Regional Gallery, May 2003, curator Rodney B. James. ABC Radio National, 28 May 2003.

115 John Shirlow, *The Pastels of Cumbrae Stewart*. Melbourne, Alex McCubbin Gallery. Exhibition catalogue, undated.

116 Pamela Gerrish Nunn, 'A View of One's Own: female artists and the nude'. *Australian and New Zealand Journal of Art*, No 1, 2000, May 2015, pp. 65–78.

117 Susan McCulloch, 'Heavenly Bodies'. *Weekend Australian*, 7–8 June 2003, p.R21.

118 Juliet Peers, 'May I re-Introduce Miss Cumbrae Stewart?', in *Janet Cumbrae Stewart; The Perfect Touch*, Exhibition catalogue, p.6.

119 Letter to Mary Cunningham, 10 August 1919, quoted in Bruce James's *Grace Cossington Smith*. Sydney, Craftsman House, 1990, p.50.

120 Unattributed, *La Robe Chinoise*. Descriptive entry, National Gallery of Australia. https://nga.gov.au/exhibition/edwardians/detail.cfm?IRN=127294.

121 Anne Gérard-Austin, 'The Greatest Voyage: Australian painters in the Paris salons, 1885–1939'.

122 Catherine Speck, 'The "Frontier" Speaks Back: Two Australian Artists Working in Paris and London', *Portal*, 2013, Vol. 10, No. 2, pp.1–16.

123 John Pigot, *Hilda Rix Nicholas: her life and art*. Melbourne, Miegunyah Press, 2000.

124 H.R. Nicholas, Letter to Meg Line in London Journal, in papers of H.R. Nicholas, National Library of Australia, MS 9817 Series 14,

Folder 4. Also in Gérard-Austin, 'The Greatest Voyage: Australian painters in the Paris salons, 1885–1939', p.12.
125 Unnamed reviewer, 'Exhibition of H.R. Nicholas'. Paris, *La Revue Moderne*, 25 April 1914, in Bertram Stevens, *The Art of Hilda Rix Nicholas*. Sydney, A. Hordern, 1919.
126 Unattributed, 'Australian Artist Returns to Sydney', *Sydney Morning Herald*, 29 October 1926, p.12.
127 Joan Kerr (ed.), *Heritage: the national women's art book, 500 works by 500 Australian women artists from colonial times to 1955.*
128 Helen Topliss (ed.), *Earth, Fire, Water, Air: Anne Dangar's letters to Grace Crowley, 1930–1951*. Sydney, Allen and Unwin, 2000.
129 Helen Topliss, *Modernism and Feminism: Australian women artists, 1900–1940*, p.108.
130 Helen Topliss, *Anne Dangar at Moly-Sabata; Tradition and Innovation.* Biography of Anne Dangar. Canberra, National Gallery of Australia, 2015, p.1. https://nga.gov.au/dangar/index.cfm.
131 Anne Loxley, Review of *Earth, Fire, Water, Air*. Sydney, *Sydney Morning Herald*, 23 December 2000.
132 Helen Topliss (ed), *Earth, Fire, Water, Air: Anne Dangar's Letters to Grace Crowley 1930–1951*, pp.46–62.
133 Anne Gérard-Austin, 'Remembering Evelyn Chapman', *Look*, Art Gallery Society of NSW, Issue 0415, April 2015, p.14.
134 Pamela Thalben-Ball, quoted in *Australian Artist Magazine*, August 2004.
135 Anne Gérard-Austin, 'The Greatest Voyage: Australian painters in the Paris salons, 1885–1939'.
136 Letters of Evelyn Chapman, Chapman papers, Box 25, Archives of Art Gallery of NSW.
137 Grace Crowley, Notebooks. Sydney, Art Gallery of NSW Archives, MS 1980.1.
138 Anne Gérard-Austin, 'The Greatest Voyage: Australian painters in the Paris salons, 1885–1939'.
139 Janine Burke, *Australian Women Artists, 1840–1940*.
140 Daniel Thomas, 'Crowley, Grace Adela Williams'. *Australian Dictionary of Biography*, Vol. 13, (MUP), 1993.
141 Grace Crowley, Notebooks, Sydney, Art Gallery of NSW Archives, MS 1980.1.

142 Janine Burke, *Australian Women Artists 1840–1940*.
143 *Grace Crowley: Being Modern*, Edited by Elena Taylor (Canberra: National Gallery of Australia, 2006), Exhibition catalogue.
144 Helen Topliss, *Modernism and Feminism: Australian Women Artists, 1900–1940*.
145 *Moral Censorship and the Visual Arts in Australia*, Edited by Alison Carroll (curator) (Melbourne: Australian Centre for Contemporary Art, 1989), Exhibition catalogue.
146 Helen Topliss (ed.), *Earth, Fire, Water, Air: Anne Dangar's letters to Grace Crowley, 1930–1951*.
147 Robert Hughes, *The Art of Australia*. Melbourne, Penguin, 1970.
148 Anne Gérard-Austin, 'The Greatest Voyage: Australian painters in the Paris salons, 1885–1939'.
149 Elizabeth Howell, 'Dorrit Black: her early influences and adoption of modernism' (master's thesis, ANU, 2013).
150 Ian North, *The Art of Dorrit Black*. Melbourne, Macmillan, 1979.
151 Dorrit Black, *Account of Travel and Work, 1927–29*. Adelaide, Art Gallery of SA, 1979.
152 *Dorrit Black: Unseen Forces*, Edited by Tracey Lock-Weir (Adelaide: Art Gallery of South Australia. December 2014), Exhibition catalogue.
153 ibid, pp.45–46.
154 Shirley Cameron Wilson, *From Shadow into Light: South Australian women artists since colonisation*. Adelaide, Delmont Pty Ltd, 1988.
155 Dorrit Black, Letter to Graham Young, Macquarie Galleries. Sydney, Art Gallery of NSW Archive, dated 16 February 1929.
156 Ian North, 'Black, Dorothea Foster'. *Australian Dictionary of Biography*, Vol. 7, (MUP), 1979. And: www.artgallery.sa.gov.au/ages/home/learning.2104.
157 Sarah Thomas, 'The Modern Art Centre'. *Art and Australia*, Vol. 44, No. 1, Spring 2006.
158 Stella Bowen, *Drawn from Life: a memoir*. London, Collins, 1941.
159 *Stella Bowen: Art, Love and War*, Edited by Lola Wilkins (curator) (Canberra: Australian War Memorial Gallery, 2002), Retrospective exhibition catalogue notes.
160 Julia (Julie) Loewe, Introduction to *Drawn from Life*.
161 Alan Judd, *Ford Madox Ford*. Cambridge, Mass., Harvard University Press, 1991, p.314.

162 Stella Bowen, *Drawn from Life*, pp.99–100.
163 ibid, pp.108–11.
164 Julia (Julie) Loewe, Introduction to *Drawn from Life*.
165 Unattributed, 'Review of Stella Bowen exhibition', *The Bulletin*, Vol. 5, No. 3, January 1944.
166 *Stella Bowen: Art, Love and War*, Exhibition Catalogue.
167 George Speirs, quoted in 'Frances Margot Freeman', https://www.australian-art-gallery.com/australian-artists/Frances-Margot-Freeman-A378.htm.
168 Joan Kerr, 'Frances Margot Freeman', *Design & Art Australia Online*, 1 January 1995.
169 From https://www.australian-art-gallery.com/australian-artists/Frances-Margot-Freeman-A378.htm.
170 National Library of Australia, see trove.nla.gov.au/newspaper/article/79475258
171 Erif Vincent, 'Biography of Madge Freeman', Madge Freeman papers. Archives of Bendigo Art Gallery, 1988.
172 *Madge Freeman* (Retrospective Exhibition) (Bendigo: Bendigo Art Gallery, 1981), Exhibition catalogue notes, p.6.
173 From www.australian-art-gallery/australian-artists/Francis-Margot-Freeman-A378htm.
174 Unattributed, 'Madge Freeman', *The Herald* (Melbourne), 9 July 1934.
175 Lucilla Wyborn d'Abrera, *Constance Stokes: Art & Life*. Melbourne, Hill House Publishers, 2015.
176 Anne Gérard-Austin, 'The Greatest Voyage: Australian painters in the Paris salons, 1885–1939'.
177 Andrea Lloyd, 'Constance Stokes: Her Life and Art'. (B.A. Honours Thesis, University of Melbourne, 1991).
178 Lucilla Wyborn d'Abrera, *Constance Stokes: Art & Life*, p.44.
179 Anne Summers, *The Lost Mother: a story of art and love*. Melbourne University Press, 2009.
180 Anne Summers, *An Artist Lost: rediscovering Constance Stokes*. Canberra, National Gallery of Australia, 2009, pp.10–11.
181 Hazel de Berg, Constance Stokes interviewed by Hazel de Berg, 2 December 1965. Canberra, National Library of Australia, Hazel de Berg Collection, www.nla.gov.au/nla.obj-214473739.
182 Anne Summers, *An Artist Lost*, p.2.

183 Ursula Hoff, 'Constance Stokes's Still Lifes', *Bulletin*, National Gallery of Victoria, Melbourne, November 2014, Vols 1–12, 1945–58, Vol. V11, No. 11, 1953.
184 Patricia Anderson, 'Constance Stokes Exhibition', *Weekend Australian*, Review section, 23 August 2015.
185 Andrea Lloyd, 'Constance Stokes: A Determined Career', *Gallery* (monthly magazine of the NGV), March 1993, p.10.
186 *Travels with My Art: Moya Dyring and Margaret Olley*, Edited by M.J. Boyde (Murwillumbah, Tweed Regional Gallery, 2015), Exhibition catalogue, pp.1–12.
187 George Johnston, *My Brother Jack*. Melbourne, Collins, 1964.
188 Gaynor Cuthbert, *Paintings from Paris: The life and art of Moya Dyring*. Kerrimuir, Rose Library Publications, 2014, p.28.
189 *Travels with My Art: Moya Dyring and Margaret Olley*, Edited by M.J. Boyde (Murwillumbah, Tweed Regional Gallery, 2015), Exhibition catalogue.
190 ibid.
191 M.J. Boyde, 'Moya Dyring: An Australian Salon in Paris'. Heide Museum of Modern Art, Media Release, October 2015.
192 Gaynor Cuthbert, *Paintings from Paris: The life and art of Moya Dyring*, p.79.
193 Unattributed, 'She paints in Paris'. *The Australian Women's Weekly*, 7 January 1953, p.3.
194 Gaynor Cuthbert, *Paintings from Paris: The life and art of Moya Dyring*.
195 Bronwyn Watson, 'Surf's up, outrage is down'. The *Australian*, 24 November 2012, p.1.
196 Unattributed, *Biography of Betty Quelhurst*. Brisbane, *Artlines* magazine, Queensland Art Gallery, No. 4, 2002.
197 Glenn A. Cooke, 'A Time Remembered: Art in Brisbane 1950 to 1975'. Brisbane, Queensland Art Gallery, 1995.
198 Barry Pearce, *Margaret Olley*. Sydney, The Beagle Press, 2012.
199 Christine France, *Margaret Olley*. Sydney, Craftsman House, 1990.
200 Meg Stewart, *Far from a Still Life*. Sydney, Random House, 2005, pp.237–8.
201 Tweed Regional Art Gallery, *Biography of Margaret Olley*. Margaret Olley Art Centre, September 2016, p.1.
202 Barry Pearce, *Margaret Olley*.

BIBLIOGRAPHY

d'Abrera, Lucilla Wyborn. *Constance Stokes: Art and life*. Hill House Publishers, Melbourne, 2015.

Allen, Christopher. 'Heart of the River'. *Weekend Australian*, Sydney, 2–3 November 2013, p.2.

Allen, Woody. *Midnight in Paris* (feature film). Gravier Productions, New York, 2011.

Ambrus, Caroline. *Australian Women Artists: First Fleet to 1945*. Irrepressible Press, Canberra, 1992.

Anne Dangar at Moly-Sabata: Tradition and Innovation. Canberra: National Gallery of Australia, 2001. Exhibition catalogue.

Art Gallery of NSW. 'Guide to papers of Grace Crowley', Access. No. MS 1980.1. AGNSW Library, Sydney.

Art Gallery of NSW. 'Notes on Bessie Gibson in the Old Salon', Access No. MS. 2014.11, Bag 24. AGNSW, Sydney.

Art Gallery of NSW. Evelyn Chapman papers. Box 25 Archives, AGNSW, Sydney.

Art Gallery of NSW. Grace Crowley notebooks. AGNSW Library, Sydney.

Art Gallery of WA. 'Profile, Kathleen O'Connor 1876–1968'. AGWA, Perth, 1967.

Art Gallery of WA. Kathleen O'Connor correspondence, Call No. MN 1403, Stacks AU4417A. Archives of AGWA, Perth.

Ashe Archive. *Researching Textiles*. Online blog, July 2012.

Bendigo Art Gallery. The Goodsir Archive, Bendigo Art Gallery, Bendigo.

Benko, Nancy. *Art and Artists of South Australia*. Lidums, Adelaide, 1996.

Benstock, Shari. *Women of the Left Bank: Paris, 1900–1940*. University of Texas Press, Austin, 1986.

Biven, Rachel. *Some Forgotten, Some Remembered: women artists of South Australia*. Sydenham Gallery, Norwood, 1976.

Black, Dorrit. *Account of Travel and Work*. Art Gallery of SA, Adelaide, 1979.

Bloem, Marja & Browne, Martin (eds). *Colin McCahon: A Question of Faith*. Craig Potton Publishing, New Zealand, 2002; Stedelijk Museum, Amsterdam, 2002.

Bowen, Stella. *Drawn from Life*. Collins, London, 1941.

Burke, Janine. *Australian Women Artists, 1840–1940*. Greenhouse Publications, Melbourne, 1980.

Burke, Janine. *Field of Vision: a decade of change: women's art in the seventies*. Penguin, Melbourne, 1990.

Butel, Elizabeth. *Margaret Preston: The art of constant rearrangement*. Penguin, Melbourne, 1985.

Calderwood, Kathleen. 'Frenemies: how Friendship and Rivalry Defined Modern Art'. Radio National, 'Books and Arts', 20 September 2016.

Carroll, Alison, editor. *A History of Moral Censorship and the Visual Arts in Australia*. Melbourne: Australian Centre for Contemporary Art, 1989. Exhibition catalogue.

Christesen, C. B. 'Bowen, Esther Gwendolyn (Stella)'. *Australian Dictionary of Biography*, Vol. 7, (MUP), 1979.

Coates, Dora Meeson. *George Coates: His Art and His Life*. J. M. Dent, London, 1937, pp.12–17.

Cody, Morrill & Ford, Hugh. *The Women of Montparnasse: The Americans in Paris*. Cornwall Books, New York, 1984.

Cruthers, John & Kinsella, Lee (eds). *Into the Light: The Cruthers Collection of Women's Art*. UWA Publishing, Perth, 2012.

Curtin, Tansy, 'Australian Artists in France' in *The Long Weekend: Australian Artists in France 1918–1939*. Edited by Karen Quinlan. Bendigo: Bendigo Art Gallery, Bendigo, 2009. Exhibition catalogue.

Cuthbert, Gaynor. *Paintings from Paris: The Life and Art of Moya Dyring*. Rose Library Publications, Kerrimuir, 2014.

Day, Gregory. Review of *Seeing Ourselves: Women's Self-Portraits* by Frances Borzello. *Australian Review*, 6 August 2016.

de Berg, Hazel. Interview with Constance Stokes. National Library of Australia, Canberra, 1965, http://www.nla.gov.au/nla.obj-214473739.

de Berg, Hazel. Interview with Kathleen O'Connor. National Library of Australia, Canberra, 1965, http://nla.gov.au/nla.obj-214365783.

de Berg, Hazel. Interview with Vida Lahey. National Library of Australia, Canberra, 1965, http://nla.gov.au/nla.obj-214438572.

de Vries, Susanna. *Ethel Carrick Fox: Travels and Triumphs of a Post-Impressionist*. Pandanus Press, Brisbane, 1997.

Di Sciascio, Peter. 'Australian Lesbian Artists of the Early Twentieth Century' in *Out Here: Gay and Lesbian Perspectives VI*, Yorick Smaal and Graham Willett (eds). Monash University Publishing, Melbourne, 2011.

Dorrit Black: Unseen Forces. Edited by Tracey Lock-Weir. Adelaide: Art Gallery of SA, 2014. Exhibition notes.

Downey, Georgina. 'Reading Rooms: Domesticity, identity and belonging in the paintings of Bessie Davidson, Margaret Preston and Stella Bowen in Paris and London 1910s–1930s'. PhD thesis, University of Adelaide, 2004.

Engledow, Sarah. *Paris to Monaro: Pleasures from the studio of Hilda Rix Nicholas*. National Portrait Gallery, Canberra, 2015.

France, Christine. *Margaret Olley*. Craftsman House, Sydney, 1990.

Gérard-Austin, Anne. 'The Greatest Voyage: Australian painters in the Paris salons, 1885–1939'. Postgraduate thesis, University of Sydney, 2014.

Gleeson, James (interviewer). Interview with Grace Crowley (sound recording). National Gallery of Australia, Canberra, 1978.

Gooding, Janda. *Chasing Shadows: The art of Kathleen O'Connor*. Craftsman House, Sydney, with Art Gallery of WA, Perth, 1996.

Goodsir, Agnes (interview). *British Australasian* magazine, London, 6 December 1906.

Grace Crowley: Being modern. Edited by Elena Taylor. Canberra: National Gallery of Australia, 2006. Exhibition catalogue.

Grishin, Sasha. *Australian Art: A history*. Miegunyah Press, Sydney, 2013.

Hammond, Victoria. *A century of Australian women artists, 1840s–1940s*. Deutscher Fine Art, Melbourne, 1993.

Harding, Lesley & Cramer, Sue. *Cubism and Australian Art*. Miegunyah Press, Melbourne, 2009.

Harding, Lesley & Morgan, Kendrah. *Sunday's Kitchen: food and living at Heide*. Miegunyah Press, Sydney, 2011.

Hazan, Eric. *The Invention of Paris: A history in footsteps*. Verso, New York, 2011.

Hels. 'Dora Meeson: an Australian expat artist in London'. *Art and Architecture mainly*, online blog, 5 November 2013 (see http://melbourneblogger.blogspot.com/2013/11/dora-meeson-australian-expat-artist-in.html).

Hoff, Ursula. 'Stokes's *Still Life*'. *NGA Bulletin*, Vols 1–12, 1945–58, National Gallery of Australia, Canberra.

Holland, Clive. 'Lady Art Students' Life in Paris'. *International Studio*, Paris, January 1904.

Howell, Elizabeth. 'Dorrit Black: Her Early Influences and Adoption of Modernism' (masters thesis, ANU, Access no. SLSA PT 25838, in State Library of SA, Adelaide).

Hughes, Robert. *The Art of Australia*. Penguin, Melbourne, 1970.

Hutchings, P.A.E. & Lewis, Julie. *Kathleen O'Connor: Artist in exile*. Fremantle Arts Centre Press, Fremantle, 1987.

Hylton, Jane. *Modern Australian Women: Paintings and prints 1925–1945*. Art Gallery of SA, Adelaide, 2000.

In a Picture Land over the Sea: Agnes Goodsir 1864–1939. Edited by Karen Quinlan. Bendigo: Bendigo Art Gallery, 1998. Exhibition catalogue.

Ingram, Terry. 'Iso Rae', *The Age*, 12 November 2002, pp.48–49.

Ioannou, Noris. 'Reynell, Gladys'. *Australian Dictionary of Biography*, Vol. 11, (MUP), 1988.

Jacobs, Jane. *The Economy of Cities*. Vintage Books, New York, 1970.

Janet Cumbrae Stewart: Perfect Touch. Edited by Rodney James (curator). Victoria: Mornington Peninsula Regional Gallery, 2003. Exhibition catalogue.

Joel, Grace. 'Australian artists in London: a reminiscence'. *Art and Architecture*, Vol. 3, No. 3, May–June 1906.

Johnston, George. *My Brother Jack*. Collins, Melbourne, 1964.

Judd, Alan. *Ford Madox Ford*. Harvard University Press, Cambridge, MA, 1990.

Kerr, Joan (ed.). *Heritage: The national women's art book, 500 works by 500 Australian women artists from colonial times to 1955*. Craftsman House, Sydney, 1995.

Kerr, Joan: *A Singular Voice: Essays on Australian art and architecture*. Power Publications, Sydney, 2009.

Lee, Mary Alice. 'An Australian Student of Frank Brangwyn: Jessie C. A. Traill in London and Belgium, 1907–1908'. *Art Journal*, No. 30, 1989.

Lee, Mary Alice. 'Traill, Jessie Constance Alicia'. *Australian Dictionary of Biography*, Vol. 12, (MUP), 1990.

Little, Penelope. 'The Beauty of Common Things: The Rediscovery of Bessie Davidson'. *Art + Australia*, Vol. 36, No. 4, 1999, pp.481–3.

Little, Penelope. *A Studio in Montparnasse: Bessie Davidson: an Australian artist in Paris*. Craftsman House, Melbourne, 2003.

Lloyd, Andrea. 'Constance Stokes: A Determined Career'. *Gallery* Magazine, National Gallery of Victoria, Melbourne, 1993.

Margaret Preston, Edited by Deborah Edwards & Rose Peel. Sydney: Art Gallery of NSW, 2005. Exhibition catalogue.

McCulloch, Alan & McCulloch, Susan, *The new McCulloch's Encyclopedia of Australian Art*. Carlton, Miegunyah Press, 2006.

McDonald, John. 'Fine Art of a Happy Marriage'. Review of *Art, Love and Life* (exhibition) at Queensland Art Gallery, 3 April–7 August 2011. *Sydney Morning Herald*, Sydney, 30 April 2011.

McDonald, John. *Art of Australia, Vol. 1: Exploration to Federation*. Pan Macmillan, Sydney, 2008.

Moya Dyring: An Australian Salon in Paris. Edited by Melissa J. Boyde. Melbourne: Heide Museum of Modern Art, October 2014. Media release.

Musée d'Orsay. Margaret Preston notes. Archives of the Musée d'Orsay, Paris, sourced 2015.

National Library of Australia. Letter from Hilda Rix Nicholas to Dorothy Richmond, 4 July 1939. National Library of Australia Archive, Canberra.

National Library of Australia. Letter from Hilda Rix Nicholas to Meg Line in *London Journal*. Papers of H.R. Nicholas, MS 9817 Series 14, Folder 4, National Library of Australia, Canberra.

Nicholas, Hilda Rix. *An Artist's Life in France*. Lecture to Women Painters Society, Rix Nicholas Archive, Art Gallery of New South Wales, Sydney.

Nicklin, Lenore. 'Grace Crowley Looks Back on Life and Art'. *Weekend Magazine, Sydney Morning Herald*, Sydney, 10 May 1975, p. 11.

North, Ian. *The Art of Dorrit Black*. Macmillan, Melbourne, 1979.

Osborne (Reynell), Gladys. 'Knowledge or Feeling in Art'. *Art in Australia*, Sydney, 15 August 1935.

Ottley, Diane. *Grace Crowley's Contribution to Australian Modernism and Geometric Abstraction*. Cambridge Scholars Publications, Cambridge, 2010.

Out of the West: Western Australian art 1830s to 1930s. Edited by Anne Gray. Canberra: National Gallery of Australia, 2011. Exhibition catalogue.

Painted Women: Australian artists in Europe at the turn of the century. Edited by Anne Gray. Perth: Lawrence Wilson Art Gallery, University of WA, 1998. Exhibition catalogue.

Panero, James. 'Why Paris?'. *Humanities*, Vol. 31, No. 6, Nov/Dec 2010.

Pearce, Barry. *Margaret Olley*. The Beagle Press, Sydney, 2012.

Peers, Juliet. 'A.M. Plante'. In *The Melbourne Modernists*, Edited by Nathan Paramanathan. Melbourne: Victorian Artists' Society, 1990. Exhibition catalogue.

Peers, Juliet. 'Dyring, Moya Claire'. *Australian Dictionary of Biography*, Vol. 14, (MUP), 1996.

Peers, Juliet. 'I Love Paris Every Moment'. In *The Long Weekend: Australian artists in France 1918–1939*. Edited by Karen Quinlan. Bendigo: Bendigo Art Gallery, 2007. Exhibition catalogue.

Pesman, Ros. *Duty Free: Australian women abroad*. Oxford University Press, Melbourne, 1996.

Phipps, Jennifer. 'Plante, Ada May', *Australian Dictionary of Biography*, Vol. 11, (MUP), 1988.

Pigot, J. *Hilda Rix Nicholas: Her life and art*. Miegunyah Press, Sydney, 2000.

Pizzichini, Lilian. *The Blue Hour: A life of Jean Rhys*. W.W. Norton & Co., New York, 2009.

Preston, Margaret. 'From Eggs to Electrolux'. *Art in Australia*, Preston edition, 3rd series, No. 22, December 1927.

Preston, Margaret. 'Why I Became a Convert to Modern Art'. The *Home* magazine, Vol. 4, No. 2, June 1923.

Reason, Robert. *Gladys Reynell: The most delightful thing on earth*. Ready Reader Books, Adelaide, 2007.

Robertson, J. 'Marie Tuck', in 'Personalities Remembered' (radio program), 19 December 1971. Manuscript, State Library of SA, Adelaide.

Robertson, Shannon. *Five Queensland Artists* (booklet). Queensland Art Gallery, Brisbane, 1975.

Siegel, Jerrold E. *Bohemian Paris: Culture, politics, and the boundaries of bourgeois life, 1830–1930*. Johns Hopkins University Press, Baltimore, 1999.

Smee, Sebastian. *The Art of Rivalry: Four friendships, betrayals, and breakthroughs in modern art*. Random House, New York, 2016.

Smith, Bernard. *Place, Taste, and Tradition; A study of Australian art since 1788*. Ure Smith, Sydney, 1945.

Snowden, Betty. 'Iso Rae in Etaples: another perspective of war'. *Wartime* magazine, Issue 8, Summer 1999, Australian War Memorial, Canberra.

Songs of Colour: The Art of Vida Lahey. Edited by Bettina MacAulay. Brisbane: Queensland Art Gallery, 1989. Exhibition catalogue.

South Australian Women Artists, 1890s–1940s, Edited by Jane Hylton. Adelaide: Art Gallery of SA, 1994. Exhibition catalogue.

Speck, Catherine. 'The "Frontier" Speaks Back: Two Australian Artists Working in Paris and London'. *PORTAL*, Vol. 10, No. 2, July 2013, pp.1–16.

Stars in the River: the prints of Jessie Traill. Edited by Roger Butler. Canberra: National Gallery of Australia. 2013. Exhibition catalogue.

State Library of NSW. Grace Crowley papers, Y1289, CY 1284B. SLNSW, Sydney.

State Library of South Australia. Marie Tuck papers, SA Periodicals, No. 709.9423 K146. SLSA, Adelaide.

State Library of Victoria, Evelyn Chapman notes. Access No. SLTF 052.9 L84. SLV, Melbourne.

State Library of Victoria. Jessie Traill papers, MS. 7975 Box 795. SLV, Melbourne.

Stella Bowen: Art, Love and War. Edited by Lola Wilkins. Canberra: Australian War Memorial 2002. Exhibition catalogue.

Stevens, Bertram. *The Art of Hilda Rix Nicholas*. Anthony Hordern & Sons Ltd., Sydney, 1919.

Stewart, Meg. *Margaret Olley: Far from a still life*. Random House, Sydney, 2005.

Stuart, Andrea. *Josephine: The Rose of Martinique*. Pan Macmillan, London, 2003.

Summers, Anne. 'An Artist Lost: Rediscovering Constance Stokes'. Talk at National Gallery of Australia, 17 November 2009. NGA, Canberra.

Summers, Anne. *The Lost Mother: A Story of Art and Love*. Melbourne University Press, Melbourne, 2010.

Taylor, Elena. 'Mary Cockburn Mercer's *"Ballet"*'. *Art Journal* 49, National Gallery of Victoria, Melbourne, 2010.

The Art of Margaret Preston. Edited by Ian North, authors Ian North, Humphrey McQueen & Isobel Seivl. Adelaide: Art Gallery of SA, 1980. Exhibition catalogue.

The Art Student in Paris, Boston Art Students' Association, Boston, 1887.

The Melbourne Modernists. Edited by Nathan Paramanathan. Melbourne: Victorian Artists' Society, 1990. Exhibition catalogue.

The Printmakers: Mainly of the Thirties. Melbourne: Important Women Artists Gallery, Melbourne, 1977. Exhibition catalogue.

Thomas, Daniel. *Project Four: Grace Crowley*. Art Gallery of NSW, Sydney, May 1975.

Thomas, Sarah. 'A Wider Vision: Dorrit Black's Modern Art Centre'. *Art and Australia*, Vol. 44, No. 1, Spring 2006.

Topliss, Helen. *Earth, Fire, Water, Air: Anne Dangar's letters to Grace Crowley, 1930–1951*. Allen and Unwin, Sydney, 2000.

Topliss, Helen. *Modernism and Feminism: Australian women artists, 1900–1940*. Craftsman House, Sydney, 1996.
Travels with My Art: Moya Dyring and Margaret Olley. Edited by Melissa J. Boyde (curator). Murwillumbah: Tweed Regional Gallery, 2015. Exhibition catalogue.
Tuck, Ruth. 'Marie Tuck'. *Kalori* magazine, Vol. 2, No. 14, March 1964, pp.3–6.
Tuck, Ruth. 'Tuck, Marie'. *Australian Dictionary of Biography*, Vol. 12, (MUP), 1990.
Unattributed. 'Biography of Betty Quelhurst'. *Artlines* magazine, Brisbane, 4 November 2004.
Unattributed. 'She paints in Paris'. *Australian Women's Weekly*, Sydney, 7 January 1953, p.3.
Unattributed. 'The Art of the Year'. *Lone Hand* magazine, Sydney, 1 April 1910.
Underhill, Nancy. 'Bessie Gibson 1868–1961'. *Art and Australia*, Vol. 17, No. 1, Spring 1979, pp.59–65.
Vincent, Erif. '*Frances Margot Freeman*'. Australian Art Gallery Online, undated. https://www.australian-art-gallery.com/australian-artists/Frances-Margot-Freeman-A378.htm
Vincent, Erif. 'Biography of Madge Freeman'. Madge Freeman papers. Archive of Bendigo Art Gallery, Bendigo, 1988.
Watson, Bronwyn. 'Surf's up, outrage is down'. *Weekend Australian*, 24 November 2012.
Wikipedia. 'Paris in the Belle Époque'. https://en.wikipedia.org/wiki/Paris_in_the_Belle_Époque#The_arts.
Wilson, Shirley Cameron. *From Shadow into Light: South Australian women artists since colonisation*. Delmont Pty Ltd, Adelaide, 1988.
Wright, Clare. *You Daughters of Freedom*. Text Publishing, Melbourne, 2018.
Young, Marisa. 'Drawn to New Perspectives in the Public Sphere. Female art, design and craft students and their cultural connections in nineteenth century South Australia'. *Outskirts Online*, Vol. 28, May 2013.
Zubans, Ruth & Rich, Margaret. 'Biography of Ethel Carrick'. Geelong: Geelong Art Gallery, 1979. Catalogue, retrospective exhibition.

ABOUT THE AUTHORS

Clem Gorman pioneered experimental theatre in Australia before working as an arts administrator in London. Nine of his plays have been staged professionally and he has written nine books of non-fiction. He has taught at universities in Australia and the US and now writes on the visual arts.

Therese Gorman wrote stage plays in the 1970s with her late husband. With husband Clem she co-authored *Sydney Harbour: A Guide from North Head to South Head*.

Therese and Clem are currently working on a biography of Sydney artist Wendy Sharpe.